Three ~~two~~
week loan

Please return on or before the last
date stamped below.
Charges are made for late return.

Middle East Oil Crises
Since 1973

About the Book and Author

The production and consumption of oil has emerged as a major factor in international economics in general and in regional and national development in particular. The struggle for access to oil and gas resources has become even more fierce, affecting the long-range strategic planning of the superpowers and causing a shift in the world balance of trade. *Middle East Oil Crises Since 1973* is the logical sequel to Dr. Shwadran's classic, *The Middle East, Oil and the Great Powers*. In this new work, Dr. Shwadran delineates the changes in the power equation, the political atmosphere, and the resources of the participants since 1973. He marshals persuasive evidence to show that economic forces, narrow vision, and the absence of strategic planning were the major contributing factors for the oil crises of the past decade, rather than the Arab-Israeli war.

Benjamin Shwadran is professor of modern Middle East history, Tel Aviv University. His many publications include *Middle East Oil: Issues and Problems* (1977); *Middle East Policies of the Great Powers* (1982); and *The Middle East, Oil and the Great Powers* (1973; Westview, 1985).

For Aiton and Dov

Middle East Oil Crises
Since 1973

Benjamin Shwadran

Westview Press / Boulder and London

Copyright © 1986 by Westview Press, Inc.

Published in 1986 in the United States of America by Westview Press, Inc.; Frederick A. Praeger, Publisher; 5500 Central Avenue, Boulder, Colorado 80301

Library of Congress Cataloging-in-Publication Data
Shwadran, Benjamin.
  Middle East oil crises since 1973.
  Bibliography: p.
  Includes index.
  1. Petroleum industry and trade—Near East.
2. Petroleum industry and trade. I. Title.
HD9576.N36S546 1986   338.2'7282'0956   85-12316
ISBN 0-8133-0150-5

Printed and bound in the United States of America.

The paper used in this publication meets the minimum requirements of the American National Standard for Permanence of Paper for Printed Library Materials Z39.48-1984.

10   9   8   7   6   5   4   3   2   1

CONTENTS

TABLES AND MAPS

Tables

Maps

PREFACE

This work, which details the rapid, dramatic, and revolutionary development of Middle East oil since the 1973 energy crisis, is a companion volume to *The Middle East, Oil and the Great Powers* (third edition, 1973; Westview Encore Edition, 1985). The three editions of that book—1955, 1959, 1973—were based on available primary and official sources. Needless to say, a great number of very important documents of the governments involved and of the major international oil companies were kept secret for many years. The complete story of the development of the Middle East oil industry could not, therefore, be presented. However, since the early 1970s a number of U.S. congressional committees—House of Representatives, Senate, and joint—and other government agencies have investigated practically every energy issue, and especially that of Middle East oil, in all their multifarious aspects. The investigations have brought to light an avalanche of hitherto secret documents. These, together with the testimony of many experts and specialists, but especially of the actors in the drama—government and company representatives—elucidated some of the underlying issues that were obscure or totally hidden before.

The probes, however, changed the essential facts of the evolution of the oil industry in the Middle East very little. These facts, as presented in *The Middle East, Oil and the Great Powers,* are still valid, and that book remains a basic work in the history of the modern Middle East. This book, therefore, refrains from repeating material covered in the previous volume, except that which was necessary for the explication and reevaluation of issues and analyses that had to be reassessed in light of new revelations. For a full treatment of events before 1973, the reader should consult *The Middle East, Oil and the Great Powers.*

The introductory chapter summarizes the oil story from the beginning of the century to the first crisis in the light of the results of the new investigations and of historical perspective. From then until the present emerge three major crises. The first two caused economic and financial disturbances in the consuming countries—developing and developed—and friction and tensions among the Western allies. The third crisis negatively affected the producing countries economically and financially and to some extent weakened them politically. We are still in the midst of this last crisis. The concluding chapter is an analysis of possible solutions to the energy problem.

This book follows the style and pattern of the previous one in treating the topics in their historical, economic, political, intraregional, regional, and global aspects—an interdisciplinary approach. The volume is meant to be used in colleges and universities in courses in these fields. It is hoped that it will be consulted as a source book by all professionals in the petroleum industry and the Middle East in general. It is also meant as a reference book for the general reader interested in the Middle East and the role of its oil in the superpowers' struggle.

I wish to express my gratitude first and foremost to my students for their many penetrating questions, which deepened my own search for the possible answers, and for their seminar papers, which widened the horizons and ramifications of all the issues. Thanks also go to Professor Itamar Rabinovich, director of the Shiloah Center for Middle East and African Studies of Tel Aviv University, for graciously providing the assistance of the center in the typing of the manuscript.

Getting the research materials for the book became a major problem, as practically all publications of the various congressional committees were issued in Washington, D.C., and all of them were out of print. I am, therefore, very grateful to the staff of the U.S. Cultural Center library in Jerusalem for help in obtaining some of the reports and documents. Similarly, a long-time friend, Mr. Macey Kronsberg, and my brother, William Z. Schwadron, obtained for me some copies of the reports and other materials in Washington. To both of them I am grateful.

Last but not least, I am thankful to my wife, Helen, for encouraging me to undertake the project, constantly urging me to complete it, and typing a major portion of the final draft.

B. S.

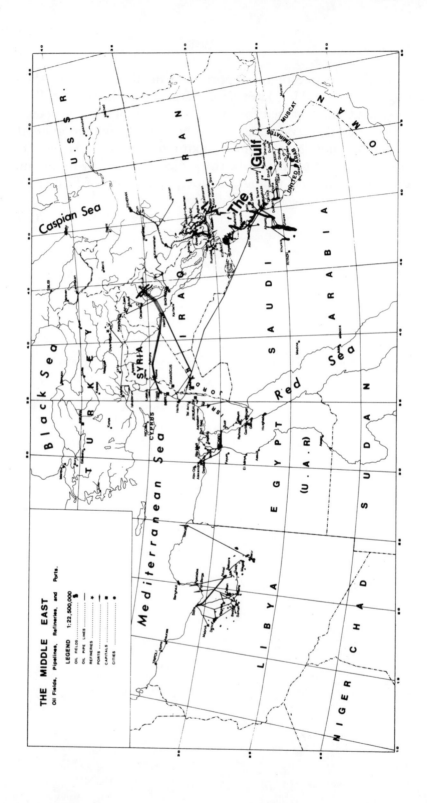

THE MIDDLE EAST
Oil Fields, Pipelines, Refineries, and Ports.

LEGEND   1:22,500,000

OIL FIELDS ....
OIL PIPE LINES ....
REFINERIES ....
PORTS ....
CAPITALS ....
CITIES ....

U. S. S. R.

Caspian Sea

Black Sea

T U R K E Y

CYPRUS

Mediterranean Sea

SYRIA

I R A Q

I R A N

The Gulf

MUSCAT

EMIRATES

UNITED ARAB

O M A N

S A U D I   A R A B I A

Red Sea

E G Y P T

(U . A . R)

S U D A N

L I B Y A

C H A D

N I G E R

1

INTRODUCTION: 1901–1971

The development of the oil industry in the Middle East in the first seven decades of the twentieth century is marked by three major struggles. First was the battle among the powers— Germany, Great Britain, the Netherlands, France, and the United States—to obtain concessions in the area. The most outstanding contest was among the major international companies to eliminate rivalries and competition and establish an international cartel of oil supplies and prices (although the effort to unite against outside obstacles was a common objective). The third struggle, perhaps the longest, most persistent, and most decisive was the one between the oil-producing countries and the foreign companies. These struggles were not chronologically separated and will therefore be treated collectively and simultaneously.

THE STRUGGLE FOR CONCESSIONS

The general pattern of development of the Middle East oil industry was through exploitation concessions granted by the ruling authorities to foreign companies. The first major concession was obtained in Iran (then Persia) by William Knox D'Arcy in 1901. Subsequently the concession became the Anglo-Persian Oil Company in which the British government became a majority owner. Anglo-Persian (later Anglo-Iranian) remained an exclusively British company until 1954.

The contest for the concession in the territory that is now Iraq and was then part of the Ottoman Empire began during the first decade of the century. The British, German, Dutch, and Americans were vying for the concession. The three European nations united and, through their influence on the Turkish government, eliminated the Americans and obtained the concession, which became the Turkish Petroleum Company. The British obtained about 50 percent, the Dutch about 25 percent, and the Germans about 25 percent. After World War I the United States demanded a share in the spoils of war. After long and acrimonious charges and countercharges between the British Foreign Office and the U.S. State Department, the Americans were given a share of about 25 percent from the British share and the German share was transferred to France. In 1928 the Turkish Petroleum Company became the Iraq Petroleum Company (IPC).

In 1930 Standard Oil Company of California (Socal) obtained the Bahrain concession, the first full U.S. concession in the Middle East. Three years later the same U.S. oil company, because of better and more venturesome business tactics, outsmarted the British oil companies and acquired the concession in Saudi Arabia. In 1934, after protracted and difficult negotiations between British and U.S. oil companies and diplomats, the Kuwait concession was granted to an equal partnership of the U.S. Eastern Gulf Oil Corporation and the British Anglo-Iranian Oil Company. Finally, in 1954 the Anglo-American rivalry for Middle East oil concessions came to an end when the U.S. oil companies were given 40 percent of the Iranian concession, now nationalized and organized as the International Iranian Oil Consortium. The Americans emerged from this long struggle as the owners of the lion's share of Middle East oil resources: 100 percent in Bahrain and Saudi Arabia, 50 percent in Kuwait, 40 percent in Iran, and 25 percent in Iraq and in all affiliates of the Iraq Petroleum Company operating outside Iraq.

THE STRUGGLE FOR CONTROL

The first move by the oil companies to control oil production in the Middle East was made in 1914 by the three partners in the Turkish Petroleum Company in the "Red Line" agreement. In it the three partners obligated themselves not to seek oil concessions in the territories of the Ottoman Empire except jointly through the company. When the Americans became partners in the company the U.S. government objected strenuously to this monopolistic restraint of trade, which was a violation of U.S. antitrust laws. Yet, after years of discussions and deals, the United States condoned the provisions of the Red Line agreement. In 1928 the U.S. companies, Standard of New Jersey and Standard of New York, became equal partners in their new Near East Development Company and thus in the 25 percent U.S. share in the Iraq Petroleum Company, which it held.

The second, more inclusive move of the international oil companies was the Achnacarry "As Is" agreement (so called because the companies agreed to leave things as they were). Meeting in Sir Henri Deterding's castle in Scotland, representatives of Standard Oil Company of New Jersey, Anglo-Persian Oil Company, and Royal Dutch–Shell Oil Company signed an agreement on September 17, 1928, which set up six basic principles for the conduct of the oil companies. Its aim was to control world oil supplies, to eliminate competition, and to maintain prices—in other words, to become an international oil cartel. Over the years other major international oil companies joined the "As Is" group.

As the international oil companies entrenched themselves in the Middle East, they operated in accordance with the principles of the "As Is" agreement. Because the general clamor of all the Middle East producing countries was for ever-greater production levels, the companies had to decide, after assessing the size and importance of their respective concessions, from which country to restrict production in order to regulate the world oil trade. Saudi Arabia and Iran were the two largest producers, and they had been rivals as to who was first in production rate. The companies dared not offend either of them; the victim therefore was Iraq. Iraq Petroleum Company systematically held down production by misrepresenting drilling results. It was discovered in 1974–1975 that IPC drillers had found wildcat wells capable of producing 50,000 barrels of oil a day, but the wells had been plugged and had not been classified at all. Company representatives denied any knowledge of this, while Iraq constantly charged that IPC was deliberately holding down production in Iraq and increasing production in Iran. In fact, the rates of growth of oil output during 1958–1972 for Iraq and Kuwait were 5.12 percent and 5.93 percent respectively, less than half the rates for Saudi Arabia and Iran. Indeed, a U.S. State Department memorandum in 1964 supported the Iraqi contention that IPC had been using Iraqi oil production as a control mechanism to regulate the world market rather than increasing Iraqi production for the benefit of Iraq.

The question of control of production and prices also affected intercompany relations. During 1943–1945, Aramco (Arabian-American Oil Company) of Saudi Arabia, owned jointly by Standard of California and Texaco, had been frustrated by the other U.S. majors in its efforts to obtain U.S. government support in building a pipeline from Saudi Arabia to the eastern Mediterranean, or even a refinery in Saudi Arabia. It found itself with an abundance of oil from the fabulous new Saudi resources. Two options were open to the partners: either underprice the oil and develop new markets, or unite with the other U.S. majors who had markets but were supposedly short of oil supplies. One member of the Board of Directors of Standard of California favored the first alternative. He believed that the two original owners of Aramco, whose marketing outlet was Caltex, could build up world markets by lowering the price (production cost was less than ten cents a barrel). From this proposal it is obvious that Aramco was not then a member of the international cartel.[1] However, the other U.S. companies exerted pressure on the board, and in 1946 Standard of New Jersey and Standard of New York were permitted to buy shares of 30 percent and 10 percent, respectively, of Aramco. They paid very handsomely for their 40 percent share in the company. It has been suggested that the interlocking financial interests of both Standard of New Jersey and Standard of California brought about the merger.

For the two new companies to join Aramco they had to break out of the restriction of the Red Line agreement. At first it looked as if there would be an open row among the international companies. Some of the other IPC members sued the two U.S. companies in a British court. Apparently, to avoid washing their dirty linen in public the plaintiffs withdrew their complaint, and the companies were permitted to join Aramco. The Red Line agreement died. Intra-Aramco company difficulties, however, soon developed. It appeared that the new companies did not need as much oil as they had appeared to need at first. Their primary purpose in buying into Aramco had been to prevent the original partners of Aramco from selling their oil in the international market below market price. Aramco operated as a nonprofit company; the two members were charged production costs and made royalty payments to the Saudi government. The new partners insisted that Aramco become a profit-making concern and charge members the going price of oil. The profits would then be divided among the partners according to their equity shares. The newcomers were underlifters, that is, they lifted less than their percentage share in the company, for they were not in great need of additional oil supplies. The original partners became overlifters, lifting more than their equity shares. Yet, the division of profits was according to equity shares. The newcomers' profit shares were greater than the original partners at the expense of the latter. This situation created constant friction between the partners, even after 1951, when the 50/50 profit-sharing arrangement between the producers and the companies was instituted.

Through the merger of Socal-Texaco with Exxon-Mobil (formerly Standard of New Jersey and Standard of New York), all four of these major U.S. companies became integral members of the international oil cartel. In 1952 the U.S. Federal Trade Commission staff report, *The International Petroleum Cartel*, revealed the existence of this international cartel, in violation of U.S. antitrust laws. On the basis of this report the U.S.

Justice Department in 1953 instituted criminal proceedings
against the U.S. companies through a grand jury investigation.

THE STRUGGLE BETWEEN
THE PRODUCERS AND THE COMPANIES

The concessions granted by the producers to the foreign companies were very broad and sweeping, covering countrywide
areas and granting extraordinary privileges, facilities, and advantages. In return, the oil-producing countries received rather
limited benefits in the form of either 16 percent of the profits
or 4 to 6 shillings per ton of oil produced. The differences in
general knowledge and development, political experience and
maturity, economic and financial resources between the awarders
of the concessions and the receivers determined both the nature
and contents of the contracts and relations between the two
groups. The foreign companies possessed the technical ability
to develop the industry; they had the financial means to operate
and expand it; they owned the refining and transportation
facilities and the markets to dispose of the oil produced; they
had the best legal advice; and they had powerful home governments, which in some cases were partners in the undertakings,
to back and protect them. The countries that granted the
concessions possessed, at first, neither technical knowledge,
financial resources, refining and transportation facilities, nor
markets for the products; above all, they had no political or
other power to back up their demands. The inevitable result
was total and exclusive control of the industry by the foreign
oil companies.

The history of relations between the oil-producing countries
and the concessionaire companies was of a struggle between
the two, the nature of which, over the decades, was determined
by the progress made by the producing countries in the areas
listed above. When, for instance, Shah Riza of Iran compre-
hended the contents of the concession granted by his prede-
cessors, he pressed the Anglo-Persian Oil Company for modi-
fication of the concession. In 1931, when negotiations with the

company failed, he cancelled the original concession but did not nationalize the oil industry. Finally, better terms were offered that limited to some extent the powers and privileges of the company, and the Shah issued a new concession. Between 1933 and 1973, the oil-producing countries made greater demands, and with the changes in world political, economic, and financial conditions, the oil companies conceded new and better terms to the oil-producing countries.

Equal Profit Sharing

An important milestone in the struggle between the oil companies and the oil-producing countries was reached in the early 1950s. The postwar aspirations of the small and newly established nations for greater importance and power encouraged the oil-producing countries to increase their demands. At the same time, the Marshall Plan for the rehabilitation of Europe and Japan had increased tremendously the demand for Middle East oil, a major element in the plan. The result was a new pattern of payments for oil: a 50/50 profit-sharing arrangement between the companies and the producers.

The chain of events that led to this far-reaching change reveals the relations of the major U.S. oil companies with the U.S. government and the tactics used by the companies to gain their ends. The major U.S. oil company operating in the Middle East was the Arabian-American Oil Company (Aramco), which owned the concession in Saudi Arabia—the largest oil-rich concession in the world. From 1941 to 1943, Aramco had successfully convinced the U.S. government of the vital importance of the Saudi Arabian concession to the national interest and security of the United States and its allies. So thorough was the job done by the Aramco representatives that the United States was ready—indeed, anxious and determined—to take over the entire concession. At this, of course, the company stopped short, and the U.S. government was powerless to force the company's hand.

Ever since the beginning of the competition between the Soviet Union and the West for the control of the Middle East, even as long ago as during World War II, the State Department had been working hand in hand with the oil companies. On September 11, 1950, the State Department invited the major U.S. oil companies to discuss means of stabilizing U.S. oil operations in the Middle East in view of the rapidly increasing threat of Communist aggression. Company representatives were handed a policy paper that concluded with the assertion that the U.S. oil companies played a vital role in the achievement of U.S. foreign policy objectives. Royalty payments by the companies to the oil-producing countries provided the economic base for the stability of the Gulf oil states and guaranteed the oil supply on which the economic, political, and strategic security of Europe depended. The State Department urged the companies to sweeten the financial terms of their contracts with the Middle Eastern governments in order to keep their concessions.

In order to facilitate this role of the oil companies in U.S. foreign policy, new agreements would have to meet the demands of both the oil-producing countries and the oil companies and also free the U.S. government from the need to extend direct aid to those countries. How to do this was obvious—increase oil-company payments to the producing countries. Existing payments were in the form of royalties that were reported as expenses on the oil companies' U.S. income-tax returns. Should Saudi Arabia, for example, impose an income tax on the companies, it would receive a much higher revenue and the companies could then receive foreign-tax credit, dollar for dollar, on their U.S. tax returns. The only loser in this arrangement would be the U.S. taxpayer; this even the State Department admitted.

Article 21 of the 1933 Saudi Arabian concession provided that the company (Aramco) and its operations were to be exempt from all direct and indirect taxation. For Aramco, therefore, agreeing to an income tax would be surrendering this established right. Moreover, the possibility that "a change in the United States income tax law might reduce the privilege of deducting such a tax as a foreign tax credit,"[2] could place Aramco in a difficult position, as Saudi Arabia would surely resent any corresponding reduction in an established tax. Aramco was not ready to give up its rights without obtaining an ironclad guarantee that it would be fully protected. However, the U.S. government was apparently determined to change the royalty system to an income-tax system. In 1948, with the approval of the U.S. ambassador, a Treasury Department official (sent to Saudi Arabia to advise on monetary policies) explained to Saudi officials the difference between royalty and income tax.

Meanwhile, negotiations continued between the State Department and Aramco representatives. Aramco expressed doubts and hesitation, but the State Department urged acceptance of the new policy. The issue came before the National Security Council. Former assistant secretary of state for Near Eastern affairs, George McGhee, testified: "The Department, through the National Security Council, made known its views on the overall political situation, and in the Council the U.S. policy was put together which led the Treasury Department to making the tax credit concession."[3] On December 30, 1950, Aramco agreed to give Saudi Arabia a 50/50 profit-sharing tax.

The immediate results of this move were summarized by the Senate Subcommittee on Multinational Corporations: "In 1950, Aramco paid the United States $50 million in income taxes; in 1951, the company paid only $6 million. Conversely, payments to the Saudis increased from $66 million in 1950 to almost $110 million in 1951. In 1952, the net tax paid by Aramco to the United States Treasury amounted to less than $1 million. In each of the years since that time the credit has completely offset United States income tax."[4] Subsequently, all the other Middle Eastern oil-producing countries adopted the income-tax system. The British and other home governments adopted the policy of giving foreign-tax credits in order to maintain the competitive positions of their oil companies.

In 1957 and again in 1966 the foreign-tax-credit practice of the U.S. companies was challenged by some members of Congress, who requested that the Internal Revenue Service audit the tax returns of the oil companies. Since 1957 the realized price of oil has been much lower than the posted price; but the tax credit was based on the higher and artificial posted price. This system, according to the Senate subcommittee, "cost the U.S. Treasury billions of dollars in revenues, and has permitted the major multinational oil companies to pay the lowest average rate of U.S. income taxes for any major industrial grouping."[5] In 1972, the percentage of their worldwide net income paid in U.S. taxes by the major oil companies was: Exxon 6.5 percent, Texaco 1.7 percent, Mobil 1.3 percent, Gulf 1.2 percent, and Socal 2.1 percent.

In 1966, Secretary of State Dean Rusk and John J. McCloy, attorney for the five major oil companies, met to discuss the request for an audit of the tax returns of the companies at which time McCloy reminded the secretary of the foreign policy rationale of the foreign-tax-credit arrangement. On January 11, 1967, McCloy wrote a letter to Rusk that excellently summarized the issues and motivation of the companies. He declared,

> I believe that the Department of State has a particular responsibility to make known to the Treasury Department the implication of its proposed attack on crude oil prices because the present system of providing substantial revenues to the oil producing countries of the Middle East by means of a combination of royalties and of local income taxes of the producing countries (creditable under U.S. tax law) was recommended to the oil companies and to the foreign governments involved by the Department of State and the Treasury Department. These departments recognized that it was in the national interest of the United States to keep such nations stable and friendly to the United States and thereby ensure American access to the vast oil resources there located. If the oil companies did not provide the necessary revenues by paying substantial taxes to producing countries large amounts of direct foreign aid might well be required.[6]

The Iranian Nationalization

The next step in the struggle between the oil-producing countries and the concessionaire companies was the nationalization of the oil industry in Iran. On March 15, 1951, the Iranian Majlis enacted a single-article nationalization law; on April 30, it passed the nine-article Enabling Law that provided for the implementation of nationalization.

From the very beginning the British and the U.S. governments approached the problem of nationalization differently. The British were determined to protect their contractual rights and refused to recognize nationalization, even in principle; they were ready to use every means at their command to force the Iranians to restore the rights of the Anglo-Iranian Oil Company. The measures taken by the Iranians and the countermeasures taken by the British brought the oil industry in Iran to a total standstill. The Iranians put the entire oil industry on strike, shut down the Abadan refinery, and decided to confiscate all company properties in Iran. The British stopped payment of royalties, threatened to take the case to international court, withdrew their tankers, and withdrew their personnel from the refinery.

Economic conditions in Iran rapidly deteriorated; a total collapse was a possibility. Fearing a Soviet penetration, the United States resolved to bring about a compromise solution based, on the one hand, on recognition by the Anglo-Iranian Oil Company of the nationalization as a sovereign act and, on the other hand, on reactivation of the oil industry following recognition by Iran of its contractual obligations to the company, including compensation for nationalization. It soon became evident that neither the Iranians nor the British were ready to compromise. The U.S. government began to explore possibilities of enlisting the major U.S. oil companies in a joint venture with Anglo-Iranian to restore the Iranian oil industry.

When the Iranians sought other oil companies to sell the oil, the major U.S. companies had refused to purchase any. Indeed, the U.S. companies were determined to cooperate with Anglo-Iranian in its efforts to prevent the Iranians from selling oil that the British company considered its property. They warned potential buyers that they would be taken to court for buying stolen property. The U.S. majors feared the consequences to their own concessions in the area should Iran succeed in its nationalization attempt. The U.S. government, on the other hand, saw in the U.S. companies the very heart of a possible solution. On October 8, 1952, Secretary of State Dean Acheson met with the secretaries of defense and the treasury, the attorney general, and the chairman of the Joint Chiefs of Staff and outlined a plan for solving the Iranian problem. He stressed from the outset that no one other than the U.S. majors and

Anglo-Iranian had sufficient tankers to move the large quantities of Iranian oil. The main concern of the United States was to integrate Iranian oil into the world markets, to restore Iran's economic health and prevent chaos from overtaking the country.

At this point, the attorney general, James P. MacGranery, reminded those present that at issue was the antitrust laws violation with which the majors had been charged in the Federal Trade Commission's 1952 report. Nevertheless, on November 16, 1952, President Harry S. Truman ordered Secretary Acheson to proceed with his approach to finding a solution to the Iranian problem. The State and Justice departments found themselves on opposite sides of the issue. For the Justice Department, in question were the charges against the U.S. majors in the Federal Trade Commission's report, as well as the possibility of additional violation of U.S. antitrust laws in the proposed cooperation of the British and U.S. companies for the disposal of Iranian oil. Justice Department officials proceeded with a grand jury investigation of the major U.S. oil companies as members of the international oil cartel. On January 9, 1953, the issue came before the National Security Council. The departments of State, Defense, and Interior presented a position paper and recommended that the grand jury investigation be terminated.

The paper argued that Middle East oil supply was important to the free world both in times of peace and in times of war; it stressed the proximity of the Soviet Union to the Middle East and the danger involved: "The Middle East comprises one of the most explosive areas of the world." The paper maintained that the economic aspect of the rate of oil production was the means of maintaining stability there. Because the rate and terms in question were, to a large extent, under the control of the oil companies operating in the area, the "American oil operations are, for all practical purposes, instruments of our foreign policy toward these countries." Because the U.S. companies supplied oil to Europe, they were also critical to the situation in Europe. In summarizing the position paper, the Senate Subcommittee on Multinational Corporations said: "Because of their role as an instrument of our foreign policy both in Europe and the Middle East, any attack on our oil companies would be viewed in those areas as a fundamental attack on the whole American system." The position paper stated: "We cannot afford to leave unchallenged the assertion that these companies are engaged in criminal conspiracy for the purposes of predatory exploration."[7] It urged that the criminal investigation be dropped and a civil suit be instituted. Criminal investigation by the grand jury could jeopardize the cooperative relationship that existed between the State Department and the oil companies. The issue for the National Security Council was no longer Iran, but the criminal investigation of the international oil cartel.

The Department of Justice opposed dropping the criminal proceedings and advanced its arguments. It maintained that a civil suit would be inadequate and concluded that "the cartel should be prosecuted criminally if there is to be equal justice under the law and if respect for the law and its even-handed administration is to be maintained."[8] The decision was now in the hands of the president. On January 11, President Truman invited representatives of the State and Justice departments and told them that he wanted the grand jury investigation terminated and the case pursued in the civil courts. Justice thereupon dropped the grand jury proceedings and instituted a civil complaint on April 21, 1953. This resounding victory for the major U.S. oil companies was presented to them by the State Department in its efforts to involve them in its policy objectives in Iran.

But the Iranian plan was itself a violation of the antitrust laws. On August 6, 1953, at the request of President Eisenhower, the National Security Council asked the attorney general to find a solution to the Iranian problem in the following explicit terms: "It will be assumed that the enforcement of the antitrust laws of the United States against the Western oil companies operating in the Near East may be deemed secondary to the national security interests to be served by: (1) Assuring the continued availability to the free world of the sources of petroleum in the Near East, and (2) Assuring continued friendly relations between the oil producing nations of the Near East and the nations of the free world."[9] The State Department, however, was apparently not willing to entrust a primarily political task to the legal department of the government and persuaded the National Security Council, on October 27, to revoke the directive to the attorney general. The task was given to Herbert Hoover, Jr., who was appointed by the president as special assistant to Secretary of State John Foster Dulles; Hoover was to act as a special representative of the U.S. government to deal with the problems related to the Iranian crisis.

Hoover enlisted the assistance of the five major U.S. oil companies already operating in the Middle East (Mobil, Exxon, Texaco, Socal, and Gulf). His scheme, in which they would take part in an international consortium with Anglo-Iranian, Royal Dutch–Shell, and Compagnie Française des Petroles, would guarantee necessary income for the shah, would prevent a price war in Europe, and would assure an outlet for Iranian crude. But the cooperation of the U.S. companies was hampered by the cartel suit pending against them, as well as the nature of the proposal, another possible violation of the antitrust laws. When the chairman of the Board of Directors of Anglo-Iranian invited the major U.S. oil companies to join the consortium, Orville Harden, vice-president of Standard of New Jersey, sent a letter to the secretary of state informing him of the invitation and asking him for his advice about accepting. In his letter, Harden stressed that "from the strictly commercial viewpoint, our Company has no particular interest in entering such a group, but we are very conscious of the large national security interests involved. We, therefore, are prepared to take all reasonable efforts, consistent with the maintenance of a sound legal and moral position, to achieve a solution of the problem."[10] This was a clear request to drop the antitrust charges against the companies, and to remove from the consortium solution any question of antitrust violation. Texaco received the same invitation, and apparently in an effort to bring the Justice Department in line with the State Department, Texaco referred the invitation to the Justice Department for approval. The Justice Department saw in the request an attempt to prevent the attorney general from proceeding with the cartel case.

A meeting between Anglo-Iranian and the U.S. majors took place in London on January 8, 1954, with Hoover present, as requested by the State Department in its approval of the meeting. The U.S. companies, according to the Senate Subcommittee on

Multinational Corporations, "recognized that their bargaining position was very strong."[11] They informed Hoover that "further progress in the London discussions would be prejudiced if while the antitrust phases were being explored, the pending suit against them was actively pressed."[12] Hoover thereupon pressed Washington for a swift resolution of the antitrust issues. His urging that the U.S. government approve the consortium was interpreted by the subcommittee as a warning that if the attorney general failed to do so and the consortium fell through, Iran might turn to the Communists for help.[13]

On January 21, 1954, the attorney general advised the president that the consortium plan could be approved because of the National Security Council findings "that the security interests of the United States require that United States oil companies be invited to participate" in the consortium; such participation "would not in itself constitute a violation of antitrust laws, nor create a violation of antitrust laws not already existing."[14] On the same day, the president informed the State Department of the developments in London and of the attorney general's ruling and authorized the secretary of state to inform the U.S. companies. On January 28, the State Department notified the five major companies of the decisions of the National Security Council and of the president. On August 15, 1954, the consortium agreement was signed with Iran, which accepted the consortium because it recognized the Iranian nationalization of the oil industry and guaranteed the industry's reactivation and thus the flow of royalties.

With the State Department as their advocate, the major U.S. oil companies succeeded in establishing their oil concessions and their operations in the Middle East as an integral part of U.S. national security and foreign policy. The determination of the State Department to reactivate the Iranian oil industry and to prevent Iran from falling into the hands of the Soviet Union, gave the U.S. major oil companies the means of forcing the Justice Department to change the cartel charges against them from criminal to civil. By the same tactics the companies maneuvered to force the Justice Department to approve the consortium plan and free it from allegations of antitrust violation.

The international consortium solution was practically an annulment of the Iranian nationalization. Foreign companies, especially Anglo-Iranian (now called British Petroleum—BP), continued to run the industry. A 50/50 profit-sharing arrangement had been offered Iran before nationalization and was now the universal practice of the region. Nevertheless, the nationalization experience must be considered a very important advance in the struggle of the producers with the companies. The oil industry became the property of Iran, and the consortium was operating it in the name of the National Iranian Oil Company (NIOC). Emotionally it was a great victory for Iran. Although nationalization was premature under the circumstances, and may have even deterred other oil-producing countries from attempting it, it was an important milestone in the long struggle.

OPEC

In spite of the nationalization of the oil industry in Iran and its consequences, the period from 1951 to 1960 may be considered as the best in the relations between the producers and the companies. Whatever the motivation for the 50/50 profit-sharing agreements, the governments of the oil-producing countries received very large increases in their revenues. Moreover, the demand for oil rose very sharply, from a total production of 87 million tons in 1950 to 228 million tons in 1959. Most of the Middle East's economic development programs, to be financed from oil income, were inaugurated during this decade, and previously established programs were expanded. It seemed not only that the companies were satisfied with the new arrangements, but also that the producing countries were happy with their newfound riches.

However, a number of developments began seriously to upset the existing patterns. In order to protect its domestic oil industry, the United States introduced an oil import quota system—at first voluntary and later mandatory—which drastically curtailed oil imports. This was a very serious blow to the Middle East oil-producing countries, as the United States was a major market for Middle East oil, after Europe. Another factor, not of great magnitude in itself but nevertheless contributing to the cumulative drop in the demand for Middle East oil, was a considerable increase in Soviet oil exports, at below-market prices. At the same time the Italian oil company ENI (Ente Nazionale Idrocarburi) joined the international oil market in addition to many independent oil companies, who penetrated the supply sources and brought down the price of oil.

In order to maintain their dominant positions in the European and Japanese oil markets, the established international major oil companies began to cut their profits. At first they offered heavy discounts from the posted price, as high as 40 percent. Because the 50 percent share of the producers was based on the posted price, the companies' profit share shrank significantly although part of the loss was recovered in a special allowance from the posted price. When the discounts offered by the companies became too burdensome they resorted to cutting the posted price unilaterally. The first cut—of eighteen cents a barrel, about a 10 percent decrease in the income of the producers—was announced by British Petroleum on January 13, 1959; the other companies followed suit. On August 8, 1960, Standard Oil Company of New Jersey announced a second cut of ten cents a barrel, which amounted to a 6 percent loss of revenue to the producers.

Although the producing countries were affected, the individual producers felt helpless against the companies. Venezuela, the original model for the 50/50 profit-sharing pattern, took the initiative in inviting the Middle East producers to restrict production in order to maintain the original price. Such a move required that the producers organize and operate as a cartel. Although not yet ready to reduce production, for they were determined to increase output and thus augment revenue, the Middle East oil producers were ready to unite and force the companies to restore the price that had prevailed before the cuts. The major producers and Venezuela met in Baghdad on September 10–14, 1960, and established the Organization of Petroleum Exporting Countries (OPEC).

The immediate aims of the new organization were: (1) to restore the price of crude oil to what it had been before the cuts, and (2) to prevent the companies from changing prices unilaterally. It failed in the first aim, for objective conditions made it impossible for the producing countries to force the companies to restore prices. As for the second aim, there was a tacit understanding that the companies would consult with the producers before making any further changes in posted price. It should be emphasized that from the very beginning OPEC was not a political organization and had no political objectives. It was an organization with economic aims—to help the members obtain the best possible terms and greater revenue for their oil from the concessionaire companies. It refused to resort to controlled production. Although OPEC was often described as a cartel, it could not and did not operate as a cartel. Its members were all sovereign countries, and the organization had no executive power and could not force members to act against their wills.

During the first decade of its existence, OPEC obtained for its members some concessions from the companies. It reduced their contribution to the sales promotion fund (the companies had deducted .5 percent of the posted price toward the fund for promotion of oil sales). It established the principle that royalties were to be considered an expense rather than a part of the 50/50 profit share of the producers. Under the original arrangement a government's 50 percent share of the profits had consisted of two parts: 12.5 percent of posted price as royalty and the balance of up to 50 percent of the profits; the royalty was part of the 50 percent. In 1964, the companies agreed to consider the royalty as part of the production cost, to be paid to the governments in addition to the 50 percent of the profits. For example, if the posted price of a barrel of oil was $2 and cost of production $1, the net profit was $1. Under expensed royalty a government would receive 25 cents as royalty, leaving a clear profit of 75 cents. The government would then receive 37.5 cents of this for a total take of 62.5 cents, whereas the company share would be only 37.5 cents. OPEC also succeeded in gradually reducing the percentage discount from the posted price. It failed, however, to achieve the major objective of restoring prices to what they had been before the 1959 and 1960 price cuts.

The Role of Libya

After the 1946 Aramco merger embracing the four major oil companies (Socal, Texaco, Standard of New Jersey, Standard of New York), the major international oil companies were in firm control of the world oil industry and markets. Gulf Oil Corporation owned 50 percent of the Kuwait concession, Anglo-Iranian owned the entire Iranian concession and the other 50 percent of the Kuwait concession, and a U.S., Dutch, French, and British partnership owned the Iraq Petroleum Company and its affiliates. When in 1954 the International Iranian Consortium was established, the majors' hold on the world market became even stronger. In 1962, however, Libya, a newcomer to the oil-producing community, disturbed the domination of the international companies by introducing a new pattern of concession awarding. Libya granted small concession areas, rather than countrywide territories, to a great variety of companies. Intentionally and methodically, the concessions—eighty-four in number—were balanced between majors (54 percent) and independents (46 percent).

In order to attract oil companies, Libya based the tax-rate payments on realized prices rather than on posted prices. The cost of Libyan oil to the companies was therefore lower than oil from the Gulf area. In the same year Libya joined OPEC; two years later, in November 1964, the Libyan government decreed that the basis for calculating the tax payment was to be the posted price. Most of the majors, after some bickering, agreed to pay the tax based on the posted price. Libyan oil was only a small portion of their total supplies, and they could easily absorb the extra cost. The independents, for whom Libyan oil was the major, if not only, source of their supply, resisted the Libyan demand. Indeed, they charged the majors with deliberately acceding to Libya's demands in order to eliminate them, the independents, from the European market. But in the end, the independents had no choice but to agree to Libya's decree. Libya's achievement was, no doubt, a victory for OPEC because it revealed the helplessness of the companies when they were being played one group against another. This technique ultimately developed into a "leapfrogging" pattern of successfully achieving victories over the companies (in which Libya and the Gulf producers successively raised their demands).

The majors soon began to feel the impact of Libya's production growth on their relations with the two giant producers in the Gulf area: Saudi Arabia and Iran. As Libya's share of the European market grew, especially through the supply of the independents, the exports of Saudi Arabia and Iran to Europe were proportionately reduced. By 1965 Libya's daily production reached 1.2 million barrels. In 1966 Occidental Petroleum Corporation of California, an independent and a newcomer to the international oil market, obtained a very valuable concession in Libya, arousing bitter resentment among the established Libyan oil companies. By 1969 Occidental was the largest producer in Libya. The company planned to produce a million barrels a day. During the following five years the share of the majors in Libya fell from 54 percent to 45 percent, while the total daily production of the country jumped to over 3 million barrels. In August 1969 Libya opened negotiations with the oil companies to raise the posted price by ten cents a barrel. Then, on September 1, King Idris was deposed and Libya was taken over by a revolutionary group headed by Muammar Qaddafi.

• Libya immediately launched a pressure campaign against the oil companies. It demanded high increases in the posted price and made other requests, including an increment in the tax rate. To overcome the collective resistance of the companies, the government refused to deal with the companies as a group, and in February 1970 it began separate negotiations with Occidental and Exxon. After three months of fruitless negotiations, Qaddafi threatened the companies with unilateral action, but the companies continued to hold out. Libya then ordered cuts in production rates as a pressure tactic, although officially the cuts were explained as a conservation measure, not connected with the government demands. The first to suffer a cut in production, as had no doubt been expected, was Occidental, the most vulnerable, whose 800,000 barrels in daily output was reduced to 500,000. This was followed by cuts in the production rates of the other independents, and then cuts were also ordered for the majors.

From time to time Libya stopped the negotiations, accompanied by deadline warnings to accept the government demands or face a total shutdown of production. Yet the ultimata were always postponed. On July 10, 1970, in order to stand up to Libya, Occidental asked Exxon for help with replacement oil, at little more than cost. Exxon refused. The Libyan government was apparently aware of the growing tension between the majors and the independents and decided to press Occidental harder. It ordered a further cut of 60,000 barrels, down to 440,000. Total Libyan daily production was reduced from 3.6 million to 2.8 million barrels. Caught between Qaddafi's demands and Exxon's refusal, Occidental capitulated. On September 4, Qaddafi announced that the government had signed an agreement with Occidental that provided for an increase of thirty cents per barrel in the posted price, a two-cent annual increase for a period of five years, and a tax-rate increase to 58 percent. In return, Libya permitted Occidental to increase production from 440,000 to 700,000 barrels a day. Most of the other companies operating in Libya signed similar agreements.

Before the U.S. majors submitted to Libya's demands, they turned to the State Department for advice. James E. Akins, director of the Office of Fuels and Energy, stated that Libya was justified and reasonable in its demands and that the companies' resistance to the Libyan demands was unwarranted. He feared that if the U.S. companies did not meet Libya's terms, the Europeans would be ready to accede to them, and the oil would be nationalized—"the Anglo-Saxon oil companies' sojourn in Libya would have ended."[15]

Libya's achievement in increasing the posted price and raising the tax rate—even though the raise in tax was considered compensation for the lower posted price during the time since the government had made its demand—undermined established patterns in Gulf area oil. The reaction of the other producers was inevitable. The Libyan victory was an important stride forward in the long struggle with the companies and became a major factor in the next crucial battle between the producers and the companies.

The Teheran and Tripoli Agreements

The most critical if not revolutionary battle in the struggle between the producers and the companies resulted in the Teheran agreement of February 1971 and the Tripoli agreement of April 1971. As soon as the results of the Libyan victory became known, the Gulf area producers began to agitate for higher posted prices and for greater tax-rate percentages. Early in December 1970, OPEC met in Caracas and passed resolutions calling for a tax rate of 55 percent for all member states, higher posted prices, and eliminations of discounts from posted prices. OPEC set up the Gulf subcommittee and demanded that negotiations with the companies should begin in Teheran within a month. The Gulf committee was to report back to OPEC not later than seven days after the conclusion of the negotiations.

On January 2, 1971, even before negotiations between the Gulf committee and the oil companies commenced, the Libyan government requested new large increases in the posted price (above those obtained in September 1970), a further tax increase, a larger freight premium, and a stated amount per every barrel produced to be invested by the companies within Libya. This time, all the companies—majors and independents—were prepared to stand together against the government. All the companies operating in Libya entered into the Libyan Producers Agreement, which provided that if the Libyan Government forced any company to cut production, as a pressure tactic the others would replace the oil. All the companies were determined to refuse to negotiate separately; negotiations would have to be with all as a group. In such an action the U.S. companies would be subject to prosecution for violating U.S. antitrust laws. This problem was solved on January 9 when the assistant attorney general issued business review letters to the companies saying that the Department of Justice "does not presently intend to institute proceedings under the antitrust laws."[16] The companies then dispatched a message to OPEC stating the conditions of the negotiations.

In the middle of January, representatives of the major companies and their attorney, John McCloy, suggested that the State

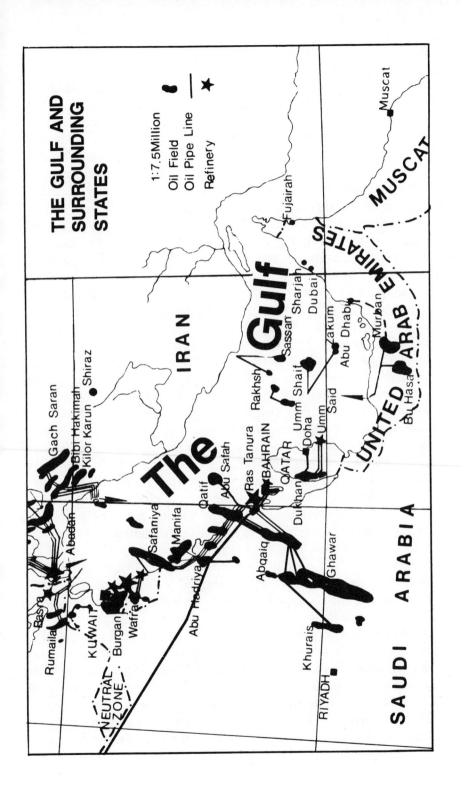

THE GULF AND SURROUNDING STATES

1:7.5Million

Oil Field

Oil Pipe Line

Refinery

Department might want to send a high-ranking diplomat to deal with the heads of government in the Middle East and thus indicate the U.S. government's interest in the issues. Under Secretary John Irwin was designated to visit the countries involved, his mission authorized by President Richard Nixon. Irwin's tasks were (1) to prevent an interruption of oil supplies; (2) to explain the reasons for the measures easing U.S. antitrust laws so that the companies could negotiate jointly; and (3) to seek assurances from the Gulf producers that they would continue to supply oil at reasonable prices to the free world. The emphasis, even at this stage, was on supplies; fear apparently persisted that there was a danger of interruption, if not total stoppage of the flow of oil to the Western world. The companies, for their part, set up a negotiating team in Teheran and two policy groups, one in London and one in New York, composed of senior executives to advise and guide the negotiations. Neither State Department nor Justice Department representatives sat in on these policy group meetings. The companies were asking for global negotiations with all OPEC members collectively and opposed separate negotiations with the Gulf group. In addition, the companies expected to negotiate as a group and not as individuals; the independents were to stand firm against pressure, for they would have the backing of the Libyan Producers Agreement. Under Secretary Irwin, in his diplomatic visits, was to back up the companies' insistence on global negotiations.

But this elaborate setup failed at its first test. Irwin arrived in Teheran on January 17 and met with the shah and his finance minister. The shah told Irwin that the companies' demand to deal with OPEC as a whole would offend the organization members; they would take the demand as a sign of bad faith. If, however, the companies agreed to negotiate separately with the Gulf group, the Gulf group was prepared to sign an agreement not to seek new terms if oil producers in other areas obtained better terms from the companies. In other words, no leapfrogging. Irwin accepted the shah's assurances that the Gulf group would not be influenced by whatever deal was negotiated with Libya. With the approval of the U.S. ambassador in Teheran, Irwin reported to the State Department that he was encouraging the companies to sign separately with the Gulf group. Secretary of State William Rogers endorsed the Irwin recommendation and informed McCloy accordingly. The State Department thus abandoned its support of the companies' message to OPEC stating that the companies would negotiate only on a global basis. Irwin and the State Department actually destroyed the elaborate plan of the companies (which had initially been supported by the State and Justice departments). This reversal of tactics was not lost on OPEC and made it more determined than ever to follow through with its demands.

In the State Department retreat, it would seem that the oil companies became victims of their own manipulations. Their main means of obtaining support and concessions from the U.S. government had been to play on the fear that the producing countries would cut off supplies to Europe and Japan and thus endanger the Western world exposing the Middle East as well as Europe to the Communist danger. This ploy had always worked. Therefore, when Irwin was told by the shah and the U.S. ambassador in Teheran that there was a real danger of OPEC cutting off supplies to the Western companies, he disregarded the carefully elaborated scheme and urged the companies to negotiate separately with the Gulf group. The companies could not repudiate their own repeated warnings and accepted the Irwin advice.

The oil companies tried a new tactic: "separate but necessarily connected" negotiations. They would have two teams negotiating simultaneously, one in Teheran and one in Tripoli and so prevent leapfrogging. But Libya was not going to be out-smarted and insisted that it would negotiate only after the Teheran negotiations were concluded. Their new scheme having failed, the companies tried another. In the negotiations with the Gulf group, they sought to commit Saudi Arabia and Iraq to their oil outlets through both the Gulf and the eastern Mediterranean, thus linking the two groups together and preventing Libya from demanding special considerations. However, the Gulf committee refused to include the eastern Mediterranean oil outlets in the negotiations. The companies were forced to negotiate on the terms dictated to them by the OPEC Gulf committee.

On February 14, 1971, an agreement between the Gulf group and the companies operating in the area was signed. Valid for five years, through December 31, 1975, the settlement provided that none of the Gulf countries should seek to obtain the more advantageous terms that might be negotiated by other states. Agreed upon were an immediate increase in the posted price of thirty cents a barrel, escalating to fifty cents by 1975 (five cents each year); a raise in the tax rate to 55 percent; and an additional 2.5 percent annual increment in the posted price to compensate for inflation and devaluation. It was estimated that added revenue to the Gulf group countries would be $1.4 billion in 1971 over 1970 and that the total increase of producer-government oil income for the five-year period would reach $11.7 billion. As justification for signing the agreement, the State Department, the president of the United States, and the oil companies all advanced stability, orderliness, and durability of oil supplies and prices during the coming five years. Yet on January 20, even before the agreement was signed, the Saudi Arabian oil minister, Ahmad Zaki Yamani, told Exxon's George T. Piercy, chief negotiator in Teheran, that he was not sure there would be five years of stability of oil supply and price.

The oil companies now turned to Tripoli for negotiations with the Mediterranean group, which consisted of Algeria, Iraq, and Saudi Arabia (for their eastern Mediterranean outlets), and Libya. Algeria, Iraq, and Saudi Arabia authorized Libya to negotiate in their behalf. After a tense and prolonged session filled with threats, interruptions, and ultimata, repeating practically the tale of 1970, the companies submitted their proposal, which was rejected by the Libyan negotiator who in turn submitted counterproposals. On March 15 the Libyan negotiator announced that unless the companies agreed to his terms by the set date, oil pumping in Libya would be totally stopped. Thus, agreements between the Mediterranean group governments and most of the operating companies were signed on April 2, 1971. The agreements were to be retroactively effective as of March 20, 1971, and five years in duration. They provided for posted prices to be increased ninety cents a barrel, from $2.55 to $3.45 (including the freight premium); an annual five-cent increase in posted prices; an additional annual 2.5 percent increase in price to compensate for inflation and devaluation; the tax rate to be raised to 55 percent (Occidental, 60 percent); and a surcharge of between eight and eleven cents a barrel for past claims. Although Libya failed to obtain a definite per-barrel amount that companies would be committed to invest in oil-industry development, the agreements provided that each company individually would commit itself to a certain minimum level of expenditure on exploration and drilling programs for each of the five years.

The achievement of the Teheran and Tripoli agreements must be marked as the end of an old era and the beginning of a new one in the relations between the producing countries and the concessionaire companies. Not only did the companies concede to all the demands of the producer governments, but the negotiations revealed the growing power, self-confidence, and inflexibility of the governments, whereas the companies appeared weaker and almost helpless. The producers emerged strengthened by their attainments and ready, with ever greater vigor, to continue the struggle to ultimate victory. The companies emerged from their experience rather timid; they realized that their power was rapidly declining. Publicly the companies expressed satisfaction with the agreements, proclaiming that five years of stability of oil supply and price had been guaranteed, but this was a face-saving device. They knew that very soon new demands would be made, and there would be no alternative but to concede to them.

In addition to the general change in the international arena, beginning after World War II, in the relations between the great powers and the small nations, which reinforced the stand of the oil producers, two major factors contributed to the reversal of positions of the producers and the companies. The demand for oil surged forward rapidly throughout the world, and the Middle East was the only source from which the demand could be supplied. The second factor was that in 1970, for the first time in U.S. history, oil production declined; of even greater significance was the very rapid decline in U.S. oil reserves. The Middle East was coming into its own.[17]

NOTES

1. In a Caltex memorandum about Aramco pricing, it was stated that before the Aramco merger, the U.S. government was given assurances that the merger would in no way limit Saudi Arabian production or erect barriers to its free movement in world commerce. On cartels, the memorandum stated: "Texaco and Socal are unalterably opposed to cartels or to the countenancing of circumstances which may give rise to cartels or which would in any way restrict trade." U.S., Congress, Senate, Committee on Foreign Relations, Subcommittee on Multinational Corporations, *Multinational Oil Corporations and U.S. Foreign Policy: Report Together with Individual Views* (Washington, D.C., 1975), p. 179 (hereafter cited as Multinationals Subcommittee, *Report*.

2. Ibid., p. 84.

3. Ibid., p. 85.

4. Ibid.

5. Ibid., p. 92.

6. U.S., Congress, Senate, Committee on Foreign Relations, Subcommittee on Multinational Corporations, *Hearings: Multinational Oil Corporations and United States Foreign Policy*, Part 9 (Washington, D.C., 1975), p. 116 (hereafter cited as Multinationals Subcommittee, *Hearings*).

7. Multinationals Subcommittee, *Report*, p. 62.

8. Ibid., p. 63.

9. Ibid., pp. 65–66.

10. U.S., Congress, Senate, Committee on Foreign Relations, Subcommittee on Multinational Corporations, *The International Petroleum Cartel: The Iranian Consortium and U.S. National Security* (Washington, D.C., 1974), p. 58 (hereafter cited as Multinationals Subcommittee, *International Cartel*).

11. Multinationals Subcommittee, *Report*, p. 68.

12. Multinationals Subcommittee, *International Cartel*, p. 60.

13. Multinationals Subcommittee, *Report*, p. 68.

14. Multinationals Subcommittee, *International Cartel*, p. 75. On September 15, 1954, Kenneth Harkins, an attorney in the antitrust division, had raised with Attorney General Robert Brownell a basic issue of law. He wrote: "If these arrangements are in fact but an extension of the cartel, it seems to me that the expressions of the Attorney General in January, the findings of the National Security

Council as to the security interest of the United States, and the desires of the State Department, are irrelevant to any consideration of the narrow legal issue of whether these arrangements disclose a violation of the antitrust laws which after all is what is now requested in an opinion from the Attorney General." Ibid., p. 91.

15. James E. Akins, "The Oil Crisis: This Time The Wolf Is Here," *Foreign Affairs* 51 (April, 1973), p. 472.

16. Multinationals Subcommittee, *Report*, p. 128.

17. As indicated in the preface, the introductory chapter attempts to elucidate, complete, and reevaluate some of the basic issues and analyses that have come to light in the multifarious congressional committees' investigations and reports. The major sources for Chapter 1 were: U.S., Congress, Senate, Committee on Finance, *World Oil Developments and U.S. Oil Import Policy* (Washington, D.C., 1973); U.S., Congress, Senate, Committee on Foreign Relations, Subcommittee on Multinational Corporations, *Chronology of the Libyan Oil Negotiations 1970-1971* (Washington, D.C., 1974); Multinationals Subcommittee, *Hearings*, Parts 4, 6, 7, 8, 9; Multinationals Subcommittee, *International Cartel*; Multinationals Subcommittee, *Report*; John M. Blair, *The Control of Oil* (New York, 1976); and *Foreign Affairs*, 1970-1980.

2

FROM THE TEHERAN
AND TRIPOLI AGREEMENTS
TO THE 1973 CRISIS

The circumstances that set the pattern for the 1971 Teheran and Tripoli agreements inevitably and inexorably led to developments that further deteriorated relations between the oil-producing countries and the concessionaire companies; the producing countries continued to grow stronger at the expense of the companies. The Tripoli agreement provided for a ninety-cent increase in the posted price; this increase was based on a basic increment in price and consideration for the preferred sulphur-light quality of Libyan oil as well as its geographic location. On the basis of the Tripoli Agreement (negotiated by Libya in Iraq's name), Iraq began to discuss with the Iraq Petroleum Company a posted-price increase for the oil of the eastern Mediterranean outlet and also demanded ninety cents. Negotiations dragged on, and on June 7, 1971, a settlement of eighty and one-tenth cents was finally agreed upon, retroactively effective as of March 20. The company was to pay Iraq a lump sum of £20.2 million for past claims; grant a four-year £10-million free loan; and undertake a new commitment to increase production. Iraq was expected to increase its revenue from $512 million in 1970 to $924 million in 1971, rising to $1.137 billion in 1975. The other conditions were the Tripoli terms. Similar negotiations were conducted between Saudi Arabia and Aramco. On June 23, agreement was reached. Posted price, effective as of March, was increased by eighty-one and one-tenth cents a barrel, bringing the price per barrel to $3.18. The other terms were derived from the provisions of the Teheran agreement.

THE MAIN ISSUES:
PARTICIPATION AND DOLLAR DEVALUATION

With the achievements of Teheran and Tripoli, OPEC launched new aims. Less than six months after the Tripoli agreement was signed, OPEC convened on September 22, 1971, in Beirut with two items on the agenda: the dollar devaluation and participation by the producer governments in the foreign con-cessionaire companies. The idea of local sharing in the ex-ploitation companies was an old one in the Middle East and can be traced back to 1912, when the Anglo-Egyptian Oil Fields, a Shell subsidiary, was organized and the Egyptian government was granted a 10 percent equity in the company. The San Remo agreement of April 20, 1920, which determined the Mesopo-tamian oil apportionment, provided that the residents of the territory were to be given the opportunity to acquire up to 20 percent of the concession. This provision was also inserted in the 1925 agreement with the Iraq Petroleum Company, and in 1971 the Iraqi government again raised the 20 percent participation issue with IPC. The original concession that Saudi Arabia granted in May 1933 to Standard Oil Company of California provided that the concessionaire company was to make it possible for Saudi Arabian subjects to buy at least 20 percent of the shares offered to the public. All these provisions, however, were never meant to be implemented. It was only when the producing countries began to gain power over the companies that government participation came up as an OPEC aim. At its June 1968 conference in Vienna, OPEC decided that members should seek participation in the ownership of the concessions. The main advocate of this demand was the Saudi Arabian oil minister, Ahmad Zaki Yamani.

OPEC leaders were not blind to the dangers inherent in the demand of participation. If the percentage demanded were too high, the companies would no doubt resist or might even surrender the concessions altogether, which the producing countries could not operate by themselves. Should the percentage be too small, the producers would be "sleeping" partners without real tangible advance in their aim of controlling the industry. Should the producers be given their percentage share in oil, they would not be able to dispose of it. How were they to pay for their shares? To find answers to all these problems OPEC adopted, at the December 1970 Caracas conference, a secret resolution that nominated the ministers of Iran, Iraq, Saudi Arabia, Kuwait, and Libya as a committee to study the implementation of the participation plan. The OPEC Vienna conference of July 1971 publicly named the participation committee and ordered it to bring recommendations to the conference to be convened in Vienna in September. The extraordinary Vienna September conference adopted two resolutions: One urged members to negotiate individually or in groups with the companies to attain adjustments in payments because of the devaluation of the dollar, an acute issue for the oil-producing countries; the other requested that members institute negotiations with their companies, individually or in groups, to attain participation.

OPEC's reasons for demanding participation were clearly and frankly stated by Nadhim Pachachi, its secretary-general, over Radio Denmark early in October 1971.

⌠ Now all over the world, in Latin America, Africa, Asia and Western Europe, the Governments of oil producing countries no longer accept the role of a sleeping partner; they want to have a direct role in the management of the exploitation of their resources so as to gain know-how and to develop national expertise in the production and marketing of oil. Remember that sooner or later all these concessions will revert to the State when the concession agreements expire. Oil exporting countries have to prepare themselves for assuming the responsibility for the management of the oil industry when the concession agreements expire. Moreover, some of these agreements originally, and specifically, provided for participation in the ownership of the concession by the granting country.[1] ⌡

George T. Piercy, vice-president of Exxon and leader of the Aramco negotiating team in Teheran, speaking in San Francisco on October 26, 1971, declared somewhat formally and timidly that the OPEC demands for participation and for compensation for dollar devaluation were "contrary to the word and the spirit of the five-year agreements so recently negotiated."[2] To this Pachachi promptly replied, challengingly if not derisively: "Really I must confess I was quite shocked by Mr. Piercy's statement. If it is pursued, such a rigid and unflexible stand can only lead to a disastrous deterioration in relations between the oil companies and the OPEC governments. As regards participation, it should be noted that the scope of the Teheran agreement was restricted to two matters: posted prices and the governments' financial take. It in no way touched on participation."[3]

On the issue of dollar devaluation, Libya again spearheaded the battle with the oil companies. In October, while the other OPEC members were discussing the issue with the companies, the U.S. Justice Department was informed by John McCloy, the companies' attorney, that Libya had taken unilateral action, by directives to the companies to make their payments in accordance with the decreed exchange rate. Iran, although it had agreed not to demand terms obtained by other producing countries, now demanded new negotiations. McCloy therefore asked the Justice Department for business review letters. The department issued the letters at the end of October. Twenty-three companies were ready to commence collective discussions. Meeting on December 7, in Abu Dhabi, OPEC decided to institute decisive talks with the companies to take place in Geneva in January 1972. On January 20, the companies met with OPEC. On the issue of the dollar devaluation the companies agreed to increase posted prices by 8.49 percent, with a formula for adjusting the price in future devaluation. This agreement became known as Geneva I. When Libya refused to accept the new arrangement, the companies agreed that the payments to the other producers would be increased to the level of the Libyan settlement.

The tough nut to crack was the issue of participation. Three elements were involved: (1) percentage of participation, (2) basis of payment for the acquired share, and (3) the disposal of the acquired share of the oil. The opinion in OPEC as to share of participation ranged from 20 percent to 51 percent, and some were even advocating a 100 percent ownership; the payment for the share was to be the net book value; and the disposal of the oil was to be accomplished by a system of buyback by the companies from the producers at current prices.

PRODUCERS' GROWING POWER

On December 7, 1971, while negotiations were being conducted, Libya nationalized British Petroleum's assets and rights, because Britain had aided and abetted Iran's occupation of three small islands in the Gulf (Abu Musa, Lesser and Greater Tonbs), which were until the occupation under British protection. In Iraq, the government's relations with the Iraq Petroleum Company had been constantly deteriorating since the 1958 revolution of Abdel Qarim Qasim. Although Qasim declared at the outbreak of the revolution, for very good reasons, that he would respect the rights of the company and that he had no intentions of nationalizing it, he immediately began to press hard. Through government fiat, the concession areas of the company were reduced to less than .5 percent of their original dimensions, and payment terms were made very burdensome. After the Teheran and Tripoli agreements, Iraq negotiated with IPC, together with the other producers, on both dollar devaluation and participation issues. On January 20, 1972, Iraq signed an agreement providing for the 8.49 percent increase in posted price. In line with the other recommendation of OPEC, Iraq demanded participation in IPC, and when the negotiations—mostly led by Saudi Arabia's Yamani—arrived at a 20 percent share, Iraq was willing to accept 20 percent.

However, relations between the company and the Iraqi government rapidly deteriorated. The closure of the Suez Canal after the Six Day War had created difficulties for the company for the oil shipped from Basrah; port cargo dues imposed by the government for oil shipped through Basrah increased the tension between the company and the government. Early in

1972, the government asked for 20 percent participation, and finally, on May 17, 1972, the government presented a number of demands to the company in the form of an ultimatum: Either meet the demands or face nationalization. On June 1, 1972, the IPC was nationalized.[4]

Under these circumstances the discussions on participation were inevitably dragged out and moved from place to place. In New York, on October 5, 1972, under the leadership of the Saudi Arabian oil minister, the oil companies and five producing countries—Saudi Arabia, Kuwait, Qatar, Bahrain, and the UAE (United Arab Emirates)—arrived at an agreement that provided for government participation in the concessionaire companies. Although Yamani had at first pushed for a 20 percent share, an immediate 25 percent share had been agreed upon; the government acquisition was to rise 5 percent in 1979 and 5 percent annually thereafter until 1982, then 6 percent in 1983, reaching 51 percent ownership in the foreign companies. Payments were to be based on updated book value, and the companies were to buy back the major portion of the governments' oil. This was a general agreement, with specific details left to each producer to work out with its companies.

A major division of objectives had emerged among the companies. Aramco partners were determined, especially as the producers' shares would be rising, to have the right to buy back the government oil share in the company so that they would retain control of the oil supply. In order to guarantee for themselves the oil supplies of the near future, the company partners provided budgetary plans to increase production capacity to 13.4 million barrels a day in 1976 and to further expand capacity to reach 20 million barrels a day in 1983. Production of such tremendous quantity would enable Aramco to dominate the world oil supply and the international world markets. For Aramco the buyback guarantee of the government share was the major consideration in the participation negotiations. The Gulf Oil Corporation, whose major oil interest in the area was its 50 percent share in the Kuwait Oil Company, was not interested in the buyback issue. Gulf Oil maintained that the determination of the companies to retain control of the participation oil undermined the companies' position on price. Gulf asked to be released from the collective negotiation and that each company be permitted to work out its own terms. Gulf's position was rejected by the other companies.

Although the original participation agreement had provided price terms for buyback oil, when Aramco company representatives met with Yamani on December 14, 1972, he demanded an immediate increase in the buyback price and gave the companies two weeks to agree to his demand. The producing countries had the upper hand and used it. The Senate Subcommittee on Multinational Corporations observed in its *Report:* "The country negotiations whipsawed the companies with consummate skill. In his conversations with the Aramco team Yamani told the companies again and again that any deal he made could be undone by deals elsewhere. In fact, the producing countries were discovering that they had the option of marketing their own oil directly at prices higher than the major companies were offering. Knowing this, the governments took the position that if the companies wanted to control the crude they would have to pay the governments' dictated price."[5]

Meanwhile, events were occurring that jeopardized the entire participation plan. The Kuwait National Assembly rejected the 25-51 percent 1972 participation plan. Libya demanded from Bunker Hunt Oil Company, British Petroleum's partner, immediate 50 percent participation. Hunt refused and offered instead to negotiate on the same basis as the Gulf companies using the 25-51 percent formula. On June 11, Libya nationalized Hunt's assets. In addition, the dollar devaluation issue came back to complicate relations between the producers and the concessionaires. On February 12, 1973, the United States devalued the dollar by 11.11 percent. In April the companies raised the posted prices in accordance with the January 1972 Geneva formula. The producers refused to accept the increases. After prolonged and hectic discussions, a new agreement was signed in Geneva on June 1, 1973, that provided for an 11.9 percent increase in posted prices with a new formula for future contingencies. This became known as Geneva II.

Although Iran was not involved in the participation issue, for theoretically the Iranian oil industry had been nationalized in 1951, the shah was determined to take advantage of the changed conditions and deprive the international consortium of its privileged position. In the middle of June 1972, the shah announced a new program for his country's oil industry: maximum output, maximum security of supply, and stability of conditions for the period of the existing agreement with the consortium, which was to expire in 1979. After that date, the shah saw far-reaching changes in the terms of operations of the consortium. He demanded that immediate production be increased to 8 million barrels a day; that the National Iranian Oil Company (NIOC) assume greater and direct responsibility in all the branches of the industry, from exploration to marketing; and that NIOC take over the Abadan refinery.

The consortium companies refused the shah's demands. He thereupon announced that, because the companies balked at his demands, when the agreement expired he would not renew it. Should they agree to his terms, however, Iran would be willing to continue supplying oil at special prices for a period of time beyond 1979. While the consortium companies were pondering the choice, the shah announced on March 20, 1973, that the Iranian government had taken over the control and operation of the oil industry; the consortium was forced to transfer operations to NIOC. The consortium surrendered and on the following day signed a new agreement the terms of which were dictated by Iran.

At the same time, negotiations between Aramco and Saudi Arabia made little progress, as the Saudis watched developments in Libya and Iran. In August 1973, Yamani met with Aramco representatives, at the company's request. He called their attention to the fact that the Teheran agreement would have to be renegotiated long before 1975 and the next change would be a huge one, imposed rather than negotiated; should the "wild ones" in OPEC insist on very high prices, the companies would be left with no choice. Yamani concluded by saying, "You will have to improve on the Kuwaiti deal if you are to avoid nationalization and then I'll have something better than Kuwait."[6] Saudi Arabia was apparently gloating on its power over Aramco. Yamani felt that he had the companies where he wanted them and that they would have to dance to his tune. On August 23, when the meeting was resumed, Prince Saud and Yamani's deputy Abdul Hady Taher were also present. Yamani stated that he would not bargain on the buyback price, it would be set by the Petromin third-party sales. He warned the company negotiators, "Don't be surprised if at any moment, I pick up the phone and instruct Brock [Powers] or Frank [Jungers] to cut production to seven million barrels a day"[7] (Powers was chairman of the board of Aramco, Jungers was president).

In Libya, in August 1973, Occidental Petroleum Corporation accepted the government order of 51 percent participation, purchase price to be new net book value. The other independent companies followed Occidental's lead. Libya then decreed 51 percent participation for all major companies as well. The U.S. State Department was greatly disturbed over this confiscatory act and urged the customers of the nationalized companies to refuse to buy oil from the Libyan government. But even a threat by President Richard Nixon to stop buying Libyan oil did not deter Libya, nor did it deter the U.S. customers of the nationalized companies from buying oil from the Libyan government.

Saudi Arabia continued to press Aramco. At a meeting on September 13 between the Aramco team and Yamani and Taher, the Saudis told company representatives that the developments of the past few weeks had drastically altered the participation problem. Kuwait would not accept even the 51 percent that Libya had decreed in August and was pressing for an immediate higher percentage. They pointed to the fact that the European governments in need of sweet crude would not support the major companies in their efforts to stand up to Libya. They also noted the shah's assertion that he had full control of the oil industry. All these facts enabled Saudi Arabia to act forcefully. The Saudis demanded that the Aramco partners immediately accept a buyback price of 93 percent of posted price. Yamani further warned the companies that if they did not agree to his terms collectively, he would deal with individual partners of the company. Only four days later, at a meeting in San Francisco, the Aramco partners accepted Yamani's terms; they agreed on a 93 percent buyback price with an escalation clause derived from the Geneva II accord providing for increases resulting from any change in posted prices. However, when Yamani left the United States the agreement had not been signed.

ASSESSMENT

A complexity of factors operated in the development of events from February through April 1971 to October 1973, which inevitably led to the greatest victory, until then, of the oil-producing countries in their struggle with the foreign concessionaire companies. The most important and decisive ingredient was the obsessive fear of the U.S. government—planted and nurtured by the major U.S. oil companies for their own selfish ends—that the producing countries might stop the flow of oil to the Western nations, the consequences of which could not even be contemplated in economic, political, and security terms. President Nixon, in reaction to Libya's unilateral 51 percent nationalization of the U.S. companies' concessions in August 1973, hinted at possible retaliation through a boycott of Middle East oil and declared: "Oil without a market, as Mr. Mossadegh learned many many years ago, does not do a country any good."[8] Nixon's reference—to the Iranian leader whose nationalization of the oil industry in Iran in 1951 failed because of Iran's inability to resist and overcome the pressures of the British oil company and the British government—was a faint-hearted, obscure hint of a possible countermove.[9] Actually, neither the U.S. government nor the U.S. companies, and certainly not the Europeans, were ready or willing to use a boycott against the oil-producing countries. All the Middle East oil producers were aware of this and acted accordingly.

A second factor was the leapfrogging technique first employed between Libya and the Gulf producers. It turned out to be such an overwhelming success that after the Teheran and Tripoli agreements the leapfrogging practitioners included as well Kuwait, Iran, and other producers, especially Saudi Arabia. The treatment meted out by Saudi Arabia to its companies was the most revealing of the tactics used. Saudi Arabia was not assumed to be among what Nixon described as "the radical elements"[10] of the Middle East producers, yet the Saudi oil minister acted as the most extreme member of the entire group, and his operation was most cleverly performed. Although Saudi Arabia accepted 20 percent at first and later 25 percent participation, the implementation was dragged on and on and not actually consummated. Yamani told the Aramco partners that he could not go through with the deal while Iran, Libya, and Kuwait were getting more and more; he had to obtain for his country an even better deal than Kuwait had gotten. There apparently was an ongoing contest between Libya, Iran, Kuwait, and Saudi Arabia as to who could get the best deal.

As the other countries gained greater advantages, negotiations became tougher and, indeed, humiliating to the companies. Toward the end of this period, in August 1973, Yamani revealed to the companies what was being prepared for them. He declared the Teheran agreement dead and indicated that a new relationship between the producers and the companies would have to replace the obsolete agreement. And he boldly told the Aramco partners that the new arrangements would not be negotiated but imposed by the producers. It was on this note that the October 1973 energy crisis was ushered in.[11]

NOTES

1. *Middle East Economic Survey* (*MEES*), October 15, 1971. Muhammad Joukhdar, deputy governor of Saudi Arabia's Petromin and former secretary-general of OPEC, on August 2, 1971, told the Beirut weekly *Risalat al-Bitrol al-Arabi:* "It is common knowledge that more than 90 percent of all the oil production is undertaken by companies which are not subject to the principle of participation. It is neither logical nor wise for oil producing countries to allow this situation to continue until the date of expiry of the agreements, with the result that—notwithstanding successive changes in the structure of exploration, drilling and production contracts since the early 'sixties—they would suddenly find themselves responsible for a complex and diverse industry. It would not be possible for them to run this industry with the necessary high standards of competence and technical skill without prior and effective experience in all aspects of the petroleum industry.

. . . The National interest is to prepare, in an effective manner, for the time when the entire industry will revert to the state."

2. *MEES,* November 5, 1971.

3. Ibid., November 12, 1971.

4. It should be noted that the Iraq Petroleum Company was the owner of a specific concession area in Iraq as well as the owner of two other areas, Mosul Petroleum Company and the Basrah Petroleum Company; the nationalization act applied only to the Iraq Petroleum Company specific concession. For further details of the nationalization see Benjamin Shwadran, *Middle East Oil and the Great Powers* (Boulder, Colo., 1985), chapter 13.

5. U.S., Congress, Senate, Committee on Foreign Relations, Subcommittee on Multinational Corporations, *Multinational Oil Corporations and U.S. Foreign Policy: Report Together with Individual Views* (Washington, D.C.), p. 137 (hereafter cited as Multinationals Subcommittee, *Report.*

6. Ibid., p. 138.

7. Ibid.

8. Ibid.

9. For further details of the 1951 events see Shwadran, *Middle East Oil,* chapters 5 and 6.

10. Multinationals Subcommittee, *Report,* p. 138.

11. The major sources for Chapter 2 were: U.S., Congress, Senate, Committee on Foreign Relations, Subcommittee on Multinational Corporations, *Hearings: Multinational Corporations and United States Foreign Policy,* Parts 5, 7, 8, 9 (Washington, D.C., 1974–1975); Multinationals Subcommittee, *Report;* OPEC, *1968 Review and Record* (Vienna).

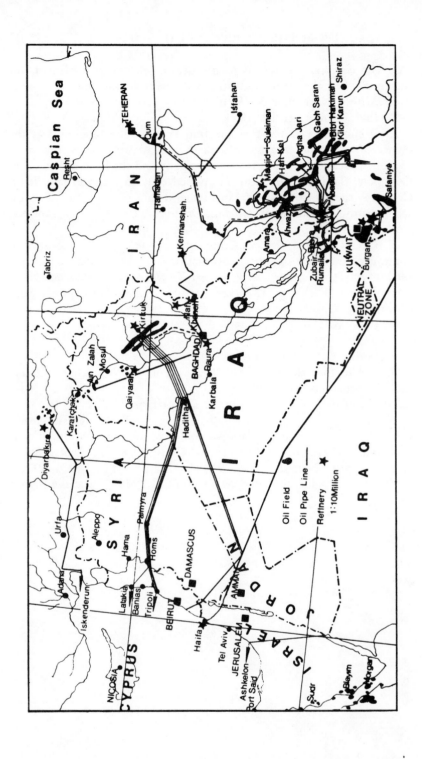

3

FIRST OIL CRISIS—
THE OCTOBER 1973 EMBARGO

The last gasp, so to speak, of the Teheran agreement before it expired occurred in Vienna at the beginning of October 1973. In the middle of September, as the oil ministers of OPEC were gathering in Vienna the Saudi Arabian oil minister, Ahmad Zaki Yamani, had publicly declared that "the Teheran agreement was dead."[1] Some OPEC members demanded the total demolition of the agreement. On September 16, OPEC decided to meet with the companies' representatives in Vienna on October 8 to work out a new oil price structure. At the meeting, the producers asked for a 50 percent increase in the posted price. The companies refused, and the meeting broke up abruptly. It was later reported that the companies might have agreed to a 25 percent increase. On October 16, 1973, Yamani's warning came true. The Gulf committee of OPEC producers met in Kuwait and unilaterally—for the first time in the history of relations between the oil-producing countries and the concessionaire companies—increased posted prices by 70 percent. This action was the greatest triumph to date of the producers over the companies.

Meanwhile the Arab-Israeli 1973 war broke out; on October 17 an Arab oil embargo was announced. It should be made distinctly clear, in spite of the great confusion in the press, in books, and, most importantly, in the public mind, that OPEC as such was not involved in the embargo. The embargo was proclaimed by the Arab oil producers' group called the Organization of Arab Petroleum Exporting Countries. Before dealing with the embargo, its operation, and its termination, we should trace the origin and development of OAPEC.

OAPEC'S ORIGIN

From the very moment that Arab League leaders realized the potentiality of Arab oil resources for realizing the political objectives of the League, they attempted to involve oil in the political struggle. The League established a Petroleum Committee in the Secretariat, and it organized the Arab Petroleum Congresses in order to demonstrate the oil power of the Arabs. But the major oil producers—Saudi Arabia, Kuwait, and Iraq—were determined to resist these attempts to turn their economic asset into a political football in a political game.

However, when the outbreak of war between Egypt and Israel in June 1967 emotionally swept the Arab world, in the electrified war atmosphere the representatives of the Arab oil-producing and -transporting countries met on June 4–5 and decided to stop the flow of oil to the markets and prevent Arab oil from reaching, directly or indirectly, any country that supported Israel. On June 6, Syria announced that it had closed all the pipelines from Iraq and Saudi Arabia that crossed Syrian territory. On the same day, Lebanon reported that it had barred the loading of Iraqi and Saudi Arabian oil into tankers within Lebanese territory. On the following day, Saudi Arabia declared that it had banned the loading of tankers bound for countries that supported Israel and prohibited the export of oil.

The negative economic consequences of these measures were soon apparent, and the producing countries rushed to revoke them. Less than a week after Saudi Arabia prohibited the export of oil, the Saudi government permitted Aramco to renew normal operations and to load tankers, except those whose destination was the United States or Great Britain. Kuwait resumed oil exports on June 14, Iraq on June 15, and Libya on July 5. It became clear to all producers, after calmer tempers prevailed, that they had suffered more from the boycott than had the

Western countries against whom it was aimed. In July the Saudi Arabian oil minister announced that as a result of the boycott his government's oil revenue had been seriously reduced, and it was necessary to cancel a number of economic development projects and to impose, temporarily, certain taxes. With Saudi Arabia as spokesman, the major producers began, at the end of June, to call for the revocation of the boycott. Algeria accused Saudi Arabia of permitting its oil to reach countries that supported Israel and expressed grave doubts that Kuwait had ever enforced the boycott. Libya openly demanded the calling off of the embargo because it did not affect the European countries; they obtained their oil from other Arab countries. These differences of opinion about the oil boycott reflected the antagonism between Arab countries that marked this period.

The official revocation of the embargo became the subject of a major battle between the big oil producers and the radicals in the Arab League, especially Egypt. Only after Saudi Arabia, Kuwait, and Libya promised an annual payment of $135 million to Egypt and Jordan, the victims of the war, did the Arab summit conference resolve in September 1967 to "resume the pumping of oil, since oil is a positive Arab resource that can be used in the service of the Arab goals."[2] Saudi Arabia, Kuwait, and Libya thus became double victims of the boycott—they suffered from lack of revenue, but also had to pay the losers. In January 1968 these three countries met in Beirut and established the Organization of Arab Petroleum Exporting Countries (OAPEC). It formulated a double objective: the protection of the economic character of oil and the protection of foreign investments in the development of oil. Membership requirements in the new organization were: The country must be Arab, its major export must be oil, and all three founding members must vote favorably on the application. The requirements that oil be the major export ruled out Algeria and Egypt and eliminated all the other members of the Arab League. Iraq would have qualified but was not, at the time, interested in joining. Because of its radical orientation, Iraq would not— had it applied—have obtained the vote of the three conservative founding members.

After the Qaddafi revolution in Libya in September 1969 the complexion of OAPEC inevitably changed. Libya was now in the radical camp against the conservatives. In Arab League councils and in OAPEC Libya pressed hard for the use of oil as a political weapon. Pressure was exerted on OAPEC to open the organization to new members and to modify its objectives. By 1970, Algeria, Bahrain, Qatar, Abu Dhabi, and Dubai had been admitted to membership. In 1971 the battle for Iraq's admission was bitterly fought. The radicals insisted that Iraq be admitted; Saudi Arabia, who at first was determined to prevent this and threatened to leave the organization should Iraq join, relented after a long and acrimonious wrangle. The admission requirements were modified, and early in 1972 Iraq, Syria, and Egypt became members, so that by March of 1972 OAPEC was transformed into the antithesis of that for which it had originally been established; OAPEC became the Arab political instrument using the oil resources as its main weapon.

As 1973 progressed it became clear that war between Egypt and Israel was inevitable and that oil would play an important role in it. King Faisal of Saudi Arabia carried on a steady consultation with President Anwar as-Sadat of Egypt about the planned war. Saudi Arabia, more and more had assumed the role of active leader in the Arab national cause, not without the intentional encouragement of Sadat. In a reversal of policy, Saudi Arabia—which had, persistently and stubbornly before the June 1967 war and with even more determination since the formation of OAPEC, tried to prevent oil from becoming a weapon in the struggle against the West, especially the United States—now became the champion of the Arab cause, ready and eager to offer Saudi oil. In April 1973, while visiting Washington, Yamani warned U.S. cabinet members of his government's determination to use the oil weapon. On May 23, King Faisal met with Aramco officials and told them that unless the United States changed its pro-Israel policy Aramco might lose their concession. The Aramco partners presented the king's message to the State and Defense departments and to the White House. They also launched a public campaign urging Aramco shareholders and other citizens to press the administration to change its policy on Israel. But, according to the companies, the U.S. policymakers did not take King Faisal's warning seriously. In a television interview broadcast on August 30, and again on September 10, in an interview with *Newsweek*, King Faisal repeated his threat to use oil as a means of forcing the United States to change its policy in regard to Israel, pointing out that the Americans risked losing their oil concession.[3]

THE 1973 EMBARGO

On October 7, 1973, war broke out between Egypt and Israel. Six days later the officers of Aramco sent President Nixon a memorandum against resupplying the Israeli army. They warned that a major production cutback of oil was imminent if the United States continued to support Israel. U.S. oil interests were threatened.

On October 17, OAPEC members met in Kuwait and decided on an immediate 5 percent production cutback from September levels. They declared that "the same percentage will be applied in each month compared with the previous one, until the Israeli withdrawal is completed from all the Arab territories occupied in June 1967 and the legal rights of the Palestinian people restored. The conferers are aware that this reduction should not harm any friendly state which assisted or will assist the Arabs actively and materially. Such countries would receive their shares as before the reduction."[4] Some Arab producers jumped the gun and cut production by more than 5 percent, and some raised the cut to as high as 10 percent. Total embargoes were imposed on the United States and the Netherlands, which also supported Israel. When OAPEC reconvened in Kuwait on November 5, it was decided to limit the total cut to no more than 25 percent from October 1, 1973, levels.

A careful analysis of the various decisions of the OAPEC conferences would reveal that there was no coherent and systematic planning either in the terms of the embargo or in the conditions for its termination. At the meeting in Vienna on November 18, after the Common Market adopted on November 6 a resolution favoring the Arab request for Israeli withdrawal to the 1967 lines, OAPEC announced that "in appreciation of the political stand taken by the Common Market countries regarding the Middle East crisis, it was decided not to implement the five percent reduction for the month of December as it applies to Europe (Common Market) only."[5] The Netherlands was not included in this exemption. But the 5 percent cut for January was to apply to all countries, including those in the Common Market. And despite the November 6 resolution, Yamani threatened in Copenhagen on November 23, while the Common Market foreign ministers were meeting there secretly to deal with the energy problem, that the cutback in oil supply might reach, should this become necessary, as high as 80 percent.

An Arab summit conference was convened in Algiers to deal with the embargo. From the very beginning Iraq did not approve the embargo. Officially Iraq explained its position by pointing out the injustice of the cutbacks for countries that were friendly to the Arabs. The proper action would have been to nationalize the foreign oil companies and drive them out from the Arab lands, as Iraq had done to the Iraq Petroleum Company concession. As an indication of consistency Iraq nationalized the Exxon and Mobil—the U.S. companies—shares in the Basrah Petroleum Company. But the real reason for Iraq's opposition to the embargo was its desperate need for markets for Iraqi nationalized oil. Ever since the nationalization, on June 1, 1972, Iraq had been unable to find markets for its oil. Should Iraq abide by the embargo, it would lose even the limited outlets it did have. Iraq consequently did not participate in the OAPEC meetings and refused to attend the Algiers summit. Libya also did not attend the Algiers summit. Neither did Libya observe the embargo provisions, although Libya was extreme in its demands, and surreptitiously sold oil to the very countries against whom the embargo was proclaimed. Both Iraq and Libya successfully took advantage of the shortage caused by the embargo to increase their sales of oil and their revenues.

It was decided at the summit meeting to classify the consuming countries according to attitude to the Middle East conflict, as "friendly," "neutral," and "hostile." Also, because of its pro-Arab resolution on the issue of Israel's withdrawal from the Arab-occupied territories, Japan was freed from an additional

5 percent cutback scheduled for December. One day after the closing of the summit meeting on November 28, Yamani announced in London that Britain, France, and Spain were classified as friendly nations and would be exempt from a January 1974 5 percent cutback.[6] From there Yamani proceeded to the United States to present the Arab case for the embargo. Then, on December 9 at a meeting in Kuwait, OAPEC decided that the January reduction of supplies would apply to all countries, hostile as well as friendly. Although the embargo caused panic and created a sense of almost hopelessness in the consuming countries, the leaders of the embargo were themselves, apparently, more than dissatisfied with the results and were seeking means to ease the embargo and even lift it altogether.

Lifting the Embargo

The rigid condition that the embargo would not be lifted until Israel had withdrawn to its 1967 borders was modified and reduced to a timetable of Israeli withdrawals guaranteed by the United States.

Oil Price shock

Price oil ↑

On December 23, 1973, the oil ministers of the Gulf OPEC members met and decided to raise the posted price of crude oil to $11.65 a barrel, an increase of more than 400 percent from the October 1, 1973, price of $2.59. Only two days later OAPEC decided that instead of cutting supplies in January 1974, it would increase them by 10 percent. OAPEC also resolved to meet in Tripoli in Libya on February 13 to deal with the embargo issue.

The developments from the time of the OAPEC meeting of December 25, 1973, to the March 18, 1974, meeting in Vienna when the decision was finally taken to lift the embargo are reflective of the nature of the Arab oil complex and the oil producers' inter-Arab relations. Saudi Arabia and Egypt made a continuous and relentless effort to convince the other Arab states to terminate the embargo. It could safely be assumed that in his peripatetic travels in the Middle East at the end of 1973, Henry Kissinger, the U.S. secretary of state, received a definite promise, among many others, that the oil embargo would be lifted and that an official announcement to that effect would be made at the OAPEC Tripoli meeting scheduled for February 13. This information was intentionally or unintentionally leaked to the press. However, instead of waiting for that date, President Richard Nixon—for his own reasons—declared in his State of the Union Address to Congress on January 30, 1974, that reliable Arab leadership sources had assured him that the oil embargo would be lifted even before the scheduled OAPEC meeting. This announcement by the U.S. president caused a furor in the Arab world, and OAPEC found itself facing a serious crisis. Whereas Saudi Arabia and Egypt strongly advocated, now more than ever, the lifting of the embargo, the radical countries—Algeria, Syria, and Libya—opposed the lifting very strenuously. As the time of the Tripoli meeting approached it became clear that the sharp differences of opinion between the advocates and the opponents of lifting the embargo might cause a breakup of OAPEC. Moreover, the United States, in whose interest the advocates pleaded, openly challenged and defied the oil-producing countries by calling a conference of all the major oil-consuming countries to meet in Washington in early February and devise plans against the danger of the embargo and against OPEC (see Chapter 5).

In order to prevent the breakup of OAPEC, a small Arab summit conference was called for February 12 in Algiers. The participants were the king of Saudi Arabia and the presidents of Egypt, Syria, and Algeria; the issues were two: the lifting of the embargo against the United States and the terms of the separation of forces between Syria and Israel. Differences persisted between advocates and opponents of lifting the embargo. It was agreed, however, to postpone the scheduled Tripoli meeting and to send a delegation of the foreign ministers of Saudi Arabia and Egypt to Washington to persuade the United States to accept the Syrian terms for the separation of forces and impose them on Israel. This would soften the opposition to lifting the embargo. But the effort of the delegation was fruitless, and it returned home without convincing the United States of the urgency of meeting Syria's demands.

Egypt was determined, as was Saudi Arabia, to lift the embargo as quickly as possible; on March 3, Egypt asked for the Tripoli meeting to convene. Five of the big oil producers were in favor of lifting the embargo, but the general opinion in the Arab countries and in the West was that lifting the embargo depended on the separation of forces between Israel and Syria (on March 3 the separation of forces agreement between Israel and Egypt was completed). Egypt was not willing to wait any longer and decided to convene the conference even in face of strong opposition from the radical countries. On March 7, Rahman al-Atiqi, Kuwaiti finance and oil minister, announced that the conference was scheduled to meet on March 10 in Cairo. Libya and Algeria, however, quickly denied both the time and place of the conference. On March 11, after a number of oil ministers had arrived in Cairo, it was decided to hold the conference in Tripoli on March 13.

The conference sessions were closed and stormy. Nevertheless, it became known that a majority of the participants wanted the embargo ended. Libya, however, refused to permit the announcement to that effect to be made on Libyan soil. It was, therefore, decided to announce the decision after a meeting in Vienna, where the ministers were gathering for an OPEC conference. An effort was to be made in Vienna to arrive at a unanimous decision. After a three-day debate, that effort failed; seven producers announced they would lift the embargo, Algeria stated that it would lift the embargo temporarily, and Syria and Libya said they would continue it. No mention was made about restoring the supply cuts, but the Saudi Arabian oil minister made it clear that supplies would be reinstated to the October 1, 1973, level. In spite of a decision to reconsider the embargo question at the June OAPEC meeting in Cairo—should U.S. policy not be satisfactory the embargo could be reimposed—it was really clearly understood by all, both advocates and opponents of the decision, that the embargo would not be renewed.

MOTIVES FOR ENDING THE EMBARGO

Why did the Arab oil-producing countries proclaim an embargo with such extreme conditions for its termination and then cancel

it after less than five months, without the fulfillment of the
stated conditions? What impelled the Egyptians to end the
embargo is obvious. Kissinger succeeded, through his tactics,
in saving Egypt from total military defeat. He brought about
the separation of forces between Egypt and Israel, and he
believed that he had extricated Egypt from the iron grip of the
Soviet Union. Egypt was in a position to exploit the United
States and demand the implementation of the commitments
that Kissinger, no doubt, had made, thus challenging the Soviet
Union. But it would be impossible to demand anything from
the United States while an Arab oil embargo was still in force
against it.

But Saudi Arabia's motives for lifting the embargo were more
complex. To understand them it is necessary to understand the
motives behind the embargo altogether. Saudi Arabia was an
active participant in the struggle between the producers and
the companies and shared in the progressive achievements of
the producing countries. During the period between February
1971 and October 1973 the gains of the producers were greatly
accelerated and culminated in the 1973 crisis. Basically the crisis
had come about because of purely economic factors, but suddenly
it assumed political aspects. Spokesmen for the most important
Arab oil-producing countries, ignoring the global strife between
the superpowers and all the international economic and financial
components of the crisis, proclaimed that the energy crisis was
a purely political issue; they reduced it to simplistic terms: The
world energy shortage was caused by Israel. All the world had
to do was to force Israel to comply with Arab demands and
it would get all the oil it wanted at former prices. The supposed
threatened disaster that Europe, Japan, and even the United
States faced could easily be avoided, the prosperity and well-
being of all could continue and blossom, if only Israel would
do the bidding of the Arabs.[7]

In view of the persistent determination of the major Arab
oil producers to prevent their oil resources from being used as
a political instrument against the Western oil-consuming countries, why did they, especially Saudi Arabia, agree to use the
embargo against the Western countries? The answer to this
question lies in the changed conditions of the producing coun-

tries. It is submitted that the underlying factors in the world energy crisis were and remained economic; the Middle East oil producers were aligned for the purpose of obtaining the highest price for their product and gaining control of the industry, aims made feasible by the fact that Middle East oil had become indispensable to the economic and industrial life of the Western countries. For the first time in the history of the Arab national movement political and economic aims coincided. The Arab leadership under Saudi King Faisal exploited the situation and assumed a political stance in proclaiming the oil embargo. Faisal utilized the political posture to reinforce the real economic factors and to rally to the side of the producer governments the loyalty and following of the Arab masses. Paradoxically, King Faisal, the arch-conservative and pro-Western Arab leader, had become the radical front-runner in the battle against the Western countries, especially the United States. Why then was Saudi Arabia so anxious to end the embargo? The decision of March 18, 1974, to lift the Arab oil embargo brought to an end the first grand attempt of the Arab producing countries to employ their oil in the political arena against the Western consuming countries. An analytical examination of the outcome of the attempt would reveal that the embargo was a failure—its political goals were not realized—except for one real achievement: tremendously large increases in the posted prices of oil, in reality the achievement of OPEC rather than OAPEC. The size of the increases alarmed Saudi Arabia, the leader of the embargo movement; the Saudis feared that in the end the increases might defeat the purpose of the undertaking.

Differences Among the Oil-Producing Countries

The failure of the embargo resulted from the very structure of the group of Middle East oil-producing countries, from the sharp differences among them, and from their various motives in proclaiming the embargo. The oil-producing countries may be divided into three categories, which determined their positions on the embargo. The first group consists of countries or emirates of the Gulf that depend heavily or exclusively on their oil revenue. They are either just on the threshold of oil development or are small and limited oil producers. They would ordinarily be ready to sell their oil according to their original contracts and concession terms without imposing special conditions. This group includes Qatar, Bahrain, Oman, and some members of the UAE. The second group consists of countries that have large populations, massive development programs, and are large oil producers. In this category are Iran, Iraq, and Algeria. They need the oil revenue to finance their current budgets and the economic projects; they would be ready to sell all the oil the consumers could purchase provided the price was high, and if possible very high. The third group consists of countries with small populations, prodigious oil resources and production records, and financial saturation. To this category belong Saudi Arabia, Kuwait, and Abu Dhabi. They would be prepared to curtail production for the industrialized nations in order to achieve their economic and financial objectives.

The Arab oil-producing countries may be further divided into two additional categories: conservative and radical nations, each group of which had opposing aims in promulgating the embargo. The conservative group had primarily economic aims; when these were fulfilled they were ready to lift the embargo without any further disturbance to international relations within the region. The radical countries, on the other hand, had political-ideological aims, and they saw in the embargo a means of changing the political, ideological, and social patterns of the Arab world; the embargo afforded an excellent opportunity to gain control of the Arab movement and the Arab social revolution. These deep differences were the cause for the struggle before and at the Tripoli conference and later at the Vienna meeting.

There could be no doubt that Saudi Arabia emerged the victor in this battle. For Saudi Arabia the embargo was a means to attain a reasonable increase in oil revenue. King Faisal never sought the aims of the Arab socialist countries. When his objective was achieved by very sharp increases in the posted prices, he hastened to resume oil shipping to the Western world and communicated to the United States his resolve to do so. The radical countries—Iraq, Syria, Algeria, and Libya—were alarmed at Faisal's decision and opposed any attempts to lift the embargo. The Soviet Union, naturally, supported the radical countries and advocated the continuation of the embargo; it accused Saudi Arabia of betraying the cause of Arab nationalism.

Another factor that made Saudi Arabia eager to lift the embargo involved the fear that the West would develop energy alternatives for Middle East oil. It should be noted that the issue of energy alternatives is not one of research and discovery. Alternatives (and they are many and varied) are already available; the problem lies only in effecting them. They have not been put into operation for reasons that are two sides of the same coin: the relatively cheap production cost of Middle East oil and the very high cost of the various possible alternatives. Iran, whose grandiose economic development projects cost hundreds of billions of dollars, was not interested in conserving oil resources. On the contrary, Iran was determined to exploit them in very huge quantities and in the shortest period of time as long as the price remained very high. Within the next ten years, Iran expected to receive sufficient funds—assuming high prices—to develop new economic resources that would make it independent of oil income. It was unlikely that any alternative could be activated within ten years that would compete with Iranian oil. Iran could use the oil remaining after that period for its own industrial needs and would not be interested in selling it in competition with the alternatives. Iran was, therefore, a consistent and persistent advocate of oil price increases, the higher the better. Saudi Arabia, in contrast, was not economically developed, and its development programs were not to be implemented within a short time or even in the foreseeable future. The Saudis expected that oil would be their major, if not exclusive, source of income during the next fifty or even hundred years. Saudi Arabia could not, therefore, risk its future by limiting supplies and by increasing prices too high. Such actions would hasten the activation of the oil alternatives. Hence Saudi anxiety and determination to lift the embargo, as well as readiness to reduce the posted prices in order to slow down or even stop completely Western efforts to activate alternatives, especially in the United States. Similar considerations prompted Kuwait and Abu Dhabi to demand the lifting of the embargo.

Saudi Leadership

In addition, Saudi Arabia was obliged to move to cancel the embargo in order to maintain its leadership position in the Arab world and for the sake of Saudi national security. Until 1973, the economic determinants of production rate and price level conflicted with Arab political objectives, and the latter was rejected for the former. Saudi Arabia did not aspire, at that time, to leadership of the Arab world, a role that was reserved for Egypt and its ruler Gamal Abdul Nasir. With the ascendance of Anwar as-Sadat in Egypt and with the approach of the 1973 war two new elements entered into the situation: Egypt abdicated its Arab leadership role to make room for Saudi Arabia, in order to bring oil into the Arab political struggle; the oil-producing countries were successful in obtaining better economic terms from the Western oil companies, which had to meet the rapidly rising demand for oil by Western consumers as supplies decreased even faster. Economic and political objectives could, for the first time, be merged to give Saudi Arabia a double advantage: higher revenue and leadership in the Arab world. In the emotionally charged atmosphere of the October 1973 war, Saudi Arabia became the leader and driving force of the Arab oil embargo. The subsequent 70 percent price increase by OPEC and the conditions for ending the embargo seemed at that time to spell total victory, economically and politically for the Arabs, and Saudi Arabia was hailed as the undisputed leader of the Arab world.

But this new position was not secure. Saudi Arabia was weak militarily. The government was exposed to internal and external dangers. Neighboring radical Arab countries were ready to undermine the conservative autocratic regime and even invade the country. The Saudis' only security was the United States, with which they had maintained, until the embargo, close relations; the U.S. oil company Aramco was the source of almost all Saudi revenue. As long as Saudi Arabia was closely connected with the United States it felt safe and well protected, but the major target of the embargo was the United States. Continuation of the embargo could have brought a total break in relations, which would have meant losing the protection of, from a Saudi point of view, the most important and powerful nation on earth. Moreover, the longer the embargo continued, the more the radical members of the Arab League—Algeria, Libya, Syria, and Iraq—would become dominant, threatening Saudi leadership and influence and even endangering Saudi Arabia's existence.

Economically, the outlook was not as bright as was originally anticipated. A 70 percent increase in price was a very impressive achievement and greatly increased revenue beyond the current needs of the country. However, when OPEC raised prices at the end of December by a total of over 400 percent, Saudi Arabia recoiled. It took immediate steps to reverse the process. The leader of the defiant proclamation of the embargo became the major force in bringing about its rapid termination, which was achieved against strenuous and bitter opposition from the radical countries in the Arab League. Putting aside the political conditions for lifting the embargo, Saudi Arabia overcame its temporary aberration, reestablished close and good relations with the United States, and, regained U.S. protection.

SHORTSIGHTED ADVANTAGE

The embargo was not a great success.[8] The companies came out the winners, together with the producers, in reaping enormous profits from the high prices, but this was a very short-range and shortsighted advantage. Technically the embargo was a failure but psychologically it gave the Arab oil-producing countries a sense of superiority and importance in both an economic and political sense. It seemed that the world was under their command and ready to do their bidding. To conclude this discussion of the Arab oil embargo, three additional aspects of the issue will be considered: (1) the impact of the embargo on the Western countries; (2) the causal relationship between the October 1973 Arab-Israeli war and the embargo; and (3) the possibility of a second embargo.

Impact of Embargo

In testimony before the U.S. House of Representatives Committee on Foreign Affairs Near East and South Asia Subcommittee on November 29, 1973, George M. Bennsky, director, Office of Fuels and Energy, Bureau of Economics and Business Affairs, Department of State, declared that the embargo of October 17, 1973, reduced overall production by at least 10 percent. Because of the embargo and subsequent cutbacks, the world's availability of oil has been reduced by over 5 million barrels a day, amounting to about 10 percent of world consumption. He estimated that U.S. imports from the Arab countries in 1973 had averaged 1,600,000 barrles a day—25 percent of all U.S. oil imports or 10 percent of total consumption.

In testimony before the Senate Subcommittee on Multinational Corporations, Standard Oil Company of California stated on March 25, 1974, that the OAPEC political move of cutting back crude production starting October 17, 1973, "effectively eliminated some 4–5 million barrels per day from available world production capacity. Arab oil production for September 1973 amounted to 20.7 million barrels per day. By November 1973, this level had been reduced by 4.8 million barrels per day (or about 25%) to a total of 15.9 million barrels per day production."[9]

In 1975, the Joint Economic Committee's Subcommittee on International Economics, basing its statements on a report by the Federal Energy Administration of August 1974 concluded: "The five-month oil embargo (1973–1974) is estimated to have cost the United States economy 500,000 jobs and a GNP loss of between $10 and $20 billion."[10] The House Committee on Interstate and Foreign Commerce reported that the 1973–1974 embargo resulted in a 2.2-million-barrel-per-day reduction of imports of crude oil and petroleum products—an interruption equal to about one-third of U.S. oil imports and about 12 percent of overall U.S. petroleum supplies. The embargo caused a 7 percent decrease in real GNP for the first quarter of 1974 and an increase in unemployment of approximately 425,000 persons for the quarter.

Some of these estimates raise a number of questions. Were the increase in unemployment and the decrease in the GNP the results of the embargo or the impact of the more than 400 percent increase in the price of oil since January 1, 1974? Moreover, as far as the Middle East as a whole was concerned, the embargo apparently had very little impact on total production. In 1973 total Middle East oil production was 6,722,168,000 barrels; in 1973 it went up to 7,765,440,000; and in 1974 it reached 7,966,810,000 barrels. The conclusion must, therefore, be drawn that the negative impact on the United States was not the shortage of supplies but the very high prices that OPEC exacted from the consuming countries.

The Embargo and the War

A recounting of the chain of events that occurred in the relations between the producers and the companies from February 1971 to October 1973 (as detailed in Chapter 2) must inevitably lead to the conclusion that the embargo was the next step in that development, which continued after the lifting of the embargo (see Chapter 4). Yet a great deal was made, especially by some of the major oil companies, of the notion that the embargo was a direct reaction to the Arab-Israeli October 1973 war. The Aramco partners, and the Saudi Arabian oil minister, tried to impress the world that the only cause for the energy crisis was the war: There were no economic factors involved, the only motive was political, and the main culprit was the U.S. government; the one way to end the crisis was for the United States to change its pro-Israel policy. The fact that the price increases were ordered by OPEC, which was not concerned with political issues, did not matter. The appeal to the United States for a change of policy promised not only a plentiful supply of oil but also a return to preembargo prices.

Statements from insiders and participants in the drama as well as from disinterested analysts refute any categorical causal relationship between the embargo and the war. In testimony before the Senate Subcommittee on Multinational Corporations, George H. M. Schuler, representing the Bunker Hunt Oil

Company, declared that he had prepared "an analysis of the events post Teheran in which one incident after another takes place. . . . and it has nothing to do with the October war. It is a chronology of demands that we retreat from and that slip away until the October war comes."[11] John McCloy, legal counsel for the oil companies, appeared before the same Senate sub-committee on February 6, 1974, and explicitly declared: "The recent oil embargo production cutbacks and subsequent cata-clysmic increases in oil prices by the producing governments, upon which so much attention had properly been centered, have been the result, not of negotiations with the companies but the unilateral fiat of the producing countries in violation of existing agreements with the companies. These increases were, it seems quite obviously, directly related to the October war."[12] This evidently contradicted the Bunker Hunt testimony.

While Saudi Arabia's minister of oil traveled throughout the United States assuring U.S. oil consumers that all that was necessary for oil prices to return to the pre-October level was for the United States to change its pro-Israel policy, the Saudi foreign minister, Omar Saqqaf, told the French press that consumers should not delude themselves into thinking that as soon as Israel conceded to Arab demands, oil prices would come down. Standard Oil Company of California, in a mem-orandum submitted to the Senate Subcommittee on Multina-tional Corporations on March 25, 1974, stated: "If a mutually acceptable solution to the Arab-Israeli problem is found, there is good reason to expect that normal competitive market forces will result in an improved balance of world supply and demand, including availability of adequate capacity for all phases of oil industry operations."[13] As guarded as this assertion is, it fails to explain why the rules of supply-and-demand balance suddenly became dependent in 1973 on the settlement of the Arab-Israeli conflict, although until 1973 they had operated effectively in spite of the conflict.

Because the companies claimed that the 1973 war had brought the sudden and unexpected cutbacks of oil supplies by the OAPEC members, and that they had been completely surprised, it is important to learn exactly when the companies realized that cutbacks might be used against them by the producers. In appearing before the Senate Subcommittee on Multinational Corporations, W. Jones McQuinn, Aramco vice-chairman, on June 10, 1974, responded to a question by saying that early in August 1973 he had made a study, at the request of the Aramco shareholders, of the possible cutbacks in supplies and "we had come even closer to the realization that a production cutback of some kind was a very real possibility." When asked by the chairman of the subcommittee whether he had the embargo in mind, he replied: "I suppose we certainly had that in mind."[14]

The Central Intelligence Agency report of 1979, *The World Oil Market in the Years Ahead,* observed that the embargo "drew attention away from underlying resource and economic problem, focusing it instead on the political activities of the Arab states and on OPEC."[15] The staff report of the Senate Committee on Energy and Natural Resources, *The Geopolitics of Oil,* concluded, "Even if the dispute [Arab-Israeli] could be resolved overnight, the problem of domestic and regional turbulence in the Middle East would remain. For many of the Arab nations, the dispute with Israel provides an opportunity to distract popular attention from pressing problems at home. . . . This willingness to use oil in pursuit of Arab political objectives means that, even with the settlement of the Arab-Israeli dispute, the potential for oil disruption and political manipulation of oil supplies will prevail."[16] Ali Khalifah al-Sabah, the Kuwaiti oil minister, explained on September 21, 1980, the cause of the 1973 embargo and the rise of oil prices: "The 1973 war was not the cause of the 1973 increase. I think that as early as January or February of 1973 we were starting negotiations with the oil companies on a new price structure."[17]

John B. Kelly, a Middle East analyst who specializes in Saudi Arabia and the Gulf states, stated in 1976,

Nor, for all the sound and fury aroused by the issue, would any amelioration of the Arab-Israeli conflict bring relief from the present dangers. It is easy to contend—which is one reason why the contention has gained universal currency—that it was the war of October 1973 which prompted the embargo on oil by the Arab oil-producing states. But the threat of an embargo had been made before, as early as the Tripoli meeting of OPEC in

December 1970, and again at the confrontation with the major oil companies at Teheran in February 1971. The object then was to force a unilateral rise in the price of crude oil, and so it was again in October 1973, when, as may be recalled, the announcement of the price rise took precedence over the promulgation of the embargo. The Yom Kippur War, in short, afforded an almost unique opportunity to the Arab oil-producing states to combine principle with profit, and at least one of those states, Saudi Arabia, apparently had advance knowledge of the impending Egyptian and Syrian attack upon Israel.[18]

The evidence from all these sources belies the claim that the embargo and its consequences were the sudden and spontaneous reaction to the 1973 Arab-Israeli war.

The Possibility of a Second Embargo

After experiencing the shocks of the 1973 embargo, whenever difficulties in the relations between the producers and the consumers arose the specter of a second embargo was raised. It should be stressed that the danger of a second embargo was first voiced not by the Arab producers but by the president of the United States and his assistants and by the representatives of the major oil companies. It was from them that the Arabs took their cue.

The ghost of the embargo was raised as a tactic, rather than a realistic appraisal of conditions, with various objectives. President Gerald Ford and his aides used it against Israel, to "persuade" Israel to agree to the harsh terms of the proposed second separation of forces between Israel and Egypt. The president asserted that if Israel assumed a rigid negotiating stance, a stalemate would be created with the attendant danger of a new war. This could only result in a second embargo, which would be more harmful and disastrous than the first one. This formula was employed whenever any U.S. administration encountered opposition to measures aimed at improving relations with the Arab producers, especially Saudi Arabia, or to prevent the enactment of measures by Congress that would antagonize the Arab producers—for example, to counter strong resistance to supplying Saudi Arabia with some of the more modern and sophisticated (and potentially offensive) weapons, or to prevent the enactment of legislation against the Arab economic boycott of Israel. In October 1976, Muhammad Mahgoub, commissioner-general of the Arab boycott of Israel, threatened that the United States would face another embargo unless U.S. firms abided by boycott regulations. Similarly, the tactic was used by the U.S. oil companies as a justification for their submission to the Arab demands and as a reason for raising oil prices. In an effort to persuade the administration to remove controls of domestic petroleum prices, the president of the American Petroleum Institute, Frank Ikard, raised the threat of a second embargo as the most vulnerable aspect of the U.S. oil industry. Only removal of controls would enable the industry to increase home production by inducing investors to invest in the domestic oil industry and thus defy the Arab producers.

The producers, watching the deep divisions that emerged among the Western countries during the first embargo, believed that they had further fragmented the Western camp. The United States adamantly adhered to its Middle East policy in spite of the efforts of the oil companies in pressing the administration to modify its policy, but the Europeans and the Japanese responded to the Arab demands. All the powerful countries of Europe competed with one another to sell the most advanced sophisticated arms to the producers in exchange for oil supplies. The producers therefore continued to threaten the consuming countries with another embargo and thereby put pressure on them to convince the United States to change its Middle East policy.

What were the realities behind the repeated threats of a second embargo? The first embargo had been far from successful and had created great internal tension within the Arab oil-producing countries. The producers actually had no means at their command to force the United States to change its policy. They could take advantage of the disagreements among the Western consuming countries, but the ability of Europe and Japan to influence the United States was limited, as were the punishments the Arabs could mete out to the Europeans and the Japanese.

A possible, though unrealistic, scenario for a second embargo may be outlined. The situation in the later 1970s has deteriorated, the efforts of negotiation between the parties failed, and a war has broken out. As a move against the consuming countries, the Arabs have instituted a second embargo. The United States continues its support of Israel and supplies Israel with the necessary military and economic aid. The embargo has been imposed on all the Western consuming countries to punish the United States, but the United States, having learned its lesson during the first embargo, adopts emergency measures, does without Middle East Arab oil, and is little affected by the embargo. In the other consuming countries—both developed and developing—anger and resentment reaches a height that drives them into the arms of the United States and together they form one solid bloc against the Arab oil producers. The Soviet Union is in no position to solve the problems of the Arab countries and certainly is not capable of meeting the needs of the consuming countries. In the producers' camp very serious difficulties and pressures develop. Iraq, Algeria, and Libya cannot hold out longer without current revenues. The consuming countries have stockpiled at least ninety days of oil supplies, and the non-Arab producers have doubled their preembargo production levels. These three Arab producers demand the lifting of the embargo. Thus, external pressure from the consuming countries and internal needs of some of the Arab producers bring about the complete collapse of the embargo and very seriously endanger the existence of OPEC. The most likely outcome is a confrontation between a strong and cohesive group of consuming countries and the producing countries, resulting in a compromise settlement in which the consumers are guaranteed a secure oil supply and the producers are granted reasonable prices.

As unrealistic as it sounds, the possibility of such a scenario could not escape the minds of the Arab oil producers. They knew that they would not dare earnestly attempt another embargo. The inevitable conclusion must be drawn that both those who threatened and those who were threatened did not take seriously the possibility of a second embargo.[19]

CONCLUSIONS

The embargo was a natural link in the chain of the struggle between the oil producers and the concessionaire companies, which after years of stalemate began in February 1971 to progress rapidly in favor of the producers. However, both the Arab producers and the companies—each for their own reasons—advanced the Arab-Israeli conflict in general and the October 1973 war in particular as the real immediate cause for the embargo. This explanation was not only inaccurate but primarily fraudulent.

When the embargo was lifted, it was not without inter-Arab tension and, perhaps unintended, exaggeration of the impact of the embargo on the consuming countries. The oil companies must be blamed, in great measure, for the acute consequences of the embargo. Out of fear of losing their concessions, the companies cooperated with the producing countries in implementing the embargo against their own governments. There can be no doubt that had the multinational oil companies cooperated instead with their governments against the producing countries, the impact of the embargo would have been very limited.[20]

As the embargo proceeded, some Arab producers, especially Saudi Arabia, realized that the embargo was more harmful than beneficial for them, and that it was imperative to terminate it as quickly as possible. This decision was definitely communicated to the United States by Egypt and Saudi Arabia; in return certain promises were given them. On the basis of these undertakings President Nixon made the announcement on January 30, 1974, at a joint session of Congress, that the embargo was about to be lifted. This announcement was not hasty and premature but was a blunt, premeditated warning to Egypt and Saudi Arabia against a possible retreat. Only eight days before, Henry Kissinger, the secretary of state, had declared: "We have every reason to believe that success in the negotiations would mark a major step toward ending the embargo. We would therefore think that failure to end the embargo in a reasonable time would be highly inappropriate and would raise questions of confidence in our minds with respect to the Arab nations with whom we have dealt on this issue."[21]

The Arab oil embargo and the conditions for ending it were a basic challenge to U.S. independence and freedom in determining its foreign policy. The existence of a strong Israel was a cardinal element in U.S. Middle East policy, hence the U.S. decision to support Israel in the war. The United States would under no circumstances submit to dictates by the Arab oil producers, especially Saudi Arabia, which was so heavily dependent for its own security on the United States. To obtain some concessions from Israel for the sake of some balance, yes, but to abandon Israel in its hour of need would mean surrender to Arab dictates. Thus at a news conference in San Clemente, California, on January 3, 1974, the secretary said, "We cannot engage in negotiations with the Arab governments about the specific terms that we will support in negotiations in order to get the embargo lifted, because it would make our foreign policy then entirely subject to the producing nations discussions."[22]

Both the president and the secretary of state stressed the fact that the negotiations for the separation of forces between Israel and Egypt were not linked to the termination of the embargo. In his address to Congress, President Nixon said, "It should be clearly understood by our friends in the Middle East that the United States will not be coerced on this issue" of lifting the embargo.[23] About a week later, Kissinger warned the Arab oil-producing countries that the United States would consider their refusal to cancel the embargo as a "blackmail tactic."[24] In testimony before the congressional Joint Economic Committee, Richard M. Gardner, an academic specialist, stated on December 13, 1973, "The most dramatic and threatening development, of course, is the Arab embargo, which has the explicit purpose of forcing the United States and its allies in Europe and Japan to change their policies on the Middle East."[25] The United States steadfastly adhered to its Middle East policy. The embargo, all its conditions for termination unfulfilled, was lifted on March 18, 1974, except against the United States and the Netherlands, because of their pro-Israel positions. The United

States was put on probation until June when its policy would be reexamined, but the embargo continued against the Netherlands.

On June 2, the Arab petroleum ministers met in Cairo and decided to maintain the embargo against the Netherlands for at least another five weeks. Saudi Arabia objected to lifting this embargo, but Algeria pleaded to end it and announced that it had already done so. Meanwhile a plan, initiated by France, for a dialogue between the Arab League and the European Economic Community, to counter U.S. efforts to unite the consuming countries, was reaching the stage of implementation. The dialogue would surely be vetoed by the Netherlands, a member of the EEC, if the embargo were continued against it. OAPEC, therefore, met again in Cairo on July 10 and cancelled the embargo on the Netherlands (see Chapter 5).

The question of a second embargo was raised by U.S. government representatives, by the oil companies' representatives, and by ministers of the producing countries. However, everyone knew that there was no substance to all the threats, that they were mere tactics. Since the embargo no attempt has been made at another. In view of the new position of OPEC oil in the world supply market since the end of 1982, an oil embargo by Arab oil producers could be contemplated only as a suicidal act. During the period from October 1973 to January 1974 OPEC made a giant step in its struggle with the companies by unilaterally increasing the price by more than 400 percent and laid the ground for new moves.[26]

NOTES

1. *New York Times,* September 8, 1973.
2. BBC, *Summary of World Broadcasts,* September 4, 1967 (Radio Cairo, September 1, 1967).
3. *New York Times,* August 31, 1973.
4. An official Saudi Arabian government version of the decision added the following proviso for the continuation of the cutback: "Or until the production for every individual country reaches the point where its economy does not permit of any further reduction without

detriment to its national or Arab obligations." Raymond Vernon, *The Oil Crisis* (New York, 1976), p. 60.

5. *Middle East Economic Survey* (*MEES*), November 23, 1973.

6. Ibid., November 30, 1973.

7. On October 3, 1974, Yamani stated in Washington: "I assure you that if we solve the Israeli problem the price of oil will come down." Ibid., October 11, 1974. Again in Washington, on April 18, 1975, Yamani told the American Society of Newspaper Editors, "The use of oil as a weapon emanated only from the Arab-Israel dispute. There is not and never has been any bilateral quarrel between Saudi Arabia and the U.S. The same can be said of the other Arab countries, and all we ask of the U.S. is its assistance in the implementation of Security Council Resolution 242 which calls for the return of occupied territories and restoration of the legitimate right of the Palestinian people. Oil as a political weapon could be diffused by reaching a peaceful solution based on Resolution 242, which guarantees the legitimate rights of all the parties concerned." Ibid., April 25, 1975.

8. In testifying before the House Committee on Government Operations, on June 21, 1979, Morris Adelman responded to a question about the embargo: "I do think the embargo of 1973–74 never happened." U.S., Congress, House, Committee on Government Operations, *Hearings: Alternatives to Dealing with OPEC* (Washington, D.C., 1979), p. 177.

9. U.S., Congress, Senate, Committee on Foreign Relations, Subcommittee on Multinational Corporations, *Hearings: Multinational Oil Corporations and United States Foreign Policy,* Part 8 (Washington, D.C., 1975), p. 657 (hereafter cited as Multinationals Subcommittee, *Hearings*). These are schematic calculations. In reality Iraq did not participate in the embargo; Iran increased its production; and Libya did not enforce the embargo.

10. U.S., Congress, Joint Economic Committee, Subcommittee on International Economics, *Report: The State Department's Oil Floor Price Proposal: Should Congress Endorse It?* (Washington, D.C., 1975), p. 16.

11. Multinationals Subcommittee, *Hearings,* Part 5, p. 124. Testimony given on January 31, 1974.

12. Ibid., p. 253.

13. Ibid., Part 8, p. 657.

14. Ibid., Part 7, p. 429.

15. United States Central Intelligence Agency, National Foreign Assessment Center, *The World Oil Market in the Years Ahead* (Washington, D.C., 1979), p. 1.

16. U.S., Congress, Senate, Committee on Energy and National Resources, *The Geopolitics of Oil: Staff Report* (Washington, D.C., 1980), p. 3.

17. *MEES,* September 27, 1982.

18. J. B. Kelly, "Saudi Arabia and the Gulf States," in A. L. Udovitch, ed., *The Middle East Oil, Conflict and Hope: Critical Choices for Americans* (Lexington, Mass., 1976), p. 457.

19. It was reported that, at the Arab summit conference that met in Rabat on October 26–29, 1974, Saudi Arabian Foreign Minister Omar Saqqaf warned the conferees that any use of Arab oil as a political weapon at this stage would have disastrous consequences. At a press conference on November 12, 1975, Henry Kissinger stated diplomatically that the West would be prepared to withstand another Arab oil embargo. "An embargo now would have a less sweeping effect" because of the cooperation of the industrialized states. In an interview with *Newsweek,* November 22, 1976, King Khalid of Saudi Arabia declared that a new oil embargo was out of the question.

20. One of the many examples of the close cooperation between the companies and the producers at the expense of their own governments was reported by U.S., Congress, Library, Congressional Research Service, in its *Congress and the Nation's Environment* (Washington, D.C., 1975), pp. 137–138. Saudi Arabia had directed Aramco to obtain data on the petroleum products delivered from Saudi Arabia and sold to the U.S. military from the Aramco shareholders' refineries to third countries. This information was apparently intended to supplement the Saudi embargo against the United States beginning in October 1973. This secondary embargo data was supplied and was used by Saudi Arabia as a basis for cutting off fuel to the U.S. military overseas. Exxon representatives claimed that they discussed the Saudi request with Defense Department officials and concluded that there was no objection to the turnover of the information to Saudi Arabia. However, Admiral W. M. Oller, director of defense, Fuel Supply Center, testified that the cable from Saudi Arabia to Aramco relating to the imposition of a secondary embargo had not been brought to his attention, and neither was the secretary of defense aware of the request. He declared that if he had seen the Saudi Arabian request, he would have attempted to prevent the information from reaching the Saudis.

21. *New York Times,* January 23, 1974.

22. United States Information Service, *Statements on the Middle East, November 29, 1973–June 24, 1974* (Washington, D.C., 1974), p. 31.

23. Ibid., p. 54.

24. *Maariv,* February 2, 1974.

25. U.S., Congress, Joint Economic Committee, Subcommittee on International Economics, *Hearings: Economic Impact of Petroleum Shortages* (Washington, D.C., 1974), p. 156.

26. The major sources for Chapter 3 were: U.S., Congress, Joint Economic Committee, Subcommittee on International Economics, *Hearings: Economic Impact of Petroleum Shortages;* U.S., Congress, House, Committee on Foreign Affairs, Subcommittee on Foreign Economic Policy and Subcommittee on the Near East and South Asia, *Hearings: Oil Negotiations, OPEC, and the Stability of Supply* (Washington, D.C., 1973); U.S., Congress, House, Committee on Interstate and Foreign Commerce, *Report: Energy Conservation and Conversion Oil Policy Act of 1975* (Washington, D.C., 1975); U.S., Congress, Joint Economic Committee, Subcommittee on International Economics, *Report: The State Department's Oil Floor Proposal;* U.S., Congress, Senate, Committee on Energy and Natural Resources, *The Geopolitics of Oil;* Multinationals Subcommittee, *Hearings,* Parts 5, 7, 8, 9; idem, *Multinational Oil Corporations and U.S. Foreign Policy: Report* (Washington, D.C., 1975); U.S. Comptroller General, *Report to the Congress: Critical Factors Effecting Saudi Arabia's Oil Decisions* (Washington, D.C., 1978); United States Central Intelligence Agency, *The World Oil Market in the Years Ahead* (Washington, D.C., 1979); U.S., Federal Energy Administration, Office of International Energy Affairs, *Report on U.S. Oil Companies and the Arab Oil Embargo* (Washington, D.C., 1974); United States Information Service, *Statements on the Middle East, November 29, 1973–June 24, 1974* (Washington, D.C., 1974); Udovitch, *The Middle East: Oil, Conflict and Hope* (Washington, D.C., 1976); Exxon Background Series, *Middle East Oil* (New York, 1980).

4

RAPID ASCENDANCY
OF THE PRODUCING
COUNTRIES

After the overwhelming achievement of OPEC members in the October and December 1973 unilateral and unprecedented oil price increases, which only whetted their appetites, a race began toward total takeover of the oil-production phase of the industry. The troubling question was: How far could the producers go before the companies would withdraw completely? Practically all the producers depended on the companies for the technological, financial, transportation, and marketing aspects of the oil operations. Should the companies suddenly withdraw, the producers did not possess the financial means for operating the industry nor the ability to compensate the companies for nationalizing their assets. As it turned out, the producers' gamble paid off. The companies took the blows one after another, each heavier than the one before, and were still willing to continue.

Three issues were involved in the takeover process, listed according to their magnitude: (1) level of producer participation in the foreign concessionaire companies; (2) percentage of the profit share (taxation rate); and (3) the royalty base. It should be noted that after the embargo ended OAPEC played no role in the struggle with the companies. The Arab producers' organization concentrated its efforts in elaborating projects and undertakings that were to serve members in technical, economic, and other mutual interests. The struggle between the producers and the companies was carried on exclusively by OPEC.

PRODUCER PARTICIPATION

Although the OPEC secretary-general and the Saudi Arabian oil minister had fully explained in October 1971 why the participation demand should be limited to 25 percent, Kuwait rejected the 25 percent agreement. Then, as early as December 1973, Saudi Arabia and Abu Dhabi demanded an immediate minimum of 51 percent participation, in spite of the agreement signed on October 5, 1972, to wait until 1982.

Kuwait

In June 1973, the Kuwaiti government announced that it was seeking a new participation agreement. At the time it was speculated that the government was seeking a total takeover. However, Robert Dorsey, chairman of Gulf Oil Corporation, who was summoned to a meeting in Kuwait, stated that "at no time was there a discussion or any suggestion of 100% ownership on the part of the Government of Kuwait."[1] Early in January 1974, the Kuwaiti government announced that it had reached agreement with the Kuwait Oil Company for a 60 percent takeover of operations. However, the Kuwait National Assembly urged the government to demand a higher percentage. Oil and Finance Minister Abd al-Rahman al-Atiqi explained to the National Assembly that the government did not demand a 100 percent takeover because it needed the continued foreign expertise and know-how in the oil industry. He stressed that it would be unwise to exaggerate Kuwait's capability to supply these factors from its own resources. On May 14, 1974, the National Assembly ratified the 60 percent participation agreement, to be effective as of January 1, 1974. About three months later the government acquired 60 percent participation in the Kuwaiti half share of the Arabian Oil Company (a Japanese company) concession in the Neutral Zone offshore area.[2]

In February 1975 the Kuwaiti government demanded total takeover. After eight long months of negotiations, Gulf Oil Corporation and British Petroleum, owners of the Kuwait Oil Company, surrendered on December 1, 1975, retroactive to March 15, their 40 percent equity in the concession for a cash payment of $50.5 million and a long-term supply guarantee. The companies were to lift, between them, 950,000 barrels a day, which was to be transported in Kuwaiti tankers. The companies were to buy the oil at current prices but were to be granted fifteen cents a barrel discount. In return for a fee, the companies were to direct all oil operations and give requested technical advice. In July 1977 Kuwait nationalized its half share of Aminoil in the Neutral Zone.

Abu Dhabi

Following a similar pattern, the government of Abu Dhabi began to negotiate with its companies in 1974 and on September 2, 1974, signed an agreement with Abu Dhabi Petroleum effective as of January 1, 1974, to increase participation from 25 percent to 60 percent. Compensation was $40.5 million. A similar agreement was signed with Abu Dhabi Marine Areas.

Abu Dhabi did not follow the other producers in total nationalization. In March 1976, the Abu Dhabi oil minister stated that his country was the only one that had not adopted total government ownership, because it was not yet capable of managing its own oil industry. But, he added, the yield was as much, if not more, as that in other oil states with 100 percent ownership.

Bahrain

At first, Bahrain (a relatively small producer and not an OPEC member) did not join the other producers in their demands for participation and so did not acquire, in 1972, a 25 percent share of Bahrain Petroleum Company. However, on September 25, 1974, Bahrain signed an agreement, retroactive to January 1, for the acquisition of 60 percent participation in the company, but including in the contract a 25 percent share as of January 1, 1973. The Bahrain refinery was not included in the deal.

In March 1975 the Bahrain government announced that the 60 percent agreement was to be considered an interim agreement until a new agreement could be concluded. On December 1975 a new one was signed transferring all oil fields, but not the refinery, to the government. On July 19, 1980, the Bahrain government acquired 60 percent participation in the refinery. (Most of the oil for the refinery came from Saudi Arabia.)

Iraq

The Iraq Petroleum Company had owned in Iraq three separate concession areas: the IPC concession in the central area, the Mosul Petroleum Company concession in the far north, and the Basrah Petroleum Company concession in the south on the Gulf. In 1972, Iraq nationalized the IPC specific concession area; then IPC voluntarily surrendered the Mosul Petroleum Company concession area to the government. The February 28, 1973, agreement between the Iraqi government and the Iraq Petroleum Company left, of the three concession areas, only the Basrah Petroleum Company in the hands of the IPC. The agreement required a production increase in 1973 to 35 million tons, in 1974 to 45 million tons, in 1975 to 65 million tons, and in 1976 to 80 million tons. (Total production from all three companies in 1972 was 72 million tons.)

On October 7, 1973, Iraq announced the nationalization of the shares of the two U.S. companies—Mobil and Exxon—in the Basrah company, as an act of punishing the United States for its Middle East policy. Two weeks later the government nationalized the Royal Dutch–Shell share in the company as a punishment of the Netherlands. On December 20, Iraq took over the 5 percent share of the Partex Foundation (Gulbenkian); this was to punish Portugal, because the foundation was located in Lisbon, for permitting the United States to refuel in the Azores the planes supplying Israel.

Although Iraq was not a signatory to the 25 percent participation agreement, it took advantage of the new participation pattern and early in March 1975 signed an interim agreement for a 60 percent arrangement with the remaining two companies, British and French, retroactive to January 1, 1974. Finally on December 8, 1975, in Baghdad, Iraqi President Hasan al-Bakr announced the nationalization of the remaining foreign interests in the company.

Libya

After Libya nationalized 51 percent of the assets of the independent oil companies in its territory, the companies formed a united resistance front and refused to comply with the demand. Soon, however, the front began to fall apart. As before, Occidental Petroleum Corporation acquiesced to the government's demand early in September 1973 on terms much harsher than those granted the companies in the Gulf area. The other independents operating in Libya followed suit very rapidly.

Six major companies refused the government decree and filed a letter of protest with the Libyan government asking for arbitration. On February 12, 1974, Libya announced that it had nationalized three U.S. companies as punishment for the provocative oil consumers' conference that had recently been convened by U.S. President Nixon in Washington. The following month, the Libyan oil minister reported that the Mobil Oil Corporation had accepted 51 percent nationalization. In July, Shell Oil Company accepted the terms of Libya's 100 percent takeover of the company's assets. In December 1974, British Petroleum reached a final settlement of all issues outstanding between itself and the Libyan government including the nationalization of its assets. Finally, in November 1977, Texaco and Standard Oil of California announced that they had reached a settlement with the Libyan government arising from the nationalization of their assets in 1973 and 1974.

Oman

In February 1974, the Oman government signed an agreement with Petroleum Development (Oman) to acquire 25 percent participation in the concern effective as of January 1, 1974. On July 17, 1974, the government raised the share to 60 percent, retroactive to January 1, 1974.

Qatar

The Qatar government signed an agreement in February 1974 raising participation from 25 percent to 60 percent retroactive to January 1, 1974, with both the Qatar Petroleum Company onshore concession and the Qatar Shell Company offshore concession. In October 1976, the government nationalized the remaining 40 percent of the two foreign companies.

Saudi Arabia

In March 1973, the Saudi oil minister, Ahmad Zaki Yamani, explained the attitude of his government on the issue of participation, "For our part, we do not want the majors to lose their power and be forced to abandon their role as a buffer element between the producers and the consumers. We want the present set-up to continue as long as possible and at all costs to avoid any disastrous clash of interests which would shake the foundation of the world oil business. This is why we are calling for participation."[3] Yet eight months later, Saudi Arabia demanded a basic change in its relationship with Aramco, to be based on a more than 51 percent government share in the company. In June 1974, when Aramco agreed to raise the 25 percent government share to 60 percent, the *Petroleum Times* noted that "with Saudi Arabia taking 60 percent control of its oil, the power of the world crude oil has virtually passed out of the hands of the oil companies into the hands of the producing state."[4]

On July 10, 1974, an Aramco spokesman announced that as of January 1, 1974, Saudi participation was to be 60 percent. It was also reported in New York that Yamani proposed a change in relationship between his country and Aramco to be based on 100 percent nationalization: The company was to pay full international market prices without discounts for the oil;

the company was to continue providing managerial and technical services, for a fee; the posted price was to be abolished; and the tax-structure base of payment was to be terminated. Full compensation to the company was to be based on updated book value.[5]

After meetings in New York, London, and Quiberon, in France, over a period of more than two years, Saudi Arabia and Aramco arrived at an agreement in October 1976. Aramco was to continue—unlike the nationalized companies in Kuwait and Iran—to handle marketing of the output of 8 million barrels a day. Terms were practically the same as had been outlined earlier by Yamani. The official announcement of the agreement was made in Riyadh in February 1979. The terms were actually agreed upon on January 1, 1976, but signature was delayed because of organizational considerations. In mid-September 1981, it was reported that Saudi Arabia paid the last installment due Aramco under the arrangements agreed upon with the transfer of $1.5 billion to the four partners of the company.

Conclusion

It is clear that between January 1973 and January 1976 practically all the Middle East oil producers—including non-OPEC members Bahrain and Oman—gained full control of the oil-production industries in their respective territories. The concessionaire companies lost, in the short period of three years, all their concessions and some of the power that went with them.

PROFIT SHARE AND ROYALTY RATE

For a better appreciation of developments in OPEC after the 1973–1974 oil crisis, the role and policies of Saudi Arabia must be clearly understood. Saudi Arabia emerged as the greatest oil producer—the possessor, by far, of the largest reserves of all the members of the organization and after the tremendous price increases, no doubt, the richest. Saudi Arabia, however, protecting its own interests, followed a consistent policy throughout the entire period in favor of reducing, if possible, the high price of oil, or at least freezing it. The Saudis maintained that the huge December 1973 increase endangered their future oil resources. The other OPEC members wished not only to keep prices high but also to examine possibilities of increasing their oil revenues.

When OPEC met in Geneva on January 7–9, 1974, it decided to freeze prices until April 1, in order to give its Economic Commission time to examine the price policy. Nevertheless, the conference decided not to abide by the Geneva II formula, which would have reduced the posted price by 6 percent because of the appreciation of the dollar. The June 1974 OPEC meeting in Quito, Ecuador, continued the price freeze but decided to raise the royalty percentage from 12.5 to 14.5 percent. The Economic Commission recommended an increase in the profit share from 55 percent to 87 percent. The Saudi Arabian oil minister, Ahmad Zaki Yamani, argued for lowering the posted price. He maintained that the existing level of crude-oil prices was ruinous to the global economy and, among other things, gave unfair advantage to the socialist bloc countries, which were relatively self-sufficient in energy resources. He therefore disassociated his country from the decision to increase the royalty on the equity crude. Algeria, on the other hand, defended the OPEC existing posted price system on purely economic grounds. The Algerian delegate declared that the October war "at the most played the role of a catalyst in taking a decision which was already well prepared and well justified on the economic level."[6]

In September, OPEC raised the royalty percentage from 14.5 to 16.7 percent and the tax rate from 55 to 65 percent. Early in November three Gulf OPEC member countries—Saudi Arabia, Qatar, and Abu Dhabi—met in Abu Dhabi and decided to: (1) lower the present posted price of marker crude from $11.65 to $11.25; (2) increase the royalty to 20 percent; and (3) increase the tax rate to 85 percent. This so-called Abu Dhabi formula was subsequently adopted by other members. This arrangement increased the averaged government revenue per barrel from $9.41 to $11.12.

Table 4.1 Middle East Oil: Cost and Profitability, 1948–1975

	1948	1951	1960	1970	1973	1974	1975
Participation, royalty, taxes (percent)							
Host government share of production	0	0	0	0	25	60	60
Host government royalty rate	—	—	12.5	12.5	12.5	20	20
Host government tax rate	0	50	50	50	55	85	85
Prices (dollars per barrel)							
Posted price	2.05	1.75	1.80	1.80	2.90	11.25	12.40
Typical sales price	2.05	1.75	1.80	1.40	2.30	10.45	11.50
Costs (dollars per barrel)							
Operating costs (explor. and prod.)	.60	.20	.20	.10	.15	.15	.25
Host government take	.25	.75	.80	.95	1.80	10.10	11.00
Profits (dollars per barrel)	1.20	.80	.80	.35	.35	.20	.25

Source: Exxon, Background Series, *Middle East Oil* (New York, 1976)

The radical OPEC members were greatly agitated over the dollar serving as the basis for payment for oil and demanded a change. In spite of the strong opposition of Iran and Saudi Arabia, the OPEC conference that took place in Libreville, Gabon, in June 1975 decided to abandon the dollar as the currency payment and to increase the posted price in October. U.S. President Gerald Ford declared on July 1, 1975, that action by OPEC to raise prices in October would be "unacceptable" to the United States. Secretary of the Treasury William Simon stated that an oil price increase was not justified on economic grounds, but added that there was little the United States could do about it until alternatives to oil were found. "They can, for a time, get away with that blackmail."[7] Secretary of State Henry Kissinger warned that an additional price increase might force the United States to take drastic action.

This was the general atmosphere when the OPEC conference opened in Vienna on September 19, 1975. After three days of heated wrangling, which threatened the unity of the organization, the oil ministers of the thirteen countries decided to increase the crude-oil price by 10 percent from October 1 until June 30, 1976, when the price would be reviewed. It was calculated at the time that the increase would cost the consumers an additional $10 billion aggregating to $110 billion a year. Arabian light oil was to go up to $12.87 a barrel. The high price of oil inevitably cut down on consumption, and as a result, total Middle East oil production fell from 1,083 million tons in 1974 to 973 million tons in 1975, an 11.1 percent drop; curiously the drop ranged from 5 percent for Abu Dhabi to 18 percent for Kuwait and 20 percent for Saudi Arabia, but Iraq increased its production in 1975 by 21.5 percent.[8] The *Petroleum Economist* of August 1975 stated that there was more than suspicion that INOC (Iraq National Oil Company) had been trimming its prices to increase sales. *World Oil* of August 15, 1976, noted that although Iraq demanded a price increase at the OPEC Bali conference, the Iraq National Oil Company reportedly cut prices (by up to $1 per barrel) to increase production. As a result, Iraq replaced Kuwait as the second largest Arab producer, after Saudi Arabia, and Iraq's revenue for 1975 was higher than that of Kuwait.

At the December 1975 OPEC conference in Vienna, Algeria's representative charged Iraq with slashing prices in order to maintain the maximum volume of exports. He accused Iraq of "not playing the game," in respect to OPEC's price aims. Iraq contended that it should be allowed a marketing leeway of some twenty to twenty-five cents below the official OPEC selling price for its nationalized crude, an amount granted as discount by the producers to their companies. To this the Algerian minister replied that adopting Iraq's contention would be tantamount to nullifying the effects of nationalization, in which case the "celebration for nationalization should be turned into a wake of mourning."[9]

In spite of the drop in demand and the consequent drop in production, and in spite of Saudi Arabia's opposition, OPEC increased royalty payments from 12.5 percent to 20 percent, the tax rate from 55 percent to 85 percent, and the posted price by 10 percent.[10] Total Middle East oil revenue increased from $9.4 billion in 1972 to $74 billion in 1975. The companies were still willing to work and cooperate with the producers.

PANIC OF SURPLUSES AND DEFICITS

The enormous jump in oil prices from 1972 to 1974 caused far-reaching financial upheavals as well as serious psychological disturbances. It upset both consumers and producers when they were overwhelmed by the tremendous, if not fantastic, transfer of wealth from the consumers (developed industrialized and developing countries) into the hands of the producers (mostly underdeveloped countries). The impact was astounding, and the magnitude of the phenomenon was difficult, if not impossible, to grasp. Those who dealt with it operated on two assumptions. One, that the prices of oil would remain high and would most likely rise to higher levels as demand also rose, while consumers would have no alternative but to pay the price decreed by the producers. The second assumption, which made the first even more frightening, was that the oil-producing countries' capacity to absorb the prodigious amounts of wealth amassed from the oil was very limited, and the bulk of the revenues would not return to the countries that paid for the oil. This meant ever-increasing accumulations of gigantic surpluses would come into the producers' hands, which would endow them with strong financial as well as political powers.

This pessimistic, almost despairing, outlook loomed heavily in the minds of the consumers and, on the other hand, beamed brightly and gleefully in the minds of the producers. The producers began to talk not only of the oil weapon but also equally of the money weapon that they had acquired as the result of their victory over the foreign concessionaires. Consumer representatives were stunned by the rapid development of events and attempted to describe and explain the ramifications of the misfortune. A very penetrating and gloomy description of the situation was presented by Gerald A. Pollack, managing director of the International Monetary Fund, in the April 1974 issue of *Foreign Affairs*. He stated that the combination of oil shortages and price increases in 1974 was likely to produce "a staggering disequilibrium in the global balance of payments . . . that will place strains on the monetary system far in excess of any that have been experienced since the war." He raised a number of searching questions, among them: (1) Could the international monetary system sustain a transfer of wealth of such unprecedented dimensions without extensive disruptions or even collapse because of the intolerable balance of payments strain? (2) Would the consuming countries be able to make the necessary internal adjustments without severe dislocations and with no lasting impairment of growth? (3) How severe would be the impact of higher prices on living standards? (4) How would the resource-poor Third World be able to cope with the oil crisis, and what would be the political consequences for the industrial countries?

Pollack estimated that the import-of-oil cost for the United States, Europe, and Japan might be $50 billion more in 1974 than it was in 1973, and by 1985 it might reach $200 billion. He believed that the OPEC investable surplus might total $100 billion by the end of 1974 and could cumulate to almost $500 billion by 1980 and more than $600 billion by 1985. These magnitudes would seem to be enough to scuttle any monetary system. Pollack asserted that "the transfer of wealth to oil-producing countries cannot fail to take its toll on the living standards of the industrial world, although even here some of the real burden could be shifted to future generations"; and concluded, with almost prophetic vision, as regards the Third World, "It seems unlikely that the industrial nations or the oil rich Arab states will be willing to provide financial support on the scale that could well be necessary to avoid violence and anarchy in these countries."

The International Monetary Fund estimated in April 1975 that the surpluses in the trade balance between the producers and the consumers had reached, in 1974, $97 billion in favor of the producers, compared to $23 billion in 1973. The accumulated deficit in the trade balance of the consuming countries during 1974 had reached $67 billion compared to $21 billion in 1973; and the developing non-oil-producing countries had amassed a deficit of $26 billion compared to $12 billion in 1973. In about August 1974, it became known that a secret study conducted by the International Bank had concluded that by 1980 the oil-producing countries would have amassed a surplus of $650 billion, and in 1985 that surplus might reach $1,200 billion. This amount was ten times larger than all U.S. investments in foreign countries and a hundred times larger than all the gold held by the United States.[11] Another study, conducted by the economic specialists of the European Economic Community, concluded that if oil prices remained stable, if oil consumption in Western Europe was drastically curtailed, and if the hopes for producers' investments were fully realized, the balance-of-payments deficit of five EEC countries—Italy, Britain, France, Denmark, and Ireland—would reach $90 billion in 1978.

The London *Economist* studied the magnitude of the revenue of the oil-producing countries during 1974. The study estimated, in typical financial terms, that OPEC could buy all companies of the world's stock exchanges in 16.6 years, all the companies of the New York stock exchange in 9.2 years, all central banks' gold in 3.2 years, all U.S. direct investments abroad in 1.8 years, all companies quoted on the stock exchanges in Britain, France, and West Germany in 1.7 years, all IBM stock in 143 days, all Exxon stock in 79 days, the Rockefeller family wealth in 6 days, 14 percent of Germany's Daimler-Benz in 2 days.[12] (Kuwait actually paid for 14 percent of Daimler-Benz with the oil revenue of 15 days.) On September 12, 1974, U.S. Secretary of the Treasury William Simon stated that it had finally dawned on the American people and the people of other oil-importing nations that the wealth of the consumers was being transferred to the producers.[13] He assumed a $53.9 billion annual surplus for the entire Middle East. In about five years the surplus would be worth the entire *Fortune* 500 corporations. On January 6, 1975, *Time* described the price increase from $1.99 per barrel before October 1973 to over $10 at the end of 1974 as "the greatest and swiftest transfer of wealth in all history." By the end of 1975, the Chase Manhattan Bank of New York estimated that the oil-exporting countries were holding more than 25 percent of the world's foreign currency reserves.[14]

The December 20, 1976, issue of *Business Week* summarized the consequences of the high oil prices:

1. The economic growth rate that was achievable by the industrial world had been permanently lowered. This intensified the unemployment-inflation dilemma. The world economy was doomed to rising unemployment if the governments refrained from stimulus, but to inflation if they resorted to demand-boosting measures.
2. The less-developed countries had piled up $170 billion in external debts—an amount far exceeding their capacity, by any standard, to repay. The only alternative would have been a massive repudiation of the Third World indebtedness, and that would have been a threat to the structure of international finance.
3. The United States and its allies had virtually acquiesced in the OPEC pricing system.

Near the end of 1976, the U.S. Treasury and Morgan Guaranty Trust Company began systematically to issue estimates and assessments that reduced the magnitude of the surpluses in the hands of the producing countries and the negative implications associated with the surpluses. Morgan Guaranty even predicted that within a few years the producers would begin to experience deficits instead of surpluses in their balance of payments.[15] Nonetheless, as late as May 1977, Robert R. Herring, chairman of the Houston Natural Gas Company, declared that about $140 billion was spent during 1976 to import mostly Middle East oil. Of the total amount, the United States paid $37 billion and Western Europe more than $70 billion. He estimated that before 1980 the investable funds controlled by the countries of the Middle East would equal or exceed the capital resources of the non-Communist world. They would include all central banks' reserves and commercial banks' holdings.[16]

From these predictions and estimates, by highly reputable international financial institutions and banks and other highly placed financial and economic experts, emerged a bleak and almost desperate picture of the Western economic situation, brought about by the oil pricing system imposed by the oil producers on the consumers. It would therefore follow that the industrial powers would be sufficiently aroused to take united measures to avert the dire predictions. What the Western nations attempted to do to meet the great challenge of the producers will be detailed in Chapter 5. Here it should be noted that despite the serious consequences of deficits in the balance of payments—increase in unemployment and high inflation, a heavy drop in economic growth, and a general economic recession—the international monetary structure did not collapse. Somehow the industrial nations learned, after awhile, to adjust to the new conditions and live with them. The victims were the non-oil-producing nations of the Third World, who did not possess the means of adjusting to the new conditions. The greater the oil prices, the greater became their indebtedness, and even greater their inability to repay.

The ability of the individual nations to adjust to the new realities stemmed not only from their basic economic strength and resources but also from the invalidity of the two assumptions made by analysts—that prices and demand would remain high and that producers would accumulate gigantic surpluses of wealth. In actuality, the high oil prices inevitably reduced consumption, as reflected in the reduced production figures of 1975 and 1978.[17] This diminished the cost for the consumers. The higher inflation in the consuming industrial countries affected the spending of the producing countries for their imports. While in Washington, the shah of Iran declared on May 18, 1975, that the oil price would probably be increased at the OPEC meeting in September because the oil-producing nations were faced with higher prices for the goods and commodities they purchased from the industrialized nations. He asserted that OPEC countries had lost about 35 percent of

Table 4.2 Middle East Oil Production: Revenue Surplus, 1974–1979

Year	Production (million tons)	Revenue (billion dollars)	Surplus (billion dollars)
1974	1,085.0	106	68
1975	975.1	99	35
1976	1,107.1	122	40
1977	1,118.4	135	33
1978	1,058.9	127	11
1979	1,076.4	175	35

Sources: British Petroleum, *Statistical Review of the World Oil Industry, 1979;*
    New York Times, June 24, 1979. The surplus figures are based on
    the estimates of the Morgan Guaranty Trust Company (as given in
    World Financial Markets, which reported on Middle East oil in either
    the March or April issue beginning with 1974; occasional references
    were made in other issues); those of the Bank of England are slightly
    higher.

their purchasing power because of inflation. Iran therefore
advocated a 35 percent increase in the price of oil.

But the most decisive factor was the erroneous assessment
of the financial absorptive capacity of the producing countries.
Although the economic development level of most of the Middle
East oil-producing countries was considerably low, as time went
on the absorptive capacity jumped by leaps and bounds, and
spending of the oil revenue on the most gigantic scale became
the order of the day. This new Middle East spending spree was
the major and redeeming means of saving the international
financial structure, the story of which will be presented in
Chapter 7.[18]

NOTES

1. *New York Times,* June 14, 1973.
2. After World War I, the boundaries between Najd (later part of
Saudi Arabia) and Kuwait were undefined. In 1922, the British, with
the consent of the two shaikhdoms, established the area—covering

250 square miles—as the Neutral Zone, in which both parties had equal rights. The zone is very rich in oil resources, and both countries shared the income from the oil. In 1964, Saudi Arabia and Kuwait decided to divide the zone administratively between themselves; the natural resources were to be shared as before. The area was renamed the Partition Zone. For further details see Benjamin Shwadran, *Middle East Oil and the Great Powers* (Boulder, Colo., 1985), pp. 423–426.

3. *Petroleum Press Service,* May 1973, p. 272.

4. *Petroleum Times,* June 14, 1974.

5. *Petroleum Economist,* July 1974, p. 251; *Middle East Economic Survey (MEES),* July 12, 1974; *Petroleum Times,* June 28/July 12, 1974.

6. *MEES,* June 21, 1974.

7. *Jerusalem Post,* July 3, 1975.

8. If the total Iraqi production of about 830,199,100 barrels were roughly divided into the total Iraqi revenue of $8.3 billion, the return per barrel would amount to $10; the averages for the other major producers amounted to over $11. *New York Times,* January 25, 1976; *World Oil,* August 15, 1976; Morgan Guaranty Trust Company, *World Financial Markets,* January 1976; British Petroleum, *Statistical Review of the World Oil Industry 1975,* p. 18. See Chapter 7.

9. *MEES,* December 26, 1975.

10. In May 1976, Oman raised the royalty rate from 16.7 percent to 20 percent; as of April 1, 1976, the tax base was raised from 65.8 percent to 80 percent. *World Oil,* June 1976; *Petroleum Economist,* May 1976.

11. *Petroleum Economist,* September 1974, p. 355; *Hadashot Haneft,* September 10, 1974.

12. Summarized in *Time,* January 6, 1975.

13. *World Oil,* November 1974, pp. 95–100.

14. *Jerusalem Post,* December 1, 1975.

15. *New York Times,* October 5, 1976; *Hadashot Haneft,* February 2, 1977.

16. *Oil and Gas Journal,* May 2, 1977.

17. *Petroleum Economist,* March 1975, noted that the high prices led to a reduction from 1973 to 1974 of about 2.5 percent in exports, as against a previously forecast increase of about 7.5 percent.

18. The major sources for Chapter 4 were: U.S., Congress, Senate, Committee on Foreign Relations, Subcommittee on Multinational Corporations, *Hearings: Multinational Corporations and United States Foreign Policy,* Part 7 (Washington, D.C., 1974); idem, *Multinational Oil Corporations and U.S. Foreign Policy: Report* (Washington, D.C.,

1975); U.S. Comptroller General, *Report to the Congress: More Attention Should Be Paid to Making the U.S. Less Vulnerable to Foreign Oil Price and Supply Decisions* (Washington, D.C., 1978); OPEC, *Annual Review and Record* (Vienna, 1974); United Arab Emirates, Department of Press and Publication, Ministry of Information and Culture, *Partners for Progress: A Report on the United Arab Emirates, 1971–1976* (n.p., n.d.); Iraq National Oil Company, *The Nationalization of Iraq Petroleum Company's Operations in Iraq: The Facts and Causes* (Baghdad, 1973); idem, *A Brief Chronicle of Major Events 1961–1973* (Baghdad, 1974); British Petroleum, *Statistical Review of the World Oil Industry 1976*; Jordan J. Paust and Albert B. Blaustein, *The Arab Oil Weapon* (Dobbs Ferry, N.Y., 1977); Exxon, Background Series, *Middle East Oil* (New York, 1980).

5

CONSUMER RESISTANCE EFFORTS

It was a well-established fact before the outbreak of the October 1973 oil crisis, and even more obvious after the resultant developments, that most of the Western European countries and Japan were heavily dependent on Middle East oil for the healthy functioning of their economies. The Middle East was the oil-producing area where quantities were large enough, production was relatively easy, quality was high, and access was free and unencumbered. It was equally clear that in spite of the many divergences in the interests of its members and the various obstacles and basic difficulties which OPEC had faced since its establishment, around 1973 it emerged as a body united and determined to attain its objectives.

CONFLICTING INTERESTS OF THE OIL-CONSUMING COUNTRIES

The oil-consuming countries, in contrast, were disunited and had no common purpose; because of individual selfish interests they were not ready to resist energetically and resolutely the mounting demands of the producers. One of the major underlying reasons for this phenomenon was the different levels of dependence of each group of the consuming countries on Middle East oil and the individual consuming countries' political interests and aims in the region.

Although the United States was the greatest consumer of oil in the world, both in absolute quantity and in per capita consumption, its dependence on Middle East oil was very limited. With a relatively easy cut of ten percent in consumption the United States could have easily freed itself, in times of emergency, from any dependence on the Middle East. In spite of its strong determination—a determination stemming from economic, political, and strategic factors—to continue and even greatly enhance its friendly relations with the Middle East producing countries, especially at the expense of the Soviet Union, the United States was willing to adopt bold measures that would free all the Western countries from the economic and political pressures of the Middle East oil-producing countries. Western European countries, conversely, depended on the Middle East oil for about 68 percent of their total energy needs. Although the countries of the European Economic Community (EEC) were planning to increase, over an extended period of time, their energy supply from local sources, they were to remain dependent on the Middle East for most of their energy supply for a long time. Japan's situation was even worse. It had been estimated that its dependence on Middle East oil had reached as high as 80–90 percent of its total energy consumption. As both Western Europe and Japan had no alternative energy sources, they were subject to OPEC pressure.[1]

The economic structures—standard of living, level of industrial development, level of technology, rate of economic growth, and quality of life and culture—of the United States, Western Europe, and Japan were all based on oil energy. Hence the radically different attitudes of Japan and Western Europe from that of the United States to the energy problem and to its possible solutions. The United States was never—until the 1973 crisis—dependent on energy sources from outside the American continent, while Western European countries and Japan were used to dependence on the Middle East and had accommodated themselves accordingly. They did not, therefore, suffer from shock at the realization of their dependence; moreover, both had suffered defeat during World War II and were better able to adjust psychologically to the inevitable change. Not so the United States. The Americans were stunned by the possibility of depending on the Middle East for supply of their future energy needs—civilian and military—and the threatening implications of such dependence for their global strategy. For a nation that came out the victor in the greatest global struggle in history, for a nation that emerged after that war unharmed, the most powerful, the richest, and technologically and scientifically the most advanced, to submit to the will of the Middle East oil-producing countries was inconceivable.

Yet, on the other hand, the Western European countries have long suffered from a complex of dependence on the United States. Throughout the period of oil development the United States dominated the oil resources of the world. It had enormous oil reserves in its own territory that for a long time supplied its own needs; it even exported oil. In addition, the United States had succeeded, since the end of World War I, in gaining control of a great part of the oil resources outside its territory, especially in the Middle East. Up to the early 1970s, the U.S. oil companies owned, as was mentioned in Chapter 1, the lion's share of the oil concessions in the region. The Western European countries were, therefore, dependent physically on the Middle East but practically on the U.S. companies for their oil supply. They, especially France, resented this humiliating situation and have attempted in different ways to extricate themselves from this, to them, oppressive dependence.

When the 1973 oil crisis broke out and the Arabs imposed an oil embargo, primarily against the United States, the Western Europeans saw a rare opportunity to rid themselves of the American yoke. France saw in the crisis a chance to become the new European leader by bringing about a new rapprochement with Arab Middle East countries and thus forging strong and renewed relations with them. France had an old score to settle with the Anglo-Saxon countries, which it believed were responsible for the elimination of France from the region. It envisioned a triumphant return to leadership and high prestige in Europe and the Middle East.

The first reaction of the United States to the oil crisis came on November 7, 1973, when President Richard Nixon announced Project Independence, whose aim was to develop "the potential to meet our own energy needs without depending on any foreign energy sources. Let us pledge that by 1980, under Project Independence we shall be able to meet America's needs from America's own energy resources."[2] Although Project Independence was featured as a major aspect in the solution of the energy crisis and was invoked many times in the years that followed—President Nixon even taunted the Arab producers, saying that they would have to drink their oil—it was realized soon after the project's presentation that it was only one element, and not an important one, in the arsenal against the producers.[3] The main effort would have to be made through uniting all the consuming nations.

The United States was ready for a match of strength between the producers and consumers in which it, of course, would be the leader of the contest. In such a test of strength lurked a danger to U.S. Middle East strategic policy, but this danger was secondary compared to the danger of retreat and surrender to the producing countries. Should the consumers succeed in winning the struggle, U.S. prestige would be greatly enhanced, as well as the prestige of the other members of the Western bloc, and the United States would be strengthened in its global struggle with the Soviet Union.

The two basic objectives of all the consuming countries were the continuous and secure supply of oil and reasonable prices; on these there was no difference of opinion. However, because of the different conditions among the consumers, fundamental differences of priorities emerged. The Europeans and the Japanese were primarily concerned with security of supplies, in response to their immediate experience of shortages caused by the embargo; the price was high, and efforts should be made to lower it, but this was of secondary importance. The United States, in contrast, was chiefly preoccupied with the price issue, and supplies for its own needs were of minor importance. These factors, in addition to political considerations (the rivalry between the Western allies), sharply divided the groups as to the steps to be taken to achieve the aims. Three attempts were made to find solutions for the consumers' oil problem.

The first attempt was initiated by the United States, which believed that the first decisive and practical step in the contest with the producers must be unification of all the consuming countries into one strong organization. The United States was convinced that the producers could not withstand a determined united front of the consumers and expressed this opinion in 1971, when the efforts of OPEC began to bear fruits of success. However, the Western European countries failed to respond. When OPEC obtained its demands from the foreign concessionaire companies, U.S. Under Secretary of State William Casey stated in June 1973 in New York: "We are interested in the development of an effective continuing mechanism among the oil-consuming nations for sharing oil in the event of an emergency curtailment of supply."[4] France, Italy, and Japan rejected this proposal. After Libya nationalized its foreign oil companies, especially the U.S. companies, the United States sent a delegation to the Organization for Economic Cooperation and Development (OECD) in Paris and again attempted to persuade the major consuming countries to adopt a program of sharing oil resources in case of a cut in supplies by the producing countries. However, the European countries steadfastly refused.

After the Arab oil embargo was imposed in October 1973, U.S. Secretary of State Henry Kissinger, on December 12, called for a cooperative move by the United States, Europe, and Japan. He proposed the naming of an energy committee that would be given instructions to prepare a practical program within ninety days. He stressed that the United States would be ready to contribute the major share of the financial and technical needs for this purpose. At a later stage the producing countries would be invited to join this committee. Kissinger also stressed that although the United States could, without difficulty, solve its energy problem alone, Europe and Japan could not hope to do so; he therefore advocated a worldwide body to deal with the world energy problems of the future.

INTERNATIONAL ENERGY AGENCY (IEA)

The president of the United States invited, on January 9, 1974, the foreign ministers of France, Britain, West Germany, Italy, the Netherlands, Norway, Canada, and Japan to a conference in Washington, D.C., to meet on February 11 to deal with the energy crisis that had resulted from the Arab oil embargo. The invitation caused internal difficulties for the European Economic Community. At a meeting of EEC foreign ministers that took place in Brussels, four days after the Nixon invitation, France attempted to block the efforts of the United States. France argued that the conference would prompt the Arab producers to impose new sanctions against the consumers, which would cause serious hardships to Europe and would hardly affect the United States; if other raw materials producers were not invited, they would adopt the same measures that the Arab oil producers had imposed. The French foreign minister proposed, instead, to call a world conference under the aegis of the United Nations, to which all consuming and producing nations would be invited for the purpose of establishing a new world order. Accepting the United States' invitation would have interfered with France's own objectives in relation to the Arabs, which France had actually achieved in the form of the November 6, 1973, EEC declaration, described openly by the French as pro-Arab. However, on January 15, the members of the EEC decided—French objection notwithstanding—to accept the Nixon invitation. France then tried to persuade the members who were to attend to restrict the conference to the formulation of general principles on the question of energy; under no circumstances was the conference to deal with tactics and measures against the oil-producing countries.

Even while these discussions on participation in the conference were going on, tension between the United States and France was growing. Early in January 1974, France announced that it had completed a deal with Saudi Arabia for purchasing 800 million tons of crude oil over a period of twenty years, for which France would supply Saudi Arabia with heavy armaments, military advanced aircraft, and other sophisticated equipment. The State Department representative plaintively noted on January 7 that although it was customary among friendly nations to inform, through advance notice, about arms deals, France had not advised the United States about its reported new twenty-year arms-oil agreement with Saudi Arabia. The French armed forces minister, Robert Galley, declared on January 24, that

France would sell arms to Arab countries without any inhibitions. French Foreign Minister Michel Jobert, visiting the Middle East, said at the end of January in Kuwait that the world energy crisis could be solved on a collective basis, "but each country has the right to work unilaterally to ensure its oil requirements."[5]

The conference opened in Washington as scheduled with a speech by the U.S. secretary of state, host of the conference. Kissinger presented a seven-point program and proposed the creation of a new body to deal with the energy problem. In spite of France's objection, the conference adopted the Kissinger proposal and decided to appoint a coordinating committee to prepare a program for a conference of consumers and producers, to be convened at the earliest possible date.

Two weeks after the conclusion of the conference, representatives of twelve countries—eight members of the EEC, Canada, Japan, Norway, and the United States—met in Washington to organize a coordinating committee. The reaction of the producers was not late in coming. The secretary-general of OPEC attacked the conference and maintained, as did France, that the proper forum for dealing with the energy problem was the United Nations. Algeria's President Houari Boumedienne called the Washington conference a "plan designed to prevent contacts between the oil producing and consuming countries." Other Arab spokesmen described the conference and its decisions as a "provocation" aimed at a confrontation between producers and consumers.[6] Because the conference proceeded with the implementation of its decisions, political commentators saw in it an impressive diplomatic victory for the United States.

The seven-member coordinating committee met in Brussels on March 13 and decided to establish three special subcommittees: one to formulate the role of the international oil companies, one to examine the state of research in the conventional sources of energy, and one to deal with atomic energy. The twelve-member Washington committee continued to deal with the energy crisis. In case of a new embargo against one of the members the others would see it as aimed at all of them, and they would share their energy resources with the embargoed country. The member states were to regulate their oil price and

supply policies in such a way as not to disturb industrial development and economic prosperity. The committee also decided that members that were producers were to increase output and that all members were to enlarge their oil stockpiles to be prepared in case of a second embargo.[7]

On October 30, Belgium, which acted as temporary secretary of the committee, announced that the United States and nine other countries of the twelve had decided to establish the International Energy Agency (IEA); it would be officially inaugurated in Paris on November 18 and would be an autonomous body within the OECD framework. Six other countries—Austria, Switzerland, Sweden, Spain, Australia, and New Zealand—indicated that they would join. On September 19, the French premier, Jacques Chirac, repeated that his country refused to join a bloc of consuming countries. He added, "France's policy has not changed. The price increases of raw materials are legitimate. France refuses to be part of a confrontation between users and sellers."[8]

In an attempt, apparently, to obtain maximum results from the efforts of the coordinating committee, the U.S. secretary of state had asked the foreign and finance ministers of France, Britain, West Germany, and Japan to a special conclave at Camp David, at the end of September, to deal with the energy problem. After these discussions no decisions had been made public. it was reported, however, that very serious differences of opinion had emerged during the meeting. Although France was the only member of the EEC that had initially opposed the U.S. proposal of a consumers' union against the producers, and although the other EEC members had attended the conference (and subsequently even became members of the International Energy Agency), they had never been ready to join an organization that committed them to a real showdown with the oil producers, as had been envisioned by the U.S. secretary of state. The Camp David meeting had exposed the gap not only between the United States and France but also between the United States and Britain, West Germany, and Japan.

The Europeans voiced their fear that a confrontation between consumers and producers might bring about an economic crisis paralleling that of the 1930s and warned the United States to abandon its fight to lower oil prices as fruitless. Instead, the United States should join in finding means of financing the higher costs of imported oil. At the annual meeting of the World Bank and the International Monetary Fund, the French delegate stated, "The fundamental problem in the present situation is not so much a decline in oil prices. That is not plausible. The problem is to adapt to the higher prices and organize our society and employment levels on a new price of oil."[9]

The Japanese finance minister, Tohio Kimura, had declared on September 27 that "confrontation must be avoided at all costs between the oil producing and oil consuming countries." This was also the opinion of Germany's chancellor, Helmut Schmidt, and the French delegate to the World Bank concluded that "there is no possible way of forcing the Arabs to lower oil prices except through peaceful dialogue."[10] Secretary of State Kissinger, on the other hand, was determined to pursue his original objective of bringing down the oil prices by strong means, if necessary. Late in October he asserted that "the high price of oil is not the result of economic forces. . . . it was the result of arbitrary decisions taken with the purpose of reducing production to keep up artificial high prices." He warned, without mincing words, "Prices that went up as a result of political decisions can also come down by political decisions."[11]

It was in this tense atmosphere that the International Energy Agency was formally launched on November 18. In addition to establishing its general organizational structure and system of voting, the agency made the following decisions: First, a ten-year blueprint was to be worked out that would reduce dependence on imported oil by limiting demand and by developing alternatives; and second, the major role of the agency was defined as coordinating all the energy measures of the consuming countries including the sharing of energy sources in times of emergencies.[12]

In the first week of February 1975, the IEA met in Paris for three days and dealt with three issues: (1) Kissinger's proposal to establish a floor price of $7 per barrel of oil in order to induce investors to develop alternatives to Middle East oil; (2)

topics of discussion for the preliminary conference and later for the conference of consumers and producers; and (3) the date for the preliminary conference and the agenda of the conferences. The agency did not adopt the Kissinger price proposal; the subject of discussion was to be limited to oil; and the date of the preliminary conference was set for March. In August 1975 the *Petroleum Economist* summarized the developments in the energy crisis and the efforts of the consumers to overcome it. It noted that a lack of solidarity at the IEA and EEC Energy Council meetings stood in marked contrast to the common front put up by the OPEC countries. With no common counterstrategy to break their overdependence on OPEC oil, other than on IEA agreement on emergency oil sharing, the industrialized nations had slowly come around to the French way of thinking, which was based on the hope that economic confrontation and coercion could be avoided by bilateral contacts and by a broad dialogue between producing and consuming countries, involving oil as well as other commodities. These were the reasons for which France had not joined the IEA. The initial dynamism in dealing with the oil supply crisis had petered out, both in the IEA and the EEC.

THE EURO-ARAB DIALOGUE

The possibility of direct oil relations between the European governments and the Middle East producing countries, bypassing the U.S. companies and their concessions, had been in the minds of Middle East producers, especially Libya, for a long time and was feared by U.S. oil companies and government policymakers. Therefore, two days after Libya nationalized 51 percent of the oil companies in its territory on September 2, 1973, Libyan Premier Abdul Salam Jalud declared that the suggestion that the United States could force the European Economic Community not to buy nationalized oil from Libya was out of the question. Instead, he said, "Libya is ready to cooperate with Europe for mutual advantage in forging a new and mutual partnership based on Arab oil and European technology and experience." He expressed the hope that the Europeans would turn to the Arab countries for investment purposes.

Early in January 1974, the Algerian president, reacting to the proposed Washington conference call, stated, "The Europeans, at the present moment have the possibility of laying the basis for a long-term cooperation which would guarantee their oil supplies for 25 years in exchange for their participation in the development of the area in which they are vitally interested."

Under the leadership of France, the EEC countries had issued on November 6, 1973—after the proclamation of the embargo—a pro-Arab declaration. At a secret meeting of the foreign ministers of the EEC that took place in Copenhagen on December 14, 1973, it was decided to propose a basic program of cooperation and mutual assistance between the members of the EEC and the Arab League countries. The Europeans were to supply the necessary financial resources and assist in the economic development of the Arab countries, while the Arabs were to guarantee steady supplies of oil at stable prices to the Europeans.[13]

In the middle of December 1973, the French premier, Pierre Mesmar, called for a new oil policy based on direct contact between the producers and the consumers that would eliminate the international companies. As the producers were interested in using their oil for the economic development of their countries, they should enter into direct agreements between themselves and the consumers. He urged that the EEC adopt this new oil policy. At the end of January 1974, when the foreign ministers of the EEC met in Brussels, France tried to convince its colleagues that the U.S. proposal was dangerous and would adversely affect European interests. France advocated instead a direct relationship with the Arab producing countries. After the long effort of France, the West German foreign minister, who was the rotating chairman of the EEC Council, announced that a dialogue would be opened with the Arab countries. The United States was greatly disturbed by this decision, especially because it was concentrating, at the time, all U.S. efforts on the consumers' conference and was deeply involved in the separation-of-forces agreements between Israel and Israel's neighbors. The EEC decision could only upset and even defeat the efforts of the United States. Indeed, in a letter to Willy Brandt, President Nixon criticized the EEC decision and said that he saw it as an anti-American move.

Some members of the EEC were also disturbed by the decision; Great Britain was reported as objecting to the dialogue. The dialogue was to take the form of an examination of the possibilities of cooperation in the areas of energy, economics, and technology. However, serious differences of opinion broke out when the foreign ministers of the EEC convened in Luxembourg early in May. All the participants, including Britain, agreed in principle to the dialogue, but Britain proposed continuous consultation with the United States on the dialogue issue. France, of course, objected. Britain thereupon made consultation with the United States a condition against using its veto. The issue reached a stalemate.

At the NATO conference in June, Kissinger announced that his government no longer objected to the dialogue provided it would be restricted to economic and nonpolitical issues. But objections still persisted within the EEC. The oil embargo against the United States and most of the European countries had been lifted in March but was still in force against the Netherlands (as mentioned in Chapter 3), which objected to the dialogue as long as this embargo continued. By the end of July the embargo against the Netherlands was lifted, and the French foreign minister, as rotating chairman, began negotiating for the dialogue. Britain insisted that the dialogue must not involve political issues, while France stressed the need for cooperation by both sides. The political secretariat of the EEC prepared a "secret" document and the foreign ministers were required to abide by its guidelines in the negotiations.

The topics for discussion were to be science, technology, meteorology, ecology problems, and education. The date for the first meeting of the two sides was set for July 31, 1974. EEC participants were the French foreign minister and the chairman of the EEC Commission; Arab league participants were its secretary-general and the Kuwaiti foreign minister. It should be noted that from the very beginning, when the dialogue proposal was first broached, the major Arab oil-producing countries displayed no particular interest in it. They apparently preferred their own bilateral negotiations and agreements for cooperation with individual European countries, especially when their revenues were so prodigiously mounting and the means of cooperation was under their own control. They were not interested in becoming involved in the plans of the Arab non-oil-producing countries.

The attempt on the part of the EEC to limit the discussions to economic questions and not become involved in the current political issues of the Arab countries failed from the outset and caused embarrassment to the main negotiator, France. The Kuwaiti foreign minister declared that it was impossible to separate economics from politics, and the Arab League secretary-general supported him by pointing out that the very discussions were being conducted within a political framework, the Arab League.

The two delegations decided to establish permanent mixed committees that were to prepare long-range programs for cooperation of the two sides. Meanwhile the two sides would continue to try to establish principles for cooperation and set up a system of priorities and joint projects. After the political committee of the Arab League heard a report of the progress of the discussions from the secretary-general, it authorized him and the Lebanese foreign minister to continue with the negotiations, which were scheduled to resume on October 20 in Paris. In the meantime, representatives of both sides met in Cairo to prepare the agenda for the Paris meeting. However, when the Paris meeting opened in November, a month later than scheduled, serious difficulties developed, and the discussions reached a stalemate. The major issue was the opposition of a number of EEC countries to the participation of the Palestine Liberation Organization (PLO) as a full member of the Arab League. They insisted that representation of both the EEC and the Arab League must be by fully sovereign countries. France favored PLO participation, but others persistently objected.

On April 22, 1975, the Arab League authorized its representatives to proceed with the dialogue. On the issue of PLO representation a compromise was worked out. The delegations would not be based on countries, but on the EEC as a whole and the Arab League as a whole. The Arab League could include, should it so desire, a PLO representative in its delegation. On July 22 a conference for advancing the Euro-Arab dialogue was opened in Rome. The 150 delegates were nongovernmental specialists from the nine members of the EEC and from twenty-one Arab League delegations. Topics dealt with were economics, finances, technology, culture, and social affairs. Ironically, because of Arab objection, oil—the very reason for the dialogue—was not included in the agenda.

The third round of discussion took place on November 22–27 at Abu Dhabi and was attended by some one hundred experts from both sides. The stumbling block to progress was a difference of opinion regarding the political issues in the Middle East. A press statement at the conclusion of the meeting said: "The two sides announced that the political aspect of the dialogue must be taken into consideration to allow the dialogue to make progress in an effective manner conducive to the fulfillment of its aims."[14] However, the official negotiations between the EEC and the Arab League made no progress. The compromise on PLO representation was not enough for the Arabs; with the advance of the status of the PLO in the international forums, the Arab League demanded full official recognition of the PLO by the EEC countries.

Relations between the EEC and the Arab League were based on the pro-Arab EEC declaration of November 6, 1973, which had been adopted through the efforts of France. In order to make it possible to give the PLO full recognition and all that such recognition would imply, a number of EEC members tried to introduce an addendum to the declaration, giving full support to the PLO. Although France strongly advocated the adoption of the new addition (which was even reportedly supported by Britain and West Germany), other members objected not only to the proposed addendum but to the very raising of the issue for discussion. The Arab League continued to insist on full recognition, and the deadlock continued.

The nine EEC foreign ministers met in Luxembourg on February 25, 1976, and approved the next stage in the dialogue that was to open in May. Although the stress was still to be on the same subjects, the EEC was also willing to include political issues for discussion. When the meeting opened on May 19 in Luxembourg, the Arab League secretary-general devoted most of his statement to the practical issues of cooperation between the two sides, but the other Arab delegate, the Bahrain foreign minister, devoted his entire speech to the question of the Palestinians. The atmosphere became tense, and the meeting adjourned for a day. In the meantime France attempted to persuade the other EEC members to adopt the addendum, but without success. The issue was not resolved.

CONFERENCE ON INTERNATIONAL ECONOMIC COOPERATION (THE NORTH-SOUTH DIALOGUE)

The basic purpose of the United States in advocating and promoting the establishment of the IEA was not only to formulate measures to protect the consumers against future oil supply cuts, but above all to unite and strengthen the consumers in their struggle with the producers for reasonable guaranteed oil price levels. To this end the original Kissinger plan had called for the establishment of a consumers' group and for a producer-consumer conference—not for the purpose of confrontation but for an equal match of strength that would result in equitable solutions. As a countermove to the U.S. effort, the Saudi Arabian oil minister, Yamani, in April 1974 at the United Nations General Assembly Special Sixth Session (and before that on other occasions), proposed a dialogue between the producers and consumers. He suggested that the dialogue be between three groups of countries: producers (Iran, Algeria, Saudi Arabia, and Venezuela); consumers (the United States, the EEC countries, and Japan); and developing countries (India, Brazil, and Zaire). His aim was obvious: By including the additional participants he wished to guarantee a majority for his side, because on every issue and question the developing countries would side with the producers. Moreover, of the three groups the producers were the best organized and had clearly defined objectives and a distinct plan of action, whereas the other two groups were disunited and had no clear aims. The producers would be in absolute control. Should the Saudi Arabian proposal be accepted, the IEA would be weakened and its objectives blurred even more.

France, which had objected to the U.S. efforts, jumped on the Yamani proposal and adopted it as its own. French initiative in sponsoring the plan would gain for France prestige and influence among all three groups. On October 24, 1974, French President Valery Giscard d'Estaing proposed a conference of representatives of the oil-producing countries, the oil-consuming countries, and the developing countries to deal with economic and financial questions. France then began to press for convening the conference early in 1975 and proposed twelve countries that would represent the three groups. In November 1974 France informed its colleagues in the EEC, the United States, Japan, Saudi Arabia, and Algeria of its plans.[15]

In the middle of December, it was reported that most of the Gulf area countries, Egypt, and the Arab League supported the French plan, but the United States vigorously opposed it. The United States maintained that the planned conference could be convened only after the consuming countries who were to participate in it had organized and adopted a united plan of action. A deadlock developed. Finally, at a summit meeting between the president of France and the president of the United States on the island of Martinique on December 14–16, a vague and obscure compromise was reached that made it possible for France to continue with its efforts. A preliminary meeting of representatives of the producers and consumers was to convene in March in Paris to prepare the agenda for the conference.[16] On March 2, 1975, the president of France sent out invitations to ten countries for the preparatory conference to be held in Paris on April 7.

In the meantime, the conference of developing countries that had convened in Dakar February 4–8 to deal with the overall question of raw materials had decided that the negotiations between the oil-producing and oil-consuming nations should be expanded to include other raw materials. The main leader at the Dakar conference was Algeria, which for its own reasons (because it wished to become a world leader), demanded that the scope of the proposed conference be widened. The United States, on the other hand, was determined to oppose the expansion of the conference, limiting it to oil so that it could not be converted into a world economic struggle between the underdeveloped nations and the industrialized nations. Thomas Enders, U.S. assistant secretary of state for economic affairs, declared in Paris early in February 1975 that the United States would resist attempts by producers of raw materials, other than oil, to establish price agreements seeking "to make the cartel the legitimate means of international behavior."[17]

The preparatory conference opened on April 7. After prolonged and difficult discussions and debates lasting nine days, the conference broke up without arriving at any decision. The United States persisted in its stand that the discussions be limited to the question of energy, while Algeria equally persisted in its demand that other raw materials be included. The breakup of the preparatory conference was considered a serious setback to the French effort, but France was not ready to give up its plan and pursued its objective relentlessly. After a while the United States softened its position. Speaking before the United Nations General Assembly, U.S. Secretary of State Kissinger proposed a compromise that would make possible the resumption of the work of the preparatory conference. His proposal, that separate but parallel commissions for energy, raw materials, development, and finances be named, was supported by the EEC Commission. France, therefore, announced on September 30 that the ten countries that had been invited to the preparatory conference had responded favorably and would meet in Paris on October 13.

The major purpose of the preparatory conference was to organize a world summit meeting to deal with the question of energy and other raw materials. It was to name the twenty-seven countries that would participate in the full conference, prepare the agenda, and establish the commissions that would begin negotiations in December. However, when the preparatory conference opened as planned on October 13, basic differences of opinion appeared on the question of guidelines for the four commissions. The developing countries—which hoped that the conference would bring about revolutionary changes in the world economic order—demanded that the instructions to the commissions be specific and detailed; on the basis of these instructions the commissions would prepare practical recommendations that would be binding on the conference. The industrialized nations, on the other hand, which were not ready to change the world economic structure, insisted that the commissions be given full freedom in their choice of recommendations without committing in advance the conference and its participants. The United States came forward with a compromise, proposing that the preparatory conference adopt the nonspecific, vaguely defined functions of the commissions as formulated in Paris, but that to them be attached the various interpretations given these functions by the participants.

On October 16, the ten delegations completed their discussions, made public a general declaration, and announced that the full conference would be convened on December 16 in Paris. It would be composed of twenty-seven countries; of these, nineteen were developing nations—among them oil producers— and eight were industrialized countries. The four commissions were not given specific instructions.[18] The conference was duly opened in Paris on December 16; its official name was the Conference on International Economic Cooperation (CIEC), and its popular name was the North-South dialogue. The president of France, as host, delivered the opening speech. He stressed the importance of the conference and declared that historically it was of no less significance than the founding of the United Nations. The major idea behind the United Nations was the establishment of a new political world order, and the Paris conference was to establish a new economic world order. The French did not hide their glee at the achievement of the opening of the conference and saw in it a great French diplomatic victory.

But the central figure of the conference was, no doubt, the U.S. secretary of state. It was reported that he told correspondents flying in the plane with the U.S. delegation to Paris that U.S. aid to the developing countries would be halted if they continued to back the oil producers' policies.[19] At the conference, Kissinger minced no words in warning the producers that "higher oil prices would seriously impair the economic recovery, would hamper international trade and increase internal difficulties of many countries." Moreover, "as a result of the higher prices the ability of the developed countries to aid the developing countries would be weakened, and the pattern of international cooperation, would be harmed."[20] His speech was a direct attack on the oil producers' policies.

Intervening in the discussion, British Foreign Secretary James Callaghan pressed for the establishment of a floor price for oil in order to protect British investment in developing the North Sea oil resources. The clash among the United States, Britain, and France was more than obvious and did not bode well for the hopes and aims of the conference. The French president assailed Britain's intervention, declaring that it did not conform with the joint EEC position worked out at the summit talks in Rome.

The producing countries reacted very strongly to Kissinger's harsh words. They rejected out of hand the assertion that the rise in oil prices had caused the world inflation and the world economic crisis. The Algerian foreign minister, Abdelaziz Bouteflika, said, "It is unjust to turn notorious non-truths into truths." The Iranian delegate stated that "the West's recession has been wholly homemade."[21] They demanded that the price of all natural resources be based on an index of the prices of products that the developing countries purchase from the industrialized nations. The industrialized nations refused to base the prices of natural resources, especially oil, on an index.

The conference, however, proceeded, and chairmen were named for the four commissions, with the United States and Saudi Arabia elected co-chairmen of the energy commission. After the four commissions were established, another preparatory meeting was scheduled for January 26, 1976. The commissions were to begin their work on February 11, and they were to report back to the conference to be convened some time in February 1977. Even though the industrialized countries prevailed, and no specific instructions were given to the commissions, the developing countries demanded that the issue of instructions be taken up again at the preparatory meeting on

January 26. Indeed, representatives of the nineteen developing countries met on January 5 in Paris; they dealt with the issue of negotiations between themselves and the eight developed countries and drafted specific instructions to be given the commissions. On February 11, the conference met with the two major questions—indexation and instructions to the commissions—unresolved.

The commissions, under the guidance of the co-chairmen of the conference—Allan MacEachen, Canadian external minister, and Manuel Perez Guerrero, Venezuelan minister of state—wrestled with the issues assigned to them. But by July 1976, the bargaining between the two sides broke down. After two months of patient effort, the co-chairmen succeeded in working out a compromise formula to resume negotiations. The major issues were the heavy debts of the Third World countries and a guarantee of the purchasing power of the producers of oil and other raw materials against world inflation. The commissions met in private in September, October, and November with the aim of convening the conference in the middle of December.

While the OPEC December 1976 conference was approaching, the Saudi oil minister Yamani made it clear that the progress of the dialogue would be one of the principal factors that would influence the extent of the oil price increase to be decided upon by the OPEC ministers at their scheduled conference. The United States, which was the major power to deal with the two questions, resisted the pressure. Secretary of State Henry Kissinger sent a cable, early in December, to the European negotiators and warned them of the dangers in establishing a direct link between any concessions offered developing countries in the Paris dialogue and price moderation by oil-exporting countries at their meeting at Qatar. He declared: "We are convinced that there is no negotiable CIEC package which the industrialized countries could accept and which would also present sufficient inducement to OPEC to refrain from a substantial oil price increase over several years, given the lack of leverage by consumers over oil prices."[22] The conference meeting scheduled to open December 15 was postponed by the initiative of the United States to the following spring.

CONSUMERS' EFFORTS SINCE 1976

IEA

Since 1976 IEA has become a practical statistical service facility for member states. It collects basic information on energy consumption, sources of imports, and other pertinent data supplied by members. It also prepares estimates of projected levels of consumption and availability of energy over longer periods of time. The IEA finally accepted the Kissinger $7-a-barrel floor price as a protection measure for investments in alternative energy sources. Concentrating most of its efforts on conservation of energy devices, it has aimed at reducing consumption and thus reducing the magnitude of dependence on the producers, its first goal a daily reduction of 2 million barrels. The very high price of oil charged by the producers and an economic recession, except for panic buying, were the real decisive factors in reducing consumption. IEA established, through a revolving fund, a $25-billion "safety net" for granting loans to members for the purchase of oil.

The IEA decision to share energy resources, in time of emergency (when a member lost 7 percent of its energy supply)—an elaborate plan—was never put to the test. In January 1980, the agency, for the first time, set individual oil import quotas for its members and instituted a monitoring system to insure that the quotas were observed. OECD set a consumption target of 24.6 million barrels a day in 1985, down from the 26 million agreed upon previously. The agency members were to increase their oil stockpiles to a minimum of sixty days' consumption; this was later raised to seventy days and aimed at ninety days.

These services and measures adopted were, no doubt, beneficial to the members, but in view of the original U.S. objective they must be considered mere palliatives.

Euro-Arab Dialogue

The fifth round of discussions took place in Tunis on February 10–12, 1977. The talks did not progress beyond the rethreshing, by both sides, of their positions on the political aspects of the Palestine issue. The Saudi Arabian delegate attempted to drive a wedge between Europe and the United States when he urged, "It is time for Europe to assume its role in the management of international relations and to have the power of the Israelis tamed. We are here seeking cooperation."[23]

In September 1979, the oil ministers of seven Arab states of the Gulf area met in Taif, Saudi Arabia, and tried to revive the Euro-Arab dialogue, but the effort failed. A year later, Qatar's minister of finance, Abd al-Aziz bin Khalifa al-Thani, declared that the Western European countries had been responsible during the last two years for the failure of the dialogue between the EEC and member states of the Arab league.

North-South Dialogue

In the middle of January 1977, Robert MacNamara, president of the World Bank, proposed that a private international commission headed by West Germany's former chancellor, Willy Brandt, be established to accelerate the North-South dialogue. When the conference met on June 1, the two demands of the developing countries were rejected by the industrialized countries. On June 3, British Foreign Secretary David Owen announced the breakdown of the energy dialogue. After eighteen months of hard bargaining, the conference was largely written off as a loss by most of the delegates. The United Nations Special Session of the Conference was convened on September 13 and after six days of debate ended in failure.

When the Big Seven industrial countries' leaders met in Jamaica on December 28, 1979, the North-South dialogue was on their agenda. Finally, at an eleven-country conference in Vienna in March 1981 an effort was made to raise the dialogue issue, but on the insistence of the United States the discussion was postponed.

REFLECTIONS

By the end of 1976, more than three years after the outbreak of the oil crisis, the three attempts of the consuming countries to stem the tide of the producers' unilateral and seemingly unlimited oil price increases as well as the ever-looming threat of supply cuts had all failed. They failed because of irreconcilable differences and cross-purposes among the consuming countries. The United States was willing to face the producers by challenging their oil price control and was ready to take measures to guarantee secure supplies; France saw in the crisis the best means of furthering its own interests, and supposedly the interests of all Western European countries at the expense of the United States. True, the other members of the EEC joined the IEA, but they were not willing to face the producers and stand up to them. Instead, they tried to adapt to the high prices and to seek financial devices to pay for the oil. The Japanese were determined to avoid a confrontation at "all costs." The IEA was a weak organization with no executive power, primarily capable of making recommendations to the members. Under such circumstances no consumer organization could have hoped to form a solid front to tackle the hard issues of the crisis. Each group and each member within the groups were aiming at different objectives.

The Euro-Arab dialogue could be described as a dialogue of the deaf. The two sides were talking, but they were saying different things. Although the primary purpose of the dialogue was to deal with the energy issue—and the consumers were prepared to discuss economic, technological, and financial aspects of the energy problem for a guaranteed oil supply—the Arabs were determined to achieve political victories through the dialogue that they had failed to obtain from the embargo. Moreover, paradoxically, the Arabs eliminated the oil question from the agenda of the dialogue, and they even demanded that the technological and economic aid that the Europeans were willing to give to the Arab countries be financed not from the tremendous oil revenue they were amassing but by the consuming countries. Under such conditions the dialogue inevitably had to end in failure.

The North-South dialogue was based, from the very beginning, on conflicting objectives. The United States, after finally agreeing to participate, hoped to come to grips with the two energy issues of supply and price; the other consumer countries hoped to make progress in their relations with the various producer groups; and the oil producers and the other raw-materials producers aimed at a new world economic order that would endow them with powers and influence equal to that of the industrialized countries.

The French, attempting to restore their lost position, influence, and prestige, were more willing to go along with the demands of the producers than with the needs of the consumers and were prepared to pay any price to lead the parade. They persuaded the EEC to adopt the pro-Arab resolution in November 1973; they justified the high oil prices; they tried to persuade their colleagues in the EEC to recognize the PLO; they advocated the expansion of the original oil producers–consumers conference into the North-South dialogue to include the other raw-materials producers. It was the French who spoke of the new world economic order. But with all the concessions that the French were ready to make at the expense of their Western allies, the three consumers' efforts failed.

The United States, although determined to face the issues and struggle with them, employed unrealistic means—indeed, gimmicks—which, of course, could not work. The obscure formula agreed upon on Martinique by the presidents of the United States and France did not produce a strong united consumers' front. Even when the agreement was made public, the two presidents must have been aware that the differences between them were as wide as ever. Again, when a stalemate was reached by U.S. insistence that the conference be limited to energy, Kissinger came up with another gimmick: four parallel commissions, energy (in which the United States was interested) and three others (which were demanded by the producers). The United States and Saudi Arabia were named co-chairmen of the energy commission. But the commissions did not work; the demands of the developing countries went beyond the intended dialogue. When an attempt was made by the oil producers to link the impending OPEC price increases with the achievements of the North-South dialogue, the United States, for all practical purposes, killed the conference.

The following two quotations from U.S. congressional committee reports in 1973 and 1974 touch on the very heart of the question. The House Committee on Foreign Affairs staff, in *The United States Oil Shortages and the Arab-Israeli Conflict*, stated: "To be effective, a counterembargo against the Arab oil states would have to be a multinational effort involving a majority of the industrialized nations. The lack of cooperation among the countries of Western Europe in face of the embargo and production cuts makes such a response unlikely in the immediate future."

The Senate Committee on Interior and Insular Affairs, in its 1974 study *Implications of Recent Organization of Petroleum Exporting Countries (OPEC) Oil Price Increases,* stated: "Although there will be great temptations and occasional peccadilloes, it is essential that the oil importing nations recognize the futility and potential chaos which would result from competing among themselves. They should especially avoid competition to reduce their trade deficits by worsening the deficit of another oil importing nation, as well as competition that will have the effect of bidding oil prices up."[24]

NOTES

1. It had been reported that in a number of years the People's Republic of China might become one of the great oil producers in the world and would compete with the Middle East oil-producing countries (*New York Times,* April 4, 1976; *Hadashot Haneft,* May 2, 1976). Japan could then purchase most of its oil from China and be independent of the Middle East. Indeed, Japan had actually increased its oil purchases from China at the expense of Indonesia, whose oil prices, in line with OPEC decisions, were higher than those of China. But all the reports about China's future oil possibilities were mere speculations. Predictions about China's future production and reserves were not based on solid facts; no reliable information was available about China's future internal energy needs and whether there would be any sizable surplus for export. In fact, in spite of the many obstacles and disappointments that Japan had experienced in its cooperative efforts with some of the Middle Eastern countries, Japan signed agreements for huge investments (running into hundreds of millions of dollars) in diverse economic undertakings in the Middle East in return for oil supplies. Thus the Middle Eastern countries seemed to

have remained the major source of oil for Japan—the many predictions and speculations notwithstanding.

2. U.S., Congress, Senate, Committee on Foreign Relations, Subcommittee on Multinational Corporations, *Multinational Oil Corporations and U.S. Foreign Policy: Report Together with Individual Views* (Washington, D.C., 1975), p. 151 (hereafter cited as Multinationals Subcommittee, *Report*). The *Project Independence Report* was released in November 1973. Its conclusions are given in Multinationals Subcommittee, *Report,* pp. 151–152; U.S., Congress, Senate, Committee on Finance, Subcommittee on Energy, *Fiscal Policy and the Energy Crisis* (Washington, D.C., 1973), p. 35.

3. A careful examination of all factors involved in the project must lead to the conclusion that although from a purely technical point of view the project could have been achieved, in the process the United States would have committed both economic and political suicide.

4. *New York Times,* June 22, 1973.

5. *Jerusalem Post,* January 28, 1974.

6. *Middle East Economic Survey (MEES),* February 8, 1974.

7. The *New York Times* of September 29, 1974, reported that the coordinating committee adopted a secret decision on September 19 to establish an international energy agency whose purpose would be to oppose the producers. The official announcement was to be made in November.

8. *Jerusalem Post,* September 20, 1974.

9. *MEES,* October 4, 1974.

10. Ibid.

11. Speech before the United Nations, quoted in *Jerusalem Post,* September 24, 1974.

12. By the end of December 1974, Spain, Turkey, Austria, Switzerland, and Sweden joined the agency.

13. Henri Simonet of the EEC Commission reported that during the Copenhagen meeting Arab foreign ministers started a round of talks with their European colleagues. These talks were the source of the Arab dialogue. The Copenhagen declaration confirmed the importance of entering into negotiations with the oil-producing countries on comprehensive arrangements. Dankwart Rustow and John F. Mungo, *OPEC: Success and Prospects* (New York, 1976), p. 83. In testimony before the U.S. Congress Joint Economic Committee's Subcommittee on International Economics, it was reported that the French foreign minister, Michel Jobert, proposed that a conference be held between European Economic Community countries and the Arab states to discuss the financial, technological, and energy relationship. *Hearings:*

Economic Impact of Petroleum Shortages (Washington, D.C., 1974), p. 184.

14. *Europe*, November 28, 1975.

15. On October 24, when the French president made his proposal, he said, "This idea, incidentally, has been mooted by others apart from us. For example, it has been proposed on several occasions by Saudi Arabia." *MEES*, November 1, 1974.

16. The compromise arrived at was apparently expressed in the decision of the presidents that "the preparatory discussion will be followed by intensive consultations among consumer countries in order to prepare positions for the conference." *MEES*, December 20, 1974.

17. *Jerusalem Post*, February 9, 1975.

18. A new crisis potentially capable of exploding the conference broke out when Great Britain requested separate representation. In view of Britain's role as a future major oil producer in the North Sea, British delegates felt that Britain would be inadequately represented by the EEC delegate (in reality France). On December 3, however, it was announced in the press in London that Britain had given up this demand, and the road was cleared for the conference.

19. *Jerusalem Post*, December 12, 1976; *Maariv*, December 17, 1975.

20. *Maariv*, December 17, 1975.

21. *Jerusalem Post*, December 18, 1975.

22. *New York Times*, December 12, 1976.

23. *Jerusalem Post*, February 20, 1977.

24. U.S., Congress, Senate, Committee on Interior and Insular Affairs, *Implications of Recent Organization of Petroleum Exporting Countries (OPEC) Oil Price Increases* (Washington, D.C., 1974). Additional major sources for Chapter 5 were: U.S., Congress, House, Committee on Foreign Affairs, Staff, *The United States Oil Shortages and the Arab-Israeli Conflict* (Washington, D.C., 1973); U.S., Congress, House, Committee on Foreign Affairs, Subcommittee on Foreign Economic Policy and Subcommittee on the Near East and South Asia, *Hearings: Oil Negotiations, OPEC, and the Stability of Supply* (Washington, D.C., 1973); U.S., Congress, Joint Economic Committee, Subcommittee on International Economics, *Hearings: Economic Impact of Petroleum Shortages*; Multinationals Subcommittee, *Report*; U.S., Federal Energy Administration, *Project Independence: Blueprint Final Taskforce Report* (Washington, D.C., 1974); Rustow and Mungo, *OPEC: Success and Prospects.*

6

THE EVOLUTION
OF OPEC

Although OPEC had gained great victories over the concessionaire companies between 1971 and 1975, and the OPEC producers had practically achieved total takeover of the foreign concessions in their territories, conflicting interests between members as well as the very nature of the organization prevented OPEC from acquiring strong executive functions. It remained a collection of sovereign states on whom it could not force obedience to majority decisions. In spite of the various provisions in the organization's rules and regulations it was never clearly established what powers of action it possessed. During the history of the organization the following issues had been raised: control of production, regulation of price, uniform price, and price differentials. These issues had not been settled by constitutional decisions but came into practice as a result of experience and bitter internal struggle. All the powers thus acquired by the organization were always subject to challenge and refusal by any member.

THE ISSUE OF PRICE REGULATION

Even in 1974, differences of opinion emerged in regard to price increases. At the OPEC conference in Quito in June 1974, it was decided to freeze posted prices for three months but to increase the profit-share level by 2 to 57 percent. Saudi Arabia objected to the profit increase. Iraq and Kuwait accused Saudi Arabia of playing the game of the imperialists, to which the Saudi Arabian oil minister replied that if the conference increased prices his country would flood the market with an additional 3 million barrels a day. Iran, on the other hand, threatened to cut daily production from 6 million to 4 million barrels. Venezuela and Iran proposed a 9 percent increase in price, whereupon Yamani announced that his government would not abide by such a decision and would instead reduce prices by 20 percent. The compromise was to maintain the existing posted price but increase the profit share by 2 percent, although Yamani declared defiantly that his country would not increase the profit share. In September OPEC decided to freeze prices to the end of 1974. A meeting of OPEC oil and foreign ministers held in Algiers on January 26, 1975, approved an Algerian plan to freeze basic oil prices for the remainder of 1975. For the years 1976–1977 prices were to be based on the inflation rates of the industrialized nations.

On August 14, 1975, Ahmad Zaki Yamani stated in Rome that some OPEC members were pressing for a 35 percent price increase; he noted that "not all the members of OPEC are reasonable, not all are concerned that the world economy should not collapse. We realize that if we don't want to ruin the world economy we must oppose policies of some OPEC members. To ruin the other OPEC countries we would just need to produce as much as we could. And to ruin the consumers we would just need to cut production."[1] He emphasized that his country would do its best to keep the oil price frozen, on condition that the industrialized countries lowered the prices of their exported goods, thus reiterating the North-South dialogue demand of the developing countries for indexation.

At the same time, U.S. Secretary of State Henry Kissinger was campaigning vigorously for a reduction in the oil price. Addressing the United Nations General Assembly, he said, "Another increase would slow down or reverse the recovery and development of nearly every nation represented in this Assembly. It would erode both the will and the capacity in the industrial world for assistance to developing countries. It would, in short, strike a blow at the hopes of hundreds of millions around the world."[2]

Tension rose at the September OPEC meeting in Vienna. When Yamani left suddenly on September 25, it looked as if the conference would break down. On September 28 the *New York Times* reported that his departure was interpreted as a walkout (a tactic that later became his regular practice). OPEC was sharply divided: The extremists demanded a 25 to 35 percent price increase; the middle of the roaders called for a 10 to 15 percent increase; and Saudi Arabia, not more than 5 percent. Finally, on September 27, OPEC decided on a 10 percent increase. U.S. President Gerald Ford reacted by declaring that the increase would "worsen inflation throughout the world."[3] The helplessness of the consumers was expressed by Secretary Kissinger when he said, "It's better than it could have been."[4]

All this occurred at the same time that the North-South dialogue negotiations were being carried on between the various groups in Paris.

Bali

On April 25, 1976, OPEC met in Geneva at the request of Iraq, which claimed that members were undercutting the OPEC price. One month later, at the opening of the Bali, Indonesia, conference, the minister of petroleum and mineral resources of the United Arab Emirates (UAE), Mana Said al-Otaiba, advocated freezing oil prices to the end of the year and commented, "We cannot understand the position of some OPEC member countries which reduce their own market prices while often simultaneously calling for a general OPEC increase. This does nothing to help maintain either OPEC solidarity or the present reasonable level of prices." To make it clear at which country al-Otaiba was aiming, the Saudi Arabian oil minister charged, "Iraq is dumping its oil at cheap prices. It is the only OPEC country which raised production, while other members cut output."[5] Iraq, ignoring the charges of al-Otaiba and Yamani, advocated a 15 percent increase and in turn charged that Saudi Arabia, in advocating a price freeze, "plays into the hands of the imperialist monopolies and enables them to export their inflation."[6] The drop in the demand for oil during 1975 helped Saudi Arabia, and at the end of May the OPEC conference decided to freeze prices. This was an impressive victory for Saudi Arabia, and Yamani declared triumphantly: "Nobody can increase prices without Saudi Arabia."[7]

According to *World Oil* and other sources, the behind-the-scenes background for the OPEC decision to freeze prices and to Yamani's boast was the leverage Saudi Arabia exercised in its threat to establish its own pricing system if the hawkish members increased prices at their own discretion.[8] As the country with the largest oil production capacity and with the greatest crude reserves, such an eventuality would have disastrous effects on OPEC. To this threat, Libya declared defiantly: "We are ready to dissolve OPEC if Saudi Arabia keeps working against the interests of the oil nations. This is a good chance for an OPEC without Saudi Arabia."[9] However, the other members dropped their demands for higher prices and submitted to Saudi Arabia's warning.

Doha

Between the Bali conference and the Doha, Qatar, conference, the various OPEC members attempted to advance their positions. When the conference opened in Doha on December 15, 1976, it was expected that even Saudi Arabia would agree to increase the oil price, for in the second half of the year the demand for oil had increased considerably. The hawkish members interpreted the increase in demand as the economic recovery of the Western industrialized nations. But Saudi Arabia maintained that the increase in demand was not the result of improved economic conditions and industrial activity but of panic buying based on the fear that OPEC would raise prices; the greater demand was not a result of consumption but of stockpiling.

Most of the OPEC members pressed for a minimum 10 percent increase, Iraq urged 25 percent, and Saudi Arabia advocated freezing prices for a period of six months. Yamani (exercising his new tactic) walked out of the conference, for consultation in Jidda. He returned with a compromise of a 5 percent increase. Finally, on December 17, eleven members voted for an immediate 10 percent increase as of January 1, 1977, and an additional 5 percent to take effect in July. Saudi Arabia and the UAE decided to raise prices by only 5 percent.

From Yamani's various statements and declarations between Bali and Doha, the Saudi tactics become clear. He talked of a possible 10 percent rise but hinted, and not very subtly, that such a rise in prices could be prevented if the industrialized nations complied with the demands of the developing countries in the North-South dialogue.

THE SAUDI POSITION

But Saudi Arabia also bitterly resented the OPEC members that, Yamani asserted, were underselling their oil at the expense of Saudi Arabia. He pointed out that in 1975 Saudi production went down to 6.5 million barrels a day from 8.5 million because his country "stuck to OPEC decisions while in a country like Iraq production went up by about 30%." Yamani charged, almost vehemently, that OPEC overpriced Saudi Arabian light crude, and he therefore advocated continuing the price freezes. But when eleven members of the organization increased prices by 10 percent, Yamani stated that a Saudi 5 percent increase would bring the overpriced Saudi Arabian light in line. He openly declared that as a result of the new situation Saudi Arabia was ready to raise production to the extent that the international market demanded and said "I think this is normal."[10]

Accusations were made that the Saudi decision on price was the result of previous arrangements with the United States. Yamani has denied the existence of such an arrangement but said that his country expected to be rewarded for its helpful action. He added, "I want you to know that we expect the West to appreciate what we did, especially the United States. That appreciation has to be shown on two fronts, first in the North-South Dialogue in Paris, and second in the Arab-Israeli conflict. There must be peace in the area as a sign of appreciation." To make sure that this appreciation was forthcoming, he warned that if progress was not made on these two fronts Saudi Arabia might modify its position later in the year. He described Saudi Arabia's motivation for its action as composed of two elements: "The political part is the North-South Dialogue and the Arab-Israeli conflict. The economic part is the world economy. And we weigh things together." When pressed as to what determined his country's decision at Doha, he replied: "Well, I should say this time it is mostly, if not completely, economic."[11]

In regard to OPEC, Yamani said on December 17 that Saudi Arabia's production capacity was 11.8 million barrels a day, additional capacity was under construction, and, if circumstances demanded it, further expansion might be considered. The threat was unequivocal. In reporting in Jidda the events of Doha, Yamani said, "We refused to accept the price increase that OPEC tried to impose on us and this means that each country is now free to fix the price of its own oil. This does not mean the break-up of OPEC, it just means that the kingdom has exercised its sovereignty over its own oil."[12]

When Saudi Arabia was accused of violating the OPEC decision, Yamani challenged the power of the organization to regulate prices. He declared,

> Did you know that OPEC is not empowered to set oil prices, and that the law establishing it does not mention this subject at all? OPEC as an organization was set up to meet the problem of artificially depressed prices created by the major companies, as well as coordinate between the member countries. The subject of setting and increasing prices was not mentioned at all. By adopting our present position we are restoring matters to their original state. The question of prices is a matter of sovereignty: so this is our oil and it is our right to set the price at which we sell it.[13]

The division in OPEC created a two-tier price structure. The Saudi challenge depended on an increased production rate that would enable Saudi Arabia and the UAE to draw away oil purchasers from the higher-priced oil of the other producers. Both Saudi Arabia and the UAE openly avowed that they intended to increase their production rates.

This decision produced sharp responses from inside OPEC and from the United States. The chief Iranian delegate to OPEC, Jamshid Amouzegar, though not mentioning Saudi Arabia by name, accused the Saudis and the UAE of attempting to increase production without needing the revenue and of deliberately wanting to hurt their colleagues. The Iranian press, however, virulently attacked Yamani as being the decisive factor in keeping prices below that decided by OPEC. On December 20, the official Iranian newspaper, *Rastakhiz,* wrote: "The Third World and all the anti-colonialist elements of the world express their hatred towards Yamani for selling the interests of his nation to the imperialists." On the same day, *Kayhan* of Teheran denounced Yamani as the "stooge of capitalists circles, and a traitor not only to his own King and country but also to the Arab world and the Third World as a whole." On December 19, the Iraqi oil minister, Tayih Abd al-Karim, charged Saudi Arabia with acting "in the service of imperialism and Zionism." He claimed that his delegation had "unmasked Saudi Arabia as defeatist and compromising reactionary cell working inside and outside OPEC against the interests of the oil producing countries and other developing countries." The Algerian oil minister declared on December 18 that if Saudi Arabia increased its oil production rates, this would be an "act of direct aggression against OPEC."[14]

In the United States praise was heaped on Saudi Arabia. Some U.S. policymakers planned to persuade Saudi Arabia to increase production to 20 million barrels a day and thus guarantee a secure supply. President Gerald Ford said that the two OPEC members exercised "international responsibility and concern for the adverse impact of an oil increase on the world economy." He described the other OPEC members as taking a course of action that "can only be termed irresponsible." Secretary of the Treasury William Simon called Saudi Arabia "a true friend of the West in general and the United States in particular." He predicted that the other OPEC countries would have to reduce their prices to Saudi Arabia's level.[15]

President-elect Jimmy Carter welcomed the restraint that Saudi Arabia and the UAE had exercised. Although he stressed that his administration would enter into no commitment with Arab producers in a quid pro quo deal, he thought the decision of limiting the price increase to 5 percent was "responsible."[16] Saudi Arabia was caught between strong opposition inside OPEC and U.S. policy. Despite its praise for the Saudi and UAE action, the United States was determined not to comply with the request of the two producers for "appreciation," as Yamani had asked, on the "two fronts"—the North-South dialogue and the Arab-Israeli conflict. The question of whether or not a two-tier price structure would destroy OPEC was uppermost in the minds of producers and consumers.

On January 12, 1977, Yamani predicted that OPEC members who opted for the 10 percent increase would suffer a 25 percent drop in oil exports during the first quarter of the year. He estimated that OPEC operated on a surplus of 3 million barrels a day because of the discontinuance of stockpiling purchases by the multinational companies. Reacting to this prediction, the shah of Iran declared that if this fall in exports "is due to overproduction by Saudi Arabia and the other country following it, this would constitute an act of aggression against us."[17] Actually, during the first nine days of January, Iranian crude-oil exports dropped 38 percent compared with the previous month. The Iranian budget minister considered cutting back development spending. Kuwait reported that its operating companies were proposing a 38 percent reduction in contract lifting. *Business Week,* on the other hand, concluded in its January 10, 1977 issue that in 1977 alone, the new oil prices would cost the United States $75 billion in Gross National Product, 3 million jobs, and $90 billion in disposable income. The non-OPEC world would lose $200 billion in GNP.

As early as February 1977, the Qatari oil minister, Abd al-Aziz bin Khalifa al-Thani, as president of the Doha conference, had visited Saudi Arabia, Iraq, Libya, Algeria, and other OPEC countries in an effort to break the impasse created by the two-tier price structure. He finally came up with a compromise solution: Saudi Arabia and the UAE were to increase their prices to 10 percent, and the other eleven members were to forgo the additional 5 percent increase in July; thus a uniform price would be reestablished. Kuwaiti reports claimed that the shah of Iran was amenable to the compromise, provided the other OPEC members agreed. Active discussion was carried on among OPEC members for a solution. However, Saudi Arabia officially rejected the proposal. In an interview on March 6, in the London *Sunday Times,* Yamani asserted that the chances for an early resolution of the inter-OPEC price dispute were remote. He emphasized, "So far I do not see any possibility of an agreement. We are sticking to our guns."

In spite of the rebuffs that the Saudis received from the United States to its two demands, they were not ready to give up the attempt. Success in these would have established Saudi Arabia as the protector of the developing countries and the defender of the Arab national cause; as a result the Saudis would become the dominating power in OPEC, at a cost of 5 percent in the price of oil. Saudi Arabia was prepared to make additional basic concessions to the United States in the question of oil stockpiling from its own increased production. According to the *International Herald-Tribune,* Prince Fahd, then deputy prime minister and heir apparent to the throne, stated in the middle of May that his country's resistance to oil price increases was aimed at persuading consuming nations, especially the United States, to push for a political settlement of the Arab-Israeli conflict. Fahd reportedly said, "As long as the United States needs our oil and we need its political influence and technological expertise, then I believe we can achieve the desired cooperation."

Asked if Saudi Arabia was inclined to help the United States build its oil reserves, he replied, "Yes, we can help. We are capable of raising our production rate to gradually help the United States insure the six-month strategic reserve of oil as programmed by President Carter." But if the United States did not respond, Fahd intimated that Saudi Arabia might agree to increase the price of oil. He said in an interview, "We are eager to have a uniform price for oil to safeguard the unity of OPEC and to counter attempts of those who try to assail this organization."[18]

Saudi Arabia, however, began to realize that it had miscalculated. The threat to double production was not feasible, as the Saudis did not possess the production capacity to achieve this aim. Nor did consumers flock to Saudi Arabia's doors to purchase its cheaper oil. The Saudis aroused the bitter antagonism and resentment of fellow OPEC members. On the other hand, the United States steadfastly refused to concede either on the North-South dialogue demands or on those involving the Arab-Israeli conflict. The backtracking began.[19] Yamani had previously blamed the United States for not recognizing his country's generosity, consideration, and sacrifice for the Western world. He reiterated his warning that if his country was not compensated for its effort it would have to modify its price position.

CHANGES IN THE MARKET

As Saudi Arabia had correctly assessed, the increased demand for oil in the second half of 1976 had been the result of stockpiling rather than increased consumption because of economic recovery. Demand for oil in 1977 consequently fell for all OPEC members. Saudi Arabia was forced to return to the OPEC fold. The Saudis would have to recognize—Yamani's pontifical declaration notwithstanding—the power of OPEC to set uniform prices for all members.

A practical answer to the continuing impasse lay in the original Qatari compromise plan. Late in May it was reported that the eleven OPEC members who had voted in December 1976 to raise prices an additional 5 percent in July had agreed to forgo the extra increase in return for a pledge by Saudi Arabia and the UAE to raise their prices by 5 percent.[20] By the end of June it was reported from Vienna that nine members, except Iraq and Libya, had agreed to the Qatari plan. At the same time, word came from Riyadh that Saudi Arabia and the UAE had raised their prices to bring them in line with the OPEC majority.

As the conference opened in Stockholm on July 12, the general atmosphere was relaxed, and all agreed to freeze prices for the balance of 1977. Saudi Arabia indicated that it favored freezing oil prices for the entire year of 1978. Even Iran, which had always demanded higher prices, indicated agreement with Saudi Arabia.

When the OPEC delegates gathered for their fiftieth conference in Caracas, Venezuela, on December 20, 1977, it was evident that members would not agree to increase the price of oil. Iraq demanded a 23 percent increase to compensate for the inflation rate of world prices. This inflation figure was disputed by some members. Venezuela and Indonesia proposed a 5 to 8 percent increase; Saudi Arabia, the UAE, Qatar, and Iran urged freezing prices. Yamani stated that his country's position was based on market reality—world oil glut. This was reflected in an announcement by Algeria, Libya, and Nigeria of a reduction of twenty to thirty cents a barrel. The only way to force prices upward would have been to cut production, but because OPEC failed to control production it could not increase prices. After two days of heated discussion, the conference concluded on December 21 with a communiqué stating, "The Conference considered the question of a price readjustment, but the Member Countries were unable to reach a Common Consensus on this issue."[21] In practical terms, this meant that prices would remain frozen at least until the next conference scheduled for June 15, 1978.

The market situation had not improved, and in fact there had been a drop in demand, when the OPEC conference opened in Geneva in the middle of June 1978. Proposals to increase prices were rejected and it was decided to maintain the existing prices to the end of the year. The hawkish members succeeded, however, in passing a resolution to form a committee for protecting oil revenue paid in dollars. The extremist members accused Saudi Arabia and Iran of being agents of the United States and other Western countries; their refusal to increase prices was aimed at helping the Western countries in their economic recovery, strengthening the dollar, and solidifying their political ties with the West at the expense of the oil-producing countries.[22]

When the next OPEC conference opened in Abu Dhabi on December 16, 1978, the clouds of the Iranian revolution were already gathering. OPEC decided on a 14.5 percent price increase, spread over the year. Yamani cited the shortages caused by the difficulties in Iran as the decisive factor in the increase: from $12.70 to $14.54 a barrel.

ASSESSMENT

In the dramatic OPEC developments between 1975 and 1978 the main actor was no doubt Saudi Arabia, as personified by its minister of oil and mineral resources, Ahmad Zaki Yamani. He battled, maneuvered, explained, argued, and presented his country's positions, changes, and retreats, always acting as his country's protagonist. Consistency was not his strong point; his game was strategy and tactics. Like a skilled debater, he took advantage of every opportunity of attacking and confounding his antagonists. His methodology was expediency.

Basically, Yamani was not ready to admit that Saudi Arabia's determination to keep oil prices down was motivated by the nature and future of its oil resources. He tried to give purely altruistic reasons for Saudi policy—deep concern for the health and soundness of the Western countries' economies—but for this altruism and concern he loudly insisted that his country be handsomely rewarded by Western, especially U.S., compliance with his country's demands. In the battle with OPEC members who opposed his country's refusal to increase oil prices, Yamani bitterly complained of the fraudulent tactics of some members who ardently advocated price increases but actually practiced price reduction of their own oil. His country, by abiding by the decisions of the organization, was being victimized by the resultant overpricing of Saudi oil. According to this reasoning, it seems that if the other OPEC members abided by the organization prices, Saudi Arabia would not then be greatly concerned by the repercussions of high oil prices on the economies of the Western countries.

While Saudi Arabia threatened its OPEC colleagues with increases in Saudi production in order to keep prices down— all out of concern for the Western economies—Yamani warned the West on December 16, 1976, not to be "too happy for what happened today. Then you will be misled. We hope we will get together again and this will be in the near future . . . OPEC continues to be strong."[23] The tactic was obvious. Yamani told the Western countries that Saudi Arabia was determined to keep prices low to prevent a collapse of their economies. Yet in an interview with *Events* on January 14, 1977, hardly a month after Doha, he stated:

> The United States is principally interested now in raising the price of oil. This is for many reasons—the most important of which is that the U.S. gains economically every time the price of oil is increased. It leads to more demand for dollars, which in turn improves the balance of payments. This is simple and basic economic rule.
>
> Furthermore, the U.S. established the International Energy Agency, and the principle of a rock bottom price for oil. This means that if the price of oil should fall below a certain level, the consumer countries will impose big enough taxes on it to guarantee continued investment in searching for an alternative energy course, whether nuclear, coal or solar power. They will always guarantee that they do not face any stiff competition from the cheaper source—oil. Through such methods the consumer countries encourage research into non-oil sources of energy.
>
> The real interest for the U.S. is in higher oil prices. I do not recall that Dr. Henry Kissinger ever raised the subject of oil prices with us, although he talks to us frequently. These are well known facts. Their whole interest is in raising the price of oil. This is a political decision in the first instance, then an economic one.

If this was indeed the case, then Saudi Arabia's iron refusal to raise prices was not a service to the United States but a disservice; how then could Yamani's country ask for compensation for its actions?

Yamani accused Britain of overestimating the size of its North Sea oil reserves and of wishing to increase world oil prices in order to make the costly exploitation of the North Sea oil profitable. Was Saudi Arabia really buying itself in with the Western powers by refusing to increase the oil price? Only a few days before the opening of the Doha conference Yamani warned his OPEC colleagues that his country would not continue forever to bear the burden of supporting OPEC's pricing system while other countries "cut prices as they wish." Yet as regards OPEC he made this amazing statement: "We must avoid out-bidding each other. We must not let our work with OPEC become affected by our activities in the Arab arena, such as propaganda and media campaigns."[24]

In the middle of January 1977 Yamani explained rather frankly why Saudi Arabia was determined to keep prices down. He pointed out that for its personal interests Iran was determined to obtain as much money as possible and industrialize itself. It would not matter to Iran if the world found alternatives for oil.

> But for us, the Arabs (Saudi Arabia) who possess gigantic quantities of proven oil reserves, we will be the ones to lose heavily if the world finds new sources of energy for its factories. We will become economically weak, and worst of all, politically weak as well. If we reached such a position we, the Arabs, would be finished politically—most definitely we would be. The Palestinian cause? That would fade away as a result.
>
> The Palestine cause is alive in the world today because of oil. If it had not been for oil then the world would not give a thought to Palestine. It is painful to realize that such elementary facts regarding oil policy continue to be ignored or unknown to the Arab public.[25]

This is the oil weapon that Yamani and his Arab colleagues had been advocating to be used against the West. Yet, this same Yamani had proclaimed many times that Saudi Arabia was vitally interested in the development of alternative sources of energy.

In Saudi Arabia's tactics with both its OPEC colleagues and with the United States, Yamani insisted all the time that his country would stick to its guns and would not raise the price of its oil. Yet at that very time it was public knowledge that Saudi Arabia was ready to accept the Qatari compromise. Throughout his discussions and negotiations with the United States Yamani indicated that he considered stockpiling to be one of the major causes for the price rises and he pleaded for stockpiling to stop so that prices would drop. He never revealed that his real objection was that stockpiling was a major weapon in the hands of the consumers against the producers. At the same time, Saudi Prince Fahd was prepared to increase production and offer the United States oil for stockpiling—in defiance of the other OPEC members—in return for U.S. concessions in the two areas of the North-South dialogue and the Arab-Israeli conflict. (See Chapter 8.)

In the end, Yamani swallowed his open challenge of OPEC's power to establish oil prices, and Saudi Arabia conceded to the organization the power that it had consistently denied it. Although Saudi Arabian policy had prevailed—in Bali prices were frozen; in Doha prices were raised 10 percent by eleven members and only 5 percent by the other two; in Stockholm they were frozen at 10 percent until the end of December—Saudi Arabia ultimately failed with OPEC and failed as well in its efforts to influence the United States. At the beginning of 1979 the issue was taken out of Saudi Arabia's hands when developments in OPEC were overtaken by the Iranian revolution and its consequences.[26]

NOTES

1. *Jerusalem Post,* August 15, 1975.
2. *New York Times,* September 26, 1975.
3. *Jerusalem Post,* September 28, 1975.
4. *Maariv,* September 28, 1975.
5. *Middle East Economic Survey (MEES),* May 31, 1976.
6. *Jerusalem Post,* May 28, 1976.
7. *Middle East Economic Digest (MEED),* June 4, 1976.
8. *World Oil,* July 1976, p. 183; *MEED,* June 4, 1976; *Petroleum Times,* June 11, 1976; *Petroleum Economist,* 1976, p. 246.
9. *MEED,* June 11, 1976.
10. *MEES,* January 10, 1977.
11. Ibid.
12. Ibid., December 27, 1976.
13. *Petroleum Times,* March 18, 1977.
14. *MEES,* December 27, 1977.
15. Ibid.

16. Ibid. A different somber note was sounded by Senator Edward Kennedy in a memorandum to Congress outlining the conclusions of the Joint Economic Committee: "In summary, the OPEC split of December 1976 is not cause for rejoicing that the cartel is about to collapse, even though internal differences and tensions have been brought to the surface. Since imported oil is an unpleasant but necessary fact of life for the United States, a broad range of policies— domestic and international must be pursued to limit this dependency." U.S., Congress, Joint Economic Committee, Subcommittee on Energy, *Hearings: Energy Independence or Interdependence, The Agenda with OPEC* (Washington, D.C., 1977), p. 224.

17. *MEES*, January 24, 1977; *MEED*, January 28, 1977.

18. *International Herald-Tribune*, May 23, 1977.

19. The *Financial Times* (London) of March 8, 1977, predicted, "At the next scheduled OPEC conference in Stockholm in July, Saudi Arabia will probably be ready for a compromise, one which will be possible without any member losing face. It is likely, for instance, that the OPEC majority will drop the claim for another 5 percent in the second half of this year." The major reason for Saudi Arabia's readiness for compromise was its inability to increase production as had been expected.

20. *Business Week*, May 30, 1977; *Jerusalem Post*, May 17, 1977.

21. *MEES*, January 2, 1978; *MEED*, January 6, 1978; *Petroleum Economist*, January 1978, p. 2.

22. In an interview in the Kuwait *Al-Siyasah* of June 25, 1978, Jamshid Amouzegar explained Iran's position on prices and on the dollar as the basis of payment for oil. In a change of position on the question of price, Iran advocated freezing prices for purely economic reasons, although still maintaining that the price of oil should approximate the cost of production of alternative energy sources. An increase in oil prices would result in a drop in demand and a consequent surplus in the world oil market. This would intensify the recession in Europe and in the industrialized countries, which in turn—and here Amouzegar came to grips with the difficult internal economic situation in Iran—would damage the development programs of the OPEC countries. As to the attempt to replace the dollar by another currency or unit of account for oil, he said that it would be dangerous to abandon the dollar for another currency, as such a move would not afford sufficient protection for the producers' oil resources.

23. *Jerusalem Post*, December 19, 1976.

24. *MEES*, December 13, 1976.

25. *Events,* January 14, 1977; *MEES,* January 17, 1977. At the end of May 1976, the oil minister of the UAE listed among his country's reasons for refusing to increase prices, "thirdly, to ensure the long-term retention of their oil markets by the OPEC producers and discourage the development of substitutes by the consumers." *MEES,* May 31, 1976.

26. The major sources for Chapter 6 were: U.S., Comptroller General, *Report to the Congress: More Attention Should Be Paid to Making the United States Less Vulnerable to Foreign Oil Price and Supply Decisions* (Washington, D.C., 1978); idem, *Report to the Congress: Critical Factors Affecting Saudi Arabia's Oil Decisions* (Washington, D.C., 1978); U.S., Congress, Joint Economic Committee, Subcommittee on Energy, *Hearings: Energy Independence or Interdependence* (Washington, D.C., 1977).

7

SURPLUSES
AND RECYCLING

The efforts of the United States, after the outbreak of the 1973–1974 energy crisis, to organize the oil-consuming countries into a strong united bloc to face the Middle East oil producers failed. So did the two other attempts, with different motives and aims, made by France. Meanwhile, the tremendous transfer of wealth from the consumers—for the oil purchased—to the oil producers continued in ever-increasing amounts. The consequences were deficits in the balance of payments, depreciations of currencies, rise in unemployment, drop in economic growth, inflation, and economic recession. These affected not only the developing—other than OPEC—countries but also the Western industrialized nations.

The only remedies for these consequences of the high oil prices involved recycling the transferred wealth back to the original owners. This meant that the consumers (because they had rejected the radical solution offered by the United States of forcing oil prices down) would have to live with and adjust to the economic ills that were created by the energy crisis. One of the most frightening aspects of the newly created conditions of the energy crisis involved the assessments of possible gigantic accumulations of surpluses in the hands of the producing countries (as outlined in Chapter 4). By successful recycling, these surpluses could be returned to the consuming nations. But what about the constantly increasing oil prices? How to live with them? An important element in the recycling solution was to transfer to the producing countries the inflation that the high prices had caused in the consuming countries by charging the oil producers high prices for their imports from the industrialized countries. Plans for recycling mechanisms were discussed and debated by the international financial institutions, but not as a collective instrument of the consuming countries. Various methods were employed by each individual country, depending on the means and resources at its command, inevitably in competition with and at the expense of the other consumers.

Four main devices were used by the major consuming industrialized nations in their recycling efforts. First was investment. The producers were to be induced to invest part of their surpluses in the consumers' financial markets, such as government bonds and securities, corporate stock shares and bonds, bank deposits, and others. The more investments the oil producers made, the less would be the deficit in the balance of payments, and the more the national currency would be strengthened. The second device was trade. Because the Middle East oil-producing countries were in need of goods and services ranging from food to factories, the industrialized countries could supply those needs and thus bring back another part of the transferred wealth. The third device was the sale of arms and ammunitions of the most advanced and sophisticated types. The newly rich oil producers were eager and anxious to build up their military strength, and the major industrialized countries were the natural source of armaments to meet these needs. From an economic point of view, arms sales were the most desirable means of bringing back the wealth, because although other devices are or could be economic producers, arms and ammunitions are nonproducers. Moreover, benefits accrue from the original sale, from the continuing need for spare parts and replacements, and after a number of years the weapons become obsolete and new models have to be ordered.

The fourth device involved contracts for developing projects in the oil-producing countries. The oil producers all realized the exhaustability of their great resource and were determined to utilize the enormous revenue for economic development projects. These would enable them to maintain economic levels after the oil had been exhausted. As the revenue from oil rose astronomically, so did allotments for economic programs—from hundreds of millions of dollars before 1973 to hundreds of billions of dollars in the later 1970s. The producing countries were incapable of planning, let alone implementing, their programs themselves and needed the industrialized countries' big companies to plan and execute the projects for them. Multibillion-dollar contracts obtained by these companies could reduce balance-of-payments deficits, stabilize currency, reduce unemployment, and raise economic growth levels.

THE SCOPE OF THE SURPLUSES
AND DEFICITS

The extent of the OPEC countries' gross oil revenues after 1973, surpluses, investments and their distribution, and income from investments was almost entirely based on estimates. The estimators were not in agreement with one another, and their estimates changed from time to time. Nor were any figures available for the magnitude of the spending of the producing countries in acquiring their current goods and commodities from the industrialized countries. On the other hand, there were no accurate calculations of the actual share of the high oil prices in the balance-of-payments deficits and the other ills attributable to the prices. Nevertheless, a number of financial institutions and firms supplied estimates. The major ones, among others, were the U.S. Treasury Department, the Federal Reserve Bank of New York, the Bank of England, the World Bank, the IMF (International Monetary Fund), BIS (Bank of International Settlement), Chase Manhattan Bank, the American Petroleum Institute, Citibank, the First National Bank of Chicago, and Bankers Trust. From these estimates a picture emerges of the fiscal relations between the oil-producing and oil-consuming countries, and repercussions in the world economy, for the years between the first energy crisis, in 1973, and the second energy crisis, in 1979.

Total revenue received for the oil during the five-year period 1974–1978, averaged from the various estimates, amounted to

$573 billion. The total surpluses for the same period, averaged from the different estimates, was $219 billion. The U.S. Treasury estimated that in the four-year period 1973–1977 the surpluses amounted to from $135 to $145 billion. It noted that between 1974 and 1978, Saudi Arabia, Kuwait, and the UAE accounted for 70 percent of the aggregate OPEC surplus. Morgan Guaranty Trust Company estimated that gross OPEC net investments in foreign assets by the end of 1978 was $178 billion; the U.S. Treasury estimate reached $188 billion.

Estimates as to the distribution of the investments were made at different times. The U.S. Treasury estimated that investments by the oil producers in the United States rose from $1 billion in 1972 to $32 billion through March 1977; most of the investments were in Treasury securities ($13.8 billion), bank deposits ($9 billion), federal and corporate stocks and bonds ($8 billion). Investments in Euro-currency amounted to $22.5 billion in 1974, $8 billion in 1975, and $10.5 billion in 1976. In 1974 investments in Great Britain amounted to $7.5 billion; it fell to $250 million in 1975 and early in 1976 rose to $1 billion. Investments in unidentified developed countries were given as $22 billion, in developing countries $16 billion, in Communist countries $4 billion, and in international financial institutions $10 billion.

The Bank of England estimated early in 1978 that the U.S. share in investments had fallen by 25 percent, from $12 billion in 1976 to $8.9 billion in 1977. The British share also fell but only from $4.5 billion in 1976 to $4.1 billion in 1977. In June 1978 the U.S. Treasury estimated OPEC investments both in figures and percentages: in Europe, $43.59 billion, or 23.6 percent; all other countries, $39.5 billion, or 21.3 percent; grants, loans, and investments in underdeveloped countries, $37 billion, or 20 percent; international financial institutions, $10.25 billion, or 5 percent. The U.S. General Accounting Office estimated that by the end of 1978 OPEC investments in the United States had reached $52 billion. This was broken down: $32 billion in deposits in U.S. banks and in their branches overseas, $20 billion in government securities and other holdings.[1]

Producers' income from investments rose elevenfold from $781 million in 1972 to $8.741 billion in 1977. At the end of that year the income from foreign investments amounted to more than the OPEC countries had been receiving for their total oil exports before 1972. In 1978 the earnings from investments reached $10.926 billion, and projected earnings for 1979 were $13 billion; for 1980 they were $15.5 billion. The First National Bank of Chicago estimated that earnings from foreign investments of Saudi Arabia, Kuwait, Qatar, and the UAE would reach $15.7 billion in 1981. Saudi Arabia's $50-billion external portfolio in 1978 earned $4.5 billion, compared to $4.3 billion for total oil-export income in 1973.

This was the credit side for the producers. What was the debit side for the consumers that the recycling was to overcome? In May 1977 it was estimated that the consuming countries' deficits for the period 1974–1976 were: OECD countries, $65 billion; the developing countries, $79 billion; making a total of $144 billion. The producers' surpluses for the same period amounted to $138 billion, a rather striking relationship between the surpluses and the deficits.

The estimates and assessments of the magnitude of the OPEC surpluses and the repercussions of this transfer of wealth caused by the high oil prices ran a full gamut from the most optimistic, those of the Morgan Guaranty Trust Company, to all the others in between, to the most pessimistic, those of *Business Week*. In October 1975, even after OPEC increased oil prices by 10 percent, Morgan Guaranty estimated that the combined surplus of OPEC countries would fall in that year from $65 billion in 1974 to $36 billion and that the surplus in 1976 would further drop to $30–34 billion and decline to $28 billion in 1977. It attributed this development to a rapid growth in OPEC imports of about $80 billion a year and to a large decline in world oil demand. Indeed, the bank predicted that within four years the OPEC countries would move from surpluses to deficits in their balance of payments.

At the other extreme, *Business Week*, in its issue of December 20, 1976, estimated that since the outbreak of the energy crisis in October 1973 the consumers had paid OPEC an additional $225 billion for oil, and that they had lost $600 billion in output; the developing nations had amassed $170 billion in external debts. According to a Brookings Institution specialist, George Perry, in 1976 alone, the United States had lost more than $60 billion in gross national product and more than 2 million jobs because of the high oil price *Business Week* concluded, "To the degree that the industrial world will continue to react to OPEC-induced inflation, the 13 oil ministers have become the macro-managers of the world, superseding policymakers in even the strongest industrial nations."

On May 22, 1978, quoting William Nordhaus, a member of the President's Council of Economic Advisers, who had said that the quadrupling of oil prices in 1974 by OPEC was "the economic disaster of the post–World War II era," *Business Week* concluded that the huge price increase transferred $80 billion a year in income and investments from the oil-consuming nations to OPEC, "simultaneously plunging the world into recession while propelling inflation rates to unprecedented peacetime levels. Now, some four years later, the inflationary explosion created in OPEC's wake is still reverberating throughout the world economy."

THE CASE OF SAUDI ARABIA

Because Saudi Arabia was the greatest OPEC producer and consequently collected the largest share of the very rapidly increasing oil revenue, and because the United States was the greatest oil consumer in the world, as well as the most advanced country in technology and the richest, with large investment interests in Saudi Arabia, it naturally followed that there would be a very close economic, financial, and technological relationship between them, in addition to political and security ties. Total Saudi Arabia oil revenue in 1972 amounted to $2.7 billion. Five years later its oil revenue jumped to $37 billion. On the other hand, in 1977 the U.S. deficit in the balance of payments went up to more than $20 billion. In order to recycle its oil payments, and thus stabilize its economy, the United States had to resort to the four devices outlined above.

Events developed very rapidly that hastened the process. On April 5, 1974, Saudi Arabia and the United States initialed an agreement for close cooperation in the fields of economics, industry, and the military. Two months later, an agreement was signed in Washington, by Secretary of State Kissinger for the United States and Prince Fahd for Saudi Arabia, that established the joint U.S.–Saudi Arabian Commission for Economic Cooperation. Designed to assist Saudi Arabia's economic and technical development in any area that Saudi Arabia might request, the agreement called on the two sides to work together to "promote progress of industrialization, trade, manpower training, agriculture and science and technology." The Saudi government deposited a credit fund of $120 million with the Treasury Department in Washington to pay for the program as it developed. Oil was not mentioned, but the agreement provided for "special relations," which became a great rallying invocation in future deals.[2]

At the end of 1974 Saudi Arabia adopted the Second Five-Year Economic Development Program for 1975–1980 and allotted it $144 billion. In September 1975, the Saudi government set up the Royal Commission as an independent body in charge of the development of Jubail on the Gulf and Yanbu on the Red Sea as two great industrial cities based primarily on the petroleum industry. The Bechtel Corporation of San Francisco was asked to prepare the master plan for the Jubail industrial complex and later was contracted for the overall management of the project. The primary industries were to be refineries, petrochemical plants, steel and aluminum works, and the infrastructure for an ultimate population of 160,000. In the middle of 1976 it was estimated that the project would bring the company $9 billion and was to last twenty years. The U.S. Ralph M. Parsons Company was granted a similar contract for the Yanbu project, which was to be the terminal of the inland pipeline and was to contain, in addition to the terminal, refineries and petrochemical complexes. In 1978 the cost of the building of the two cities was estimated at $30 billion.

In 1976 the Saudi government organized the Saudi Arabia Basic Industries Corporation (SABIC) with a capital of $3 billion. This corporation was to hold the government's share of the equities of the various joint venture refineries, petro-chemical complexes, and industrial projects planned for Jubail and Yanbu. Petromin, the Saudi Arabian national oil company, was expanding very rapidly, and the government took away some of its functions and transferred them to the newly created Ministry of Industry and Electricity. Foreign companies wishing to do business with Saudi Arabia had to deal with the various ministries; if their business specifically involved the petroleum industry, they had to deal, in addition to the Ministry of Oil and Mineral Resources, with Petromin, SABIC, the Royal Commission for Jubail and Yanbu, and the Ministry of Industry and Electricity.

In dealing with the foreign companies, the Saudi government evolved two types of economic projects. One was entirely owned and financed by the government, through its companies and agencies; the other was a form of joint venture, the percentage ownership of the government and the foreign company varying from project to project. In April 1974, the U.S. Raytheon Company signed a contract with Saudi Arabia to supply the Saudis with an advanced Hawk antiaircraft missile system at a cost of $260–270 million. In May 1974, Petromin and Mobil signed an agreement to build a 2,700-barrels-a-day lubricating-oil refinery near the Jidda refinery. The equity shares were 61 percent Petromin and 39 percent Mobil. In the same month, Saudi Arabia requested Aramco to build a natural gas gathering system and facilities to generate electric power and operate these projects on behalf of the government. The projects were to cost $16 billion. Aramco was one of the major U.S. instruments for recycling. Although Aramco was totally nationalized (in 1976–1979), the four U.S. partners continued to handle the technical operation of the industry from exploration to marketing.

Early in January 1975, Saudi Arabia announced that it had concluded a $750-million arms deal with the United States for the purchase of several squadrons of model F5E warplanes. Early in 1976 it was reported to the U.S. House Appropriations Subcommittee that Saudi Arabia held the fourth largest share of the U.S. public debt after Germany, Japan, and France, with debt holdings worth $4.5 billion. In September 1976, Mobil and the Saudi Ministry of Industry and Electricity signed an agreement to build a joint venture, 50/50 ownership, major refinery and petrochemical center at Yanbu. In January 1977, the U.S. Fluor Corporation was granted a $1-billion contract to erect an ethylene-based petrochemical plant near Jubail. In August Petromin signed an agreement for the construction of a major specialized refinery at Jubail with Texaco and Socal; ownership was Petromin 50 percent, Texaco and Socal 25 percent each.

It was reported in May 1978 that the U.S. Corps of Engineers was engaged in four major programs in Saudi Arabia with a total potential cost of $26 billion. Brigadier General Richard M. Connell, director of military construction in the Office of the Chief of Engineers, listed them as: Ordnance Corps, Naval expansion, National Guard modernization, and Engineers Assistance Agreement. The Pentagon revealed, in the middle of February 1978, a $670-million plan to build military training facilities in Saudi Arabia. This would bring U.S. earnings in that country to more than $15 billion, most of which had occurred in the previous five years.[3]

Newsweek reported on March 6, 1978, that the United States obtained a big share of Saudi Arabia's investment dollars—at least $35 billion in fixed Treasury bonds alone and countless other holdings totaling billions. It quoted a U.S. businessman in the Saudi capital as saying, "They're going to fuel our industry and keep our economy afloat." The *United States Banker* estimated that from 1974 to 1978 the net inflow of Saudi Arabian capital to the United States averaged $5 billion annually.

ASSESSMENT

This by no means exhaustive but random list of developments more than proves the extraordinary success of the United States in recycling the wealth from Saudi Arabia through all the four devices. Indeed, a study conducted by the First National Bank of Chicago for the years 1977–1979 showed that the financial flow from the Middle East oil-producing countries to the United States had balanced the outflow of cash from the United States for oil imports. Theoretically, it is highly desirable that nations should develop interdependence and through commercial and economic activity maintain international peace. However, such interdependence requires some sort of equality between the parties and a high degree of stability and level of development in both. In the process of paying out huge amounts of dollars for the purchase of oil and recovery of those dollars through recycling, the United States had become dependent on Saudi Arabia in four areas: oil supply, investments, arms sales, and project contracts.

U.S. industrial and service corporations, as well as the energy and weapons sectors, exploited the Middle East oil producers' special conditions and reaped huge profits, but at the same time they became heavily dependent on their relations with Saudi Arabia. In the joint-venture undertakings, the foreign companies invested heavily in their host's great variety of projects. By this method the foreign companies acquired a strong vested interest in the undertakings. On the other hand, Saudi Arabia guaranteed for itself—especially in the gigantic petrochemical complexes—markets for the manufactured products, in sharp competition with the products of the foreign companies' home factories. As an inducement to the foreign investors, Saudi Arabia offered to sell an additional 1,000 barrels a day for every $1 million invested (later this was reduced to 500 barrels a day). In periods of oil supply shortages, this was indeed a very enticing offer and added another handicap to U.S. relations with Saudi Arabia.

The first risk of dependence on Saudi Arabia was, of course, supply. The United States was to depend for its oil supply, for both civilian and military needs, on a country that is not only far away—so that the oil has to be carried through dangerous waterways, seas, and oceans—but also a country whose very regime and internal stability were possibly subject to disturbances, upheavals, and even revolutions. The extent of U.S. dependence on Saudi Arabian oil was claimed by Saudi Arabia's agent to have averaged, in 1978, 1.6 million barrels a day. The magnitude of U.S. oil imports from Saudi Arabia, which was expected to increase rapidly, could become a weapon in the hands of the supplier. Under threat of reducing production or even total embargo, the United States could be forced to agree to demands it did not wish to meet. This is what Yamani and the other Arab leaders called the oil weapon.

The second dependence risk was investments. There always existed a possibility of sudden withdrawals of the investments—for a great variety of reasons—which could cause financial panic. Should Saudi Arabia withdraw its dollar investments and convert them, say, into German marks (such demands were heard in Saudi Arabia, especially when the dollar was weak in relation to other currencies), the disastrous consequences could not be exaggerated. Such a possibility hung as a Damoclean sword on the heads of U.S. policymakers.

The third dependence risk was the project contracts. Although it would not be logical nor in its own interests for Saudi Arabia to suddenly cancel the great economic development programs, a country like Saudi Arabia is not always guided by logic or even self-interest. A sudden debacle could bring all the projects to a complete standstill. The Iranian situation presents a frightening possibility. The fourth dependence risk was a possible decision by the Saudi authorities to change their arms suppliers. A sudden switch might not create serious difficulties to Saudi Arabia. This, therefore, could become a weapon in the hands of Saudi Arabia against the United States.

In addition, the complex recycling process exposed the U.S. government to two pressures, internal and external. The U.S. concerns supplying Saudi Arabia its various needs, through their own heavy investments in the country, became deeply dependent for their projects on Saudi Arabia. These companies could exert great pressure on the U.S. government to comply with Saudi demands and requests in order to maintain their positions and their solvency. The story of AWACS (Airborne Warning and Control System)—in which the sale of the spy plane to Saudi Arabia was battled out in the U.S. Senate—contains an excellent possibility of such pressure. Externally, the Western countries were in running competition with one another to sell Saudi Arabia their best and most advanced arms and ammunition as well as other products. All the leaders of the great Western nations had made their pilgrimages to Riyadh in search of favors and lucrative contracts. In October 1980, after a visit to Saudi Arabia, the French president came home with a $3.45-billion naval weapons contract. West Germany had offered to train Saudi air force personnel, and Chancellor Helmut Schmidt visited Riyadh with the aim of increasing trade and inducing the Saudis to invest in Germany in return for German support of Saudi political demands in the Middle East.

The British position was different from that of the United States, West Germany, and France, which were seeking oil supplies from Saudi Arabia. The British, who produced their own oil in the North Sea, were not interested in Middle East oil; their very difficult economic situation made them desperate for greater export markets. Arms exports to the Middle East had been one of Britain's major achievements, and the large loss in arms orders after the visit to Saudi Arabia of France's president Giscard d'Estaing was a serious matter. So British Prime Minister Margaret Thatcher made her pilgrimage to Riyadh and to other Middle East capitals. In this mad rush for contracts, the United States also dispatched its senior representatives with enticing offers.

There were some dissenting voices about recycling as the solution to the problem of high oil payments. In May 1977, the *Petroleum Economist* commented that the political leaders of the Western countries have been hesitant to inform their citizens that the real problem faced by the oil-importing countries was how to adapt to the transfer of wealth to the oil-exporting nations and possibly later to other developing countries. "Instead they have chosen to elaborate on the attempts to launch the so-called petrodollar recycling schemes." The U.S. Congressional Budget Office declared that the high oil price imposed a burden on oil-importing countries and called the OPEC price a cartel price. "This pricing policy causes a drop in living standards among oil-importing countries of between $50 billion and $100 billion per year, oil-importing countries cannot erase this burden by balancing their trade accounts."[4]

In spite of all the dangers and the challenges to the validity of the recycling solution, and in spite of economic difficulties during the five years from 1973 to 1978, U.S. policymakers pursued the recycling solution with ever greater vigor. They apparently felt that, under the circumstances, the advantages outweighed the disadvantages or that there was no alternative.[5]

NOTES

1. The U.S. General Accounting Office could not supply a breakdown of the shares of the various members of OPEC in the total amount. Neither the Treasury Department nor the Commerce Department would provide the necessary information. The Treasury had made "special commitments" of financial confidentiality to Saudi Arabia and possibly to some other OPEC countries for their purchasing of U.S. government securities. In 1976 Prince Fahd warned the U.S. government and U.S. banks not to be pressured into mandatory disclosure of details of Arab bank deposits and depositors. In the event of such disclosures, Saudi Arabia would immediately withdraw its deposits from such banks. The same warning was issued by the Kuwaiti minister of finance. *Middle East Economic Survey (MEES)*, July 26, 1976, and July 23, 1979.

2. U.S., Comptroller General, *Report: The U.S.–Saudi Arabian Joint Commission On Economic Cooperation* (Washington, D.C., 1979), p. I, gave the background: "The United States–Saudi Arabian Joint Commission on Economic Cooperation, established on the heels of the Arab oil embargo and price increases, fosters closer political ties between the two countries through economic cooperation; assists Saudi industrialization and development while recycling petrodollars; and facilitates the flow to Saudi Arabia of American goods, services, and technology."

3. The *Washington Post* correspondent in Dhahran reported on September 1, 1978, that the U.S. Embassy in Jidda had counted 332 U.S. firms that did business in Saudi Arabia. Their projected sales for 1978 were $3.4 billion. U.S. income from sales and services far outstripped the cost of oil that the United States bought from Saudi Arabia—estimated at $6 billion. Listed were the big U.S. construction companies engaged by Saudi Arabia: Fluor Corporation, with a $14-billion gasification contract and other works; the Bechtel Corporation of San Francisco, contracted for the Jubail project; Morrison-Knudson Company of Boise, Idaho, with a $6-billion military city contract; and the Ralph M. Parsons Company, contracted for the Yanbu project, plus a $4-billion contract to build the airport at Jidda.

4. *Petroleum Economist,* May 1977, pp. 166–167.

5. The major sources for Chapter 7 were: U.S., Congress, Congressional Budget Office, *The Effect of OPEC Oil Pricing on Output, Prices, and Exchange Rates in the United States and Other Industrialized Countries* (Washington, D.C., 1981); U.S., Comptroller General, *Report to the Congress: More Attention Should Be Paid to Making the United States Less Vulnerable to Foreign Oil Price and Supply Decisions* (Washington, D.C., 1978); idem, *Report: The U.S.–Saudi Arabian Joint Commission on Economic Cooperation*; U.S., Congress, House, Committee on Ways and Means, *Report: Energy Conservation Act of 1975* (Washington, D.C., 1975); U.S., Congress, Senate, Committee on Foreign Relations, Subcommittee on Multinational Corporations, *Multinational Oil Corporations and U.S. Foreign Policy: Report* (Washington, D.C., 1975).

8

THE SECOND
OIL CRISIS:
1979–1980

In mid-1978 it seemed that the energy crisis that began in October 1973 had stabilized. Oil prices had been frozen since July 1977, demand for oil had dropped, and production was reduced. The OPEC revenue surplus had practically reached zero, while the developed countries experienced a surplus of $8 billion. The consequences of high oil prices, which had had so great an impact since the beginning of the crisis, seemed to have lessened considerably; it looked as if the international economic pattern was slowly returning to its precrisis state.

The 1973 crisis had been the culmination of the long and continuous struggle between the oil-producing countries and the foreign concessionaire companies. During the crisis years the producers achieved total victory. At first, they were drunk with their accomplishments and were ready to continue with new conquests. But after five years, the march slowed down and some balance set in; relations between producers and consumers were normalizing.

A number of indicators of the conditions of the oil industry strengthened this assessment. The spot market, which is not a black market but rather a speculators' instrument, is one of the best indicators of the world oil supply situation. In times of shortages spot prices are much higher—the level depending on the shortage—than the OPEC set prices. In times of glut, spot prices are below OPEC set prices. And in times of balance between supply and demand, the spot market is quiescent. Credit terms are a second indicator. In times of shortfall prices naturally go up; credit time is cut, which is a means of augmenting prices. In times of glut prices fall and credit time is extended to induce purchasers. In normal times credit terms are stable.

A third indicator is the differentials structure. OPEC designated Saudi light oil as the benchmark or marker crude on which to base the price; the other oils—depending on their quality, weight, sulphur content, and geographic location— were to be priced above or below the Saudi-light price. Here, as in the other two indicators, in times of shortage the differences are very great, sometimes as much as $4 to $6 a barrel above the marker crude. In times of glut there are hardly any marked differences. In normal times there are small differences. Because OPEC did not succeed in regulating the differentials structure, it became an important instrument in the hands of the various OPEC members to manipulate the oil market. In mid-1978 all the indicators functioned as in a normal situation. The spot market was generally inactive; credit terms were stable at sixty days from date of lifting; and differentials were small.

Although Saudi Arabia had seriously challenged, at the end of 1976, the power of OPEC to set prices and had vigorously claimed that price setting was a sovereign prerogative of each member, by July 1977 the Saudis retreated and agreed to raise its prices and concede to the organization the power to determine the price structure. By the middle of 1978, the price-regulation power of OPEC was universally accepted. At the Geneva Conference in June 1978, OPEC decided to keep oil prices frozen; only at the Abu Dhabi conference, in December 1978, under the impact of the disturbances and strikes in Iran, did Saudi Arabia relent, and OPEC resolved to increase prices by 14.5 percent, to be spread over the year, reaching at the end $14.54 a barrel for Saudi Arabian light.

1979—THE DELUGE

When, early in 1979, the situation in Iran deteriorated rapidly and Iranian oil production of about 5 million barrels a day came to a total standstill, reaching a point at which it was necessary for Iran to import oil for local consumption, the Western consuming countries were thrown into a panic. The U.S. secretary of energy, James Schlesinger, declared on February 8 that the loss of Iranian oil to the free world market was potentially more serious to the West than the 1973 Arab oil embargo. His department calculated that the loss of Iranian oil led to a shortage in U.S. supplies of about 500,000 barrels daily, or 2.5 percent of consumption.

Six days after the establishment, on February 5, 1979, of the Ayatollah Khomeini government in Iran, Abu Dhabi, disregarding OPEC, unilaterally raised the price of its crude oil by 6–7 percent. All the producers of quality oil—Abu Dhabi, Qatar, Kuwait, and Iraq—notified their customers that, effective as of February 15, they had imposed a one-dollar premium charge on every barrel of oil. After touring the Gulf oil-producing countries' capitals and conferring with Saudi Oil Minister Yamani, the UAE minister of oil and industry, Mana Said al-Otaiba, declared on February 10 at a press conference that "some oil companies are exploiting market conditions in the present circumstances to reap massive profits, particularly from the developing consumer countries. These companies do not have the right to reap such huge profits which should properly go to those who by rights are entitled to them."[1] Hence the price increases.

On February 26, Kuwait notified its crude-oil customers that it had imposed $1.20 a barrel, effective as of February 20, above the basic OPEC price structure. On the same day Venezuela raised its oil prices by 15 percent. Addressing a conference on world energy economics in London, Yamani said that he expected temporary oil price increases by some OPEC members such as Kuwait, UAE, Qatar, and Venezuela and declared that these increases "will never be incorporated in the price structure as it was decided by OPEC in Abu Dhabi last December." He added that his country would play its usual "moderating" role in the upcoming conference, on March 26 in Geneva.[2] This statement marked the beginning of a long, losing battle by Saudi Arabia to hold oil prices down and maintain a uniform structure.

In view of the unilateral price increases by members of the organization, the OPEC Secretariat issued, on February 28, a statement that declared that the

> Conference decisions in setting crude oil prices do not prevent Member Countries from making an upward adjustment in the light of prevailing circumstances. Therefore, the decisions taken by Member Countries either by adjusting their prices upwards, or by choosing other courses of action or further consultations, certainly fall within the framework of the Statute of Organizations, and are strictly in accordance with their sovereign rights, afforded by the OPEC Conference as long ago as January 1961. The Statute emphasizes the "sovereign equality" of Member Countries and that "due regard shall be given at all times to the interests of the producing nations."[3]

Meanwhile steps were taken to fill the gap created by the oil supply shortfall. On February 25, Saudi Arabia increased oil production, on a three-month basis, from 8.5 million barrels a day to 9.5 million barrels a day. The Saudis charged the OPEC price for the 8.5 million barrels—$13.34 a barrel—but added a 9 percent surcharge on the extra million barrels. In mid-February it was reported that Saudi Arabia, Iraq, Nigeria, and Mexico were together producing an extra 3 million barrels daily—2.5 million barrels short of needed world market supplies.

The Saudi Arabian governor of Petromin, Abdul Hady Taher, who did not always agree with Yamani's policies, maintained at the end of February that there was no need for the proposed extraordinary OPEC conference in Geneva scheduled for March 26 to discuss prices, "because any decision taken on prices in the light of the market's instability will be neither wise nor sound." However, in view of the unilateral surcharge increases by some individual producers, the conference had to meet in an attempt to bring some order to the situation.

Geneva Conference: March 26–27

The conference simply recognized the realities of the market and its inability to compel members to abide by the price decisions, as had been clarified in the Secretariat statement. Its major decision was to increase prices by 9 percent as of April 1, raising prices on that date to levels that earlier decisions would have delayed until December. In addition, the conference permitted members to impose surcharges that would raise prices up to 27 percent. Yamani described the conference decision as a "free for all." In order to maintain high prices, some members indicated that they would keep production tight and restrict output.

After the conference, the following picture emerged. Saudi Arabia and the UAE maintained the OPEC official price and raised the price per barrel from $13.34 to $14.54. Other producers added to the new price a surcharge of $1.20. Libya, Algeria, and Nigeria, because of the high quality of their oils, added a surcharge of $4 a barrel. Because production in Iran was increasing, Saudi Arabia, Iraq, and Kuwait announced at Geneva that they would cut production to the levels that had existed prior to the Iranian revolution. To what extent that was an actual determination and to what extent this announcement was a strategy device was not clear at the time. After the conference Yamani stated, "With all modesty, if it were not for us, the minimum price for crude would have been $17.50 for barrel."[4] *Time* magazine, April 9, 1979, quoted Yamani as saying that unless the United States acted, there would be another increase in June.

In the middle of April, Abu Dhabi and Qatar raised their prices to $17.10 a barrel; Saudi Arabia raised the price of her extra-light Berri crude to $16.44; Libya, $24.80; Iraq, $16.28; Kuwait, $15.80; and Iran, $16.57. The issue of controlled production came up. Traditionally, OPEC could not establish a production control system, considered an infringement on members' sovereign powers. But under the circumstances of such high prices, controlled production might be necessary to maintain the desired levels. Some members had already announced that they had curtailed production. On April 2, when Yamani was asked about his country's production rate, he replied, "Sir, we refuse to talk about the level of production in Saudi Arabia with the OPEC members' countries. It is not their affair. It is our affair. It has been our own affair. And it has been our policy since the early 1960's to avoid any production program. Nothing has changed. We raise it or lower it—it is our affair."[5]

When it was reported that Iran was producing 4 million barrels a day, and Saudi Arabia announced that it would reduce its production level back to 8.5 million barrels a day, it was suggested in a question to Yamani that if Saudi Arabia was dissatisfied with the OPEC surcharges, it could perhaps correct the situation by raising the Saudi production ceiling. In contrast to his threat after the 1976 Doha conference of doubling production to bring prices down, Yamani replied, "I do not think I should raise my production for this. I'm not fighting OPEC; it is not my duty or my job." He rejected U.S. pressure to increase production and said, "I think you, the consumers should alter it—not Saudi Arabia—by reducing consumption."[6]

Meanwhile, the price increases and surcharges continued. On May 20, Algeria proposed a $21-per-barrel price, an increase of $2.45 as a surcharge over the previous price of $18.45. On the same day, Kuwait added sixty cents to its surcharge, making a total of $2.40. Venezuela also added sixty cents to its surcharge, and other Gulf producers followed Kuwait as well. On June 1, it was reported in Washington that Saudi Arabia had increased its price by $1.40 a barrel. NIOC had increased its surcharge by twenty cents, bringing the total price of Iranian light to $18.47 a barrel. On June 5, Ecuador increased its price by 32 percent, from $20.36 a barrel to $26.80.

Other devices were employed to augment revenue. On June 24, Iraq inserted in its oil contracts a "most-favored-seller" clause, which provided that its oil customers would pay for their oil on the basis of the "highest premium charged by any other oil sellers."[7]

Geneva Conference: June 26–28

In the midst of this chaotic situation, the ordinary midyear OPEC conference opened in Geneva on June 26. After two days of heated debate, in an attempt to unify prices, OPEC adopted a new price framework ranging from $18 to $23.50 a barrel, effective July 1 until the next December 17.[8]

The reaction in the Western world to the OPEC June decision was one of gloom. U.S. President Jimmy Carter declared that after the Geneva OPEC action "there is no one on earth who will fail to suffer from the extraordinary increases."[9] The Big Seven Western industrialized nations' representatives meeting in Tokyo declared that the "unwarranted rises in oil prices mean more worldwide inflation and less [economic] growth. That will lead to more unemployment, more balance of payment difficulty, and [will] endanger stability. We deplore the [OPEC] decision."[10] These solemn pronouncements had no possible action behind them. The hard reality was that the weighted average increase in the oil price since December 1978 had been 56 percent. Total OPEC revenues for 1979 were estimated to reach $160 billion compared to $119 billion in 1978.

Saudi Arabia faced two fronts. On the one hand, the Saudis had to resist the pressure of other OPEC members to raise prices and, on the other hand, had to resist a pressing demand by the United States to raise the production level to reduce the price. Having agreed in June to the new price structure of OPEC, Yamani placed the onus on the United States. Early in July he ominously stated, "Either the United States can compel Israel to implement U.N. resolution 242 and withdraw to the pre-1967 borders, or it can't. If it can't, then you must be prepared to face the consequences."[11]

The consequences—which had nothing to do with the UN resolution—followed. Practically all producers reduced the credit terms for all their oil customers from sixty to thirty days. On August 20, Iran increased its contract prices by twenty-one cents a barrel in lieu of reducing the credit time. On October 15, Kuwait increased its price by $1.94 a barrel to a total of $21.43 retroactive to October 1. Iran raised its price to the full $23.50, and so did Libya and Algeria. Kuwait and the other Gulf producers followed Iraq in inserting in their contracts a most-favored-seller clause. The spot market price reached the $40 to $50 mark.

Saudi Arabia's decision to increase production from 8.5 to 9.5 million barrels a day on a three-month basis had effectively been used to baffle both the other OPEC members and the United States. After the March conference, Saudi Arabia had announced that it would return to its 8.5-million-barrels level. In June, Yamani indicated that his country might increase production if there were enough inducements: high enough price for the oil, good and attractive terms for foreign investments, guarantees against confiscation and nationalization of the foreign investments, and no restriction on movement of capital. "I think if all these incentives are worked out and confirmed, may be Saudi Arabia would consider looking at the idea of exploring in the areas which are not yet explored and are not covered by the so-called Aramco concession."[12] At a news conference at Atlanta, Georgia, in the end of October, Yamani sharpened his tactic by threatening a possible cut even of the 8.5-million-barrels ceiling. He pointed out that there was in his country a "Young Turk Mafia" that advocated limiting oil production to actual current financial needs of the kingdom and raising the price of oil to the effective OPEC price. Under such circumstances Saudi Arabia would produce no more than 5 million barrels a day instead of the 9.5 million. He stressed that this approach had a strong following in his country.

The march of prices proceeded with new schemes. The major producers cut the lifting quantities from their customers' contracts by heavy percentages and sent the differences to the spot market.[13] The *Petroleum Economist* reported that by the fourth quarter of 1979 spot prices for crude were reaching as high as $45 a barrel. Although the marker crude remained at $18, unprecedented leapfrogging rounds of increases in official prices continued all the time. The result was that by early December some official prices, including those of Iran and the main African producers, were up by 80–90 percent compared with the December 1978 prices.

U.S. under secretary of the Treasury Department, Anthony Solomon, in testimony before the Senate Banking Committee on December 12, 1979, stated that oil prices since December 1978 had increased by more than 80 percent. He calculated that OPEC financial surpluses for the year would grow from zero at the end of 1978 to $60 billion at the end of 1979. He told the committee that the oil price had become "a—if not the—dominant factor" in determining both the severity of inflation and the world's ability to grow economically.[14] The developed countries had ended 1978 with a surplus of $8 billion, but they would end 1979 with a serious deficit; and the developing countries, which ended 1978 with a $20-billion deficit, would end 1979 with a $33-billion deficit. Total OPEC production in 1979 was actually 4.5 percent above total production in 1978, up from a daily average of 29.88 million barrels in 1978 to 31.22 million barrels in 1979—obviously no shortage—yet prices jumped unprecedentedly.

Caracas Conference: December 17–20

As the rate of oil price increases accelerated, Saudi Arabia was determined, more than ever, to reestablish an OPEC uniform system. Saudi readiness to increase prices in June to $18 a barrel, instead of persuading the other members to fall in line with the Saudi new high price, had encouraged them to raise their prices even higher. These new increases affected the Western economy, for which the Saudis expressed grave concern. Actually, because Saudi Arabia maintained the official $18 price, the real beneficiaries were the oil companies who reaped economic profits from the differences in price. Yamani described this absurd situation as stupid. So, four days before the opening of the Caracas conference, Saudi Arabia announced an across-the-board increase of $6 a barrel, retroactive to November 1. This 33.3 percent increase was a desperate attempt to dissuade the other OPEC members from moving up to the spot-market price level; on the other hand, it was aimed to regain for the Saudis the $6-a-barrel extra profit of the companies. One day before the opening of the conference, Libya, as if in response to Saudi

Arabia, announced an increase of $4 a barrel, bringing the price up to $30. Others followed suit.

When the conference opened, on December 17, Iran asked for higher prices and for production reductions, to which Yamani replied that his country would not increase the price beyond $24 a barrel for marker crude and would maintain the daily 9.5-million-barrel production level. After four days of acrimonious debate over price, the conference ended without adopting any overall resolution. Each member could determine its own price system. Commenting on the Caracas conference, the *Petroleum Times* of January 1, 1980, said, "It showed that OPEC countries now accept that they do not need the Organization to make crude oil prices stick. They can go it alone now. The market has taken over."

Yamani was defeated; he was looking for a scapegoat and he found it, accusing the consuming countries once again of stockpiling oil. Early in 1980 he declared that there would have been a glut of 1 million barrels a day in the market, but for political reasons the consuming countries were stockpiling oil. The surplus production was being stockpiled, and this, according to Yamani, was what had driven prices up. At the same time he announced that Saudi Arabia was expanding production capacity to 12 million barrels a day.[15]

1980—BANNER YEAR FOR OPEC

The period after the Caracas conference was characterized by accelerated leapfrogging increases unaffected by Saudi Arabia's efforts to reestablish a uniform system. On January 2, 1980, Nigeria increased the price of a barrel of oil from $31.09 to $34.48, followed by Libya, to $34.73. Saudi Arabia increased the price from $24 to $26 on January 28, retroactive to January 1. On the following day Abu Dhabi and Kuwait increased their prices by $2; two days later Iran increased its price by an additional $2 to a total of $35 a barrel.

Kuwait announced late in January that it had cut production by 500,000 barrels a day, or 25 percent of total production.

A month later, the Kuwaiti oil minister, Ali Khalifah al-Sabah, reported that his country was sending oil to the spot market. He declared that there was nothing wrong with the spot market, it "was nothing more than an indicator to us that our prices were wrong."[16] After cutting production by 25 percent, in April Kuwait cut its contracts with the three major Western companies—British Petroleum, Royal Dutch–Shell, and Gulf Oil Corporation—by 75 percent. The difference was sent to the spot market or sold through government-to-government contracts. It should be noted that, as in 1979, in spite of the weakening of the oil market as indicated by the drop in the spot market price per barrel from $40–45 to $34–35, the premiums charged by OPEC members were as high as ever: Kuwait, $5.50; Qatar, $6; and Iran, $7 a barrel in new contracts.

Saudi Arabia's efforts to reestablish an OPEC uniform system by raising its price were all failures: before Caracas, a jump of 33 percent, from $18 to $24 a barrel; at the end of January 1980, from $24 to $26 a barrel. In the middle of May, after the OPEC meeting in Taif, the Saudis raised the price again, from $26 to $28, retroactive to April 1. Yamani explained that his country had increased the price "as a step towards reunification of OPEC prices" and "to take back some of the profits currently being realized by the oil companies on Saudi oil and to narrow the gap between our Saudi price and the market price."[17] But a pattern had become well established: After each Saudi price increase the other producers raised their higher prices by a similar amount and retained the premiums.

Algiers Conference: June 9–11

The midyear OPEC conference decided to set the level of the marker crude at $32 a barrel. The differentials were limited to $5. The price structure that was to go into effect on July 1 was to be reviewed at the next fall meeting. The next ordinary meeting was set for December 15 at Bali.

Pressure in the oil market had softened and spot market prices fell, leading to a demand for reduced production. Kuwait, Libya, Venezuela, Nigeria, and Iran announced cuts in their production levels. Saudi Arabia, however, continued with its 9.5 million barrels a day, and Iraq refused to reduce its daily 3.5 million barrels. Yamani declared in Algiers that his country continued with its production level "because there is no unified price system. If we have a one price system, then Saudi Arabia will go down to 8.5 million barrels a day."[18]

Vienna Conference: September 17–18

An extraordinary OPEC meeting consisting of the foreign, finance, and oil ministers was held in Vienna on September 17–18. Again Saudi Arabia attempted to cajole all members into agreeing to a uniform price system, for which the Saudis would increase their price to $32 and reduce production to 8.5 million barrels a day. However, the others refused to be cajoled. The only outcome was Saudi Arabia's increase from $28 to $30 a barrel; but the Saudis continued to refuse to reduce output. The Saudi deputy oil minister, Abd al-Aziz al-Turki, stated, almost in the words of his superior, "Saudi Arabia has not committed herself to anything of this sort. We refuse, on principle, even to discuss the subject of production, which concerns us alone. Our decision on production derives from market conditions and Saudi Arabia's international commitments."[19]

The Vienna conference was held under the gathering clouds of the impending Iraq-Iran war. As a result of the war, three major OPEC meetings were postponed—the Quito meeting of the finance ministers scheduled for October 6, the London meeting of oil ministers to discuss production ratios, and the summit meeting of heads of state in Baghdad to celebrate the twentieth anniversary of the founding of OPEC. The outbreak of the war also eliminated from the world oil market some 5 million barrels a day. Saudi Arabia came to the rescue by adding 900,000 barrels to its daily production of 9.5 million barrels; Kuwait and other members also added to their production levels.

Bali Conference: December 15–16

As originally scheduled, the OPEC year-end conference opened in Bali on December 15, under the heavy shadows of the Iran-

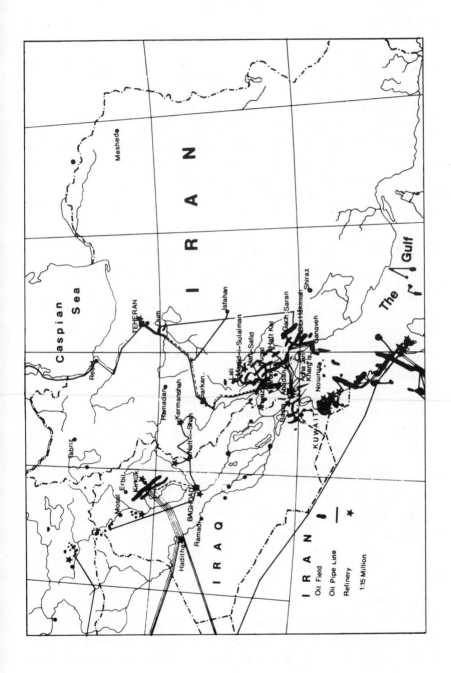

Iraq war. The conference decided to continue the existing price system, with all its anomalies, but from a higher base. The price range went from $32 a barrel, charged by Saudi Arabia, to $41. 1980 was, by all standards, the great banner year in the history of OPEC. In spite of a 14 percent drop in exports, from 30.9 million barrels a day in 1979 to 26.8 million barrels a day in 1980, OPEC members' revenues rose by 45 percent over the previous year, from $192 billion to $272 billion. OPEC surplus estimates for 1979 were $63 billion, and for 1980 they were $120 billion. External assets at the end of 1980 were $327 billion. The current account deficits of the industrialized countries were estimated as $50 billion.

Assessment

OPEC members learned a basic far-reaching lesson from their 1979–1980 experience. A sudden large-scale oil shortage—such as that caused by the heavy reduction in oil flow from Iran—not only raised the price of oil over a prolonged period to extraordinary heights, but also demonstrated, beyond any doubt, that the consuming countries were ready and able to pay high prices for oil. The consumers were in a real panic as to whether the producers would cut production; their major concern was not, it seemed, the price, but the security of supply.

The Saudi Arabian oil minister, who repeatedly maintained that his country's anxiety over the Western economy prompted it to persistently resist oil price increases, stated in a speech in London on March 25, 1980, that the growth of the gross domestic product in the OECD countries in 1979 reflected a rise of 111 percent between 1973 and 1979. The price of oil during the same period went up 103 percent. "The fact that growth in OECD countries forged ahead at rates higher than those of oil demonstrated beyond doubt the ability of the economies to absorb oil price increases without much difficulty."[20]

Saudi Arabia's real motivation for maintaining relatively low oil prices came from the state of its own economy and its projected long-term dependence on oil revenue (see Chapter

3). The Saudis, therefore, had to maneuver continually between OPEC members and the United States. Although the United States, of all the Western alliance countries, was the least dependent on the Middle East for oil, it was almost obsessively disturbed by fear of a shortfall of oil supplies, much more so than were the European countries and Japan. The United States thus pressured Saudi Arabia to increase production. Such an increase would reduce the danger of oil shortages and reduce oil prices, and in the process Saudi Arabia's prestige would rise, and its leadership in OPEC and throughout the Middle East would be firmly established. Saudi Arabia was to be the United States' major ally in the Middle East in the struggle against the other superpower, the Soviet Union.

STOCKPILING

Yamani, aware of U.S. fears of oil shortages, hoped to obtain from the United States concessions that would enhance Saudi Arabia's position with the Arabs and among OPEC members. He constantly demanded that the United States change its policy on Israel in favor of the Arabs, and he also hammered away against oil stockpiling by the consumer countries.

Oil stockpiling by consuming countries is a measure of self-protection against possible supply shortfalls, for whatever reason. After the 1973 embargo, stockpiling became a vital weapon in the hands of the consumers against a possible cutoff of supplies or a huge price increase. The IEA made stockpiling a basic element of its program (see Chapter 5). On the other hand, producers saw in stockpiling a real threat to their power. When the United States adopted, in 1975, the Strategic Petroleum Reserve (SPR) plan for stockpiling up to 1 billion barrels of oil at a cost of $14 billion, OPEC viewed the program as a barefaced confrontation maneuver against the oil exporters. The OPEC secretary-general, Ali Attiga, harshly denounced the U.S. decision. The Bali conference of May 1976 issued a communiqué stating that the conference "took notice of actions being taken by certain consuming countries against the interests of member countries of the Organization, and decided to take appropriate measures, if necessary, to protect the legitimate interests of member countries."[21]

The importance of stockpiling was clearly understood in the United States. A year after the Bali conference, Senator Edward M. Kennedy stated before the Joint Economic Committee's Subcommittee on Energy, "There is a general agreement that the existence of an adequately stocked strategic petroleum reserve would greatly advance the bargaining power with OPEC and protect us from the political threat of another oil supply interruption."[22] A committee that had visited the Middle East reported before the Senate Committee on Energy and Natural Resources that "both the Iraqi and Saudi Oil Ministers opposed stockpiling by consuming nations. Their ostensible reason was that inventory building creates uncertainty in the world oil market and prevents OPEC from agreeing to a unified structure."[23] The committee reported that Yamani opposed stockpiling and was quoted as saying, "Saudi Arabia cannot be expected to keep production high and prices low so that the U.S. can store oil, especially since the Saudi Government is under a lot of pressure to cut production to no more than 8.5 million barrels per day."[24]

On March 4, 1980, at the completion of a three-day visit by the U.S. secretary of energy, Charles Duncan, to Saudi Arabia, Yamani denied reports that the secretary had approached the Saudis with a request to purchase Saudi crude for stockpiling purposes or had asked his country to maintain output at the current level of 9.5 million barrels a day for the fourth quarter of the year. Yamani emphasized that it was "the policy of the Saudi Government to meet real consumer demand in the world and not for the purpose of stockpiling."[25] In an interview with the Zurich *Weltwoche* at the end of November 1980, Yamani repeated his old theme that the greatest danger to world oil supplies remained the Arab-Israeli conflict. He stressed that "unless the Arab-Israeli conflict is solved the flow of oil from our countries will shrink suddenly and drastically, we will deal that blow to you, I promise that."[26] As far as the short-term outlook was concerned, Yamani repeated his warning that unless the consumers reviewed their stockpiling policies, a price of $50 per barrel of oil would be instituted the following spring.

Late in February 1981, Saudi Arabia's Petromin governor, Abdul Hady Taher denied reports that the Saudis would cut production or increase the oil price, but he warned the consuming countries against stockpiling. He declared, "If a country like Saudi Arabia is producing oil beyond its financial needs, it is making a big sacrifice, instead of storing oil in expensive facilities in consuming countries, it is better to store it where God put it in the first place—in the ground." (See Chapter 6.)

But stockpiling paid off. After the outbreak of hostilities between Iraq and Iran, the oil ministers of the EEC met in Brussels on November 27, 1980, and agreed to draw down oil stocks to meet the shortfall in supplies. Indeed, the general impact of the war was not felt in the international oil market, not even in the more sensitive spot market.

Yamani had failed (and perhaps never really expected to succeed) in his attempts to influence U.S. policy on Israel, but he did have some success in the issue of stockpiling. In the United States, the Strategic Petroleum Reserve program had been adopted in 1975, but the government, despite congressional resolutions, had not proceeded energetically with stockpiling. Four years after the establishment of SPR only about a hundred million barrels had been pumped into the salt caverns. When the Iranian revolution broke out, President Carter stopped stockpiling for two reasons: the high cost and his desire to maintain good relations with Saudi Arabia. However, after prodding by Congress to resume stockpiling, the secretary of energy, Charles Duncan, was sent to Saudi Arabia in March 1980 to sound out the Saudis about maintaining their extra million barrels a day to help fill SPR—Yamani's denial notwithstanding. After the enactment of the Energy Act in July 1980, President Carter reactivated the stockpiling program, thereby risking Saudi Arabia's ill will. The program intensified after the outbreak of the Iran-Iraq war. At first President Ronald Reagan was ready to continue with the stockpiling program.

In his budget message he called for the purchase of 80 million barrels at a cost of $3 billion.

Taking advantage of the rivalry among the Western countries for favored positions in the Middle East, particularly in their relations with the producer countries, the major oil producers prevailed on the IEA members to draw down their oil stock. The agency's executive director, Ulf Lantzke, reported at the end of November 1980 that the twenty members had complied with the producers' request. During the final quarter of 1980 they had reduced their oil stocks by 32 million tons. Early in December, a meeting of the agency's board of directors was held in Paris to establish policy for reducing oil stocks during the first half of 1981. Members were expected to reduce their stocks at a rate of 30 to 40 million tons a quarter. Only the United States held out against reducing its stocks. But the United States was as determined as the Europeans to maintain its position with the Middle East producers—particularly Saudi Arabia—and the Reagan administration retreated from its resolution to continue stockpiling oil.

SAUDI ARABIA'S PRODUCTION CAPACITY

Saudi Arabia's strategy had been to threaten to increase or even double production in order to bring oil prices down. The ability of Saudi Arabia to increase production and the limits of that capacity were thus of great importance to the Saudis in their relations with the other OPEC members. It was also of great significance to the other OPEC members to assess the reality of the threats. And it was of vital importance for the United States to know the true potential of Saudi production capacity, not merely as a Saudi tactical device in the game of international politics, but as the basis for energy and political policies. Once the actual facts of Saudi production capacity were established, should they be made public? These facts would inevitably affect U.S. relations with Saudi Arabia, with the other Middle East oil producers, with the Western countries, and even with the

Soviet Union. Or should they be kept secret? The U.S. State Department, as would be expected, was against making public the extent of Saudi Arabia's oil production capacity.[27]

In February 1976, it had been reported that although Saudi Arabia was capable of producing 11 million barrels of oil a day, the country was planning to expand capacity by an additional 5 million barrels a day over the next five years. The Saudi government planned to invest some $143 million in the exploration of new areas. In August 1978, Saudi Arabia found itself on the horns of a dilemma. On the one hand, production was being held down in the face of the worldwide oil glut, and prices were frozen; on the other hand, production capacity was being expanded at a vast cost. The United States hoped that the production capacity expansion would continue, because U.S. oil import predictions were based largely on Saudi Arabian capacity. Later in the month a CIA report declared that Saudi Arabia could expand production to 19 million and 23 million barrels a day. Yamani immediately discounted the report. In an interview in *Al-Medina* on August 20, he said that he did not believe that his country could attain such an output capacity at any time in the future and added, "There are several question marks concerning the report which is full of exaggerations." He estimated that Saudi Arabia might gradually increase its oil production capacity to 14 million barrels a day from the current level of about 11 million barrels.

The U.S. Senate Committee on Foreign Relations Subcommittee on International Economic Policy studied the question of Saudi Arabia's oil production capacity. On April 19, 1979, it released *The Future of Saudi Arabian Oil Production: A Staff Report*. After a year of study, the staff had concluded that because of a combination of technical and financial restraints as well as the strong conservationist concerns of the Saudi government, "it would be imprudent for the United States to plan on . . . Saudi Arabia's oil production plan to increase" above 12 million barrels a day. The *Report* stressed that 12 million barrels a day was the government target for maximum sustainable capacity by 1987, based on a facility capacity of 14 million barrels a day. It also stated that the overproduction efforts of Aramco in the later part of 1977 in some fields caused irreparable damage and reduced ultimate recovery. Consequently, allowable production levels were swiftly reduced in some fields. The publication, which included secret data gathered from documents obtained under subpoena from the Aramco partners, caused shock and embarrassment to the oil companies, to Saudi Arabia, and above all to the State Department. The State Department quickly issued a statement stressing that the *Report* did "not represent the Administration views."[28]

In an interview in the *New York Times* on June 21, 1979, Prince Fahd responded to a question about a temporary rise in Saudi production: "The Saudi Government has not decided, so far, to increase production beyond the present 8.5 million b/d. I believe the capacity of the Kingdom may not enable it to increase production beyond 8.5 b/d." As for reports that Saudi Arabia would set a long-term capacity on a production of 12 million barrels a day, Prince Fahd said that these were inaccurate and that there were no plans to go that far. But only seven days later in Geneva, at a press conference after the OPEC meeting, Yamani said, "It is known that we have a plan which will bring the Saudi maximum capacity to 14 million b/d, which means sustained capacity will be less than that, of 12 million b/d."[29] In July 1979, the U.S. Central Intelligence Agency (CIA) lowered its estimate of Saudi maximum sustained capacity from its May 7 estimate of 10 million barrels a day to 9.5 million barrels a day. At a press conference after the OPEC Caracas meeting on December 20, 1979, Yamani stated, "We have under construction an increase in the sustained capacity of our production up to 12 million b/d."[30]

From all these conflicting statements it becomes obvious that the plans of U.S. policymakers to make Saudi Arabia the main source of oil supply for the Western world by increasing its production capacity to 20 million barrels a day—as well as to base U.S. oil and Middle East policies on Saudi production capacity—were, to say the least, premature and highly exaggerated.

THE OPEC LONG-TERM
STRATEGY COMMITTEE

At the OPEC ministerial meeting in Taif, Saudi Arabia, in May 1978, it was decided to set up a long-term strategy committee, to be chaired by Ahmad Zaki Yamani of Saudi Arabia; committee members would represent Algeria, Iran, Iraq, Kuwait, and Venezuela. The committee was to prepare recommendations to be submitted to the plenary. After meeting in various places for eighteen months, the Long-Term Strategy Committee (LTSC) prepared—actually written by Saudi Arabia and Venezuela—a forty-four-page working paper. The final draft was taken up by the extraordinary OPEC meeting held in Taif on May 8, 1980. The recommendations—criticized by Libya, Iran, and Algeria— called for the establishment of a floor price for crude oil, to be adjusted on a quarterly basis, which would be based on an index reflecting the impact of inflation on international trade, an exchange rate based on a basket of currencies, and an increase of the floor price in real terms proportionate to the growth of GNP of the OECD countries. In order to maintain the price structure, appropriate means would have to be taken by all members to restrict production.

In addition, the proposals stated that if there should be a decision to hold a dialogue with the industrialized countries, OPEC should demand and obtain: free access to the markets of the developed countries for refined products and petrochem-icals; access to existing and new advanced technology and know-how needed by OPEC countries for exploration activities, enhanced oil recovery, and the development of industries; plus increased involvement of industrialized countries in exploration activities in OPEC countries. OPEC countries were to win participation in joint research development programs; the lo-cation of energy-intensive industries in areas of natural-gas production in OPEC countries; the removal of economic sanc-tions against OPEC countries by some industrialized countries;

and the lifting of trade barriers on non-oil exports from oil-producing countries. The consumers were to be given assurances with respect to security of supply. Some members felt that the proposals were behind the times and were too mild.

These recommendations were the major item on the agenda of the September 16–17, 1980, Vienna OPEC conference. It was decided to submit them to the summit meeting in Baghdad in November, but no final action was taken on them.

CONCLUSIONS

During the 1979–1980 period, OPEC members made tremendous advances in terms of oil prices, in marketing, and in enormous revenues that endowed them—in Yamani's words—with money power in addition to oil power, huge surpluses in income that became a major source of power and influence in the financial world. They were courted by the most powerful nations in the world. But they were more than ever divided among themselves, in both aims and methods to achieve these aims; they were working at cross-purposes. For two full years Saudi Arabia was frustrated in its efforts to restore the uniform price. After almost three years of meetings, debates, discussions, and wrangling, the Long-Term Strategy Committee had failed to achieve acceptance of its program, which it was hoped would stabilize, if not firmly institutionalize, the producer oil industry.

Although a drop in the demand for oil was already noticeable at the end of 1980, OPEC members still believed that consumers had no alternative but to pay the ever-increasing prices exacted by the producers. It was only a matter of time for the consumers to adjust to the high prices. They, the producers, could afford to wait. In spite of the constant protestations of Yamani that his country was gravely concerned about the impact of the high oil prices on the Western economies, Saudi Arabia also believed that the consuming countries would adjust, in time, to the higher oil prices. They had done so in the past without any serious consequences.

Although OPEC had sustained many shocks and much battering during the period of the second energy crisis, 1979–

1980, and despite the foreboding predictions of some specialists and analysts, the organization survived. This was primarily because of the nature of OPEC: Its members, sovereign states, were free to act; they would take whatever suited them and refuse what did not suit them. But above all, the division of the consumers was their strength. (See Chapters 1 and 6.) The consuming countries, indeed, were as divided and as helpless as ever. They paid the high oil prices and protested through solemn descriptions of the magnitude of the consequences of the high prices to their economies, but made no countermoves.[31]

NOTES

1. *MEES,* February 19, 1979.
2. *International Herald-Tribune,* February 27, 1979.
3. *Middle East Economic Survey (MEES),* March 12, 1979.
4. *Newsweek,* April 9, 1979.
5. *MEES,* April 2, 1979.
6. Ibid.
7. Ibid., June 25, 1979.
8. The *Petroleum Times* of July 15, 1979, noted that traditionally prices laid down by OPEC conferences had always been minimum prices. At Geneva in June of 1979, OPEC decided, for the first time, on a maximum price. OPEC's failure to hold prices would mean that the market had taken over, to the detriment of its function as the instrument of world crude-oil pricing.
9. *Time,* July 9, 1979; *Newsweek,* July 9, 1979.
10. *Newsweek,* July 9, 1979.
11. *International Herald-Tribune,* July 2, 1979.
12. *MEES,* June 25, 1979.
13. On producers sending their oil to the spot market, *MEES,* October 22, 1979, noted: "What is interesting is that two distinct levels of crude spot trading seem to be emerging—one operating within the traditional traders and brokers, and the other with OPEC governments themselves as the direct source of supply. While quotes among the former are still within the $37–39/barrel range, companies (Japanese mainly but also some smaller U.S. refiners) are actually paying over $40/barrel for spot deals with OPEC Governments (Iran and others) with the extra premium being regarded as a sort of

insurance for a better guarantee of delivery and as an entry fee for the future regular contracts."

14. *International Herald-Tribune,* December 13, 1979.

15. On November 4, 1979, in response to a report in the October 20, 1979, *Economist* that Saudi Arabia intended to increase output to 10.5 million barrels a day, Yamani firmly denied such reports. He said, "I don't think the question is one of increasing supply. The question is one of reducing consumption drastically so that you, the consumers can correct the balance, stop this upward trend and reduce the price of oil." *MEES,* November 5, 1979. Earlier, on October 25, in a lecture at the University of California at Berkeley, Yamani predicted that OPEC would again have a unified price structure for crude oil the next year.

16. In February, when asked whether Kuwait received a higher price for oil sold to noncontract purchasers than that charged in the spot market, al-Sabah answered, "Definitely, there was about two to three dollars a barrel difference between the prices some of the consumers were offering to traders and the prices they were prepared to pay the government suppliers. And rightly so. An engagement of a government supplier to deliver oil in a month hence is a commitment that he is obliged to honor, come what may. Whereas the trader could disappear tomorrow. So if the buyer pays a premium for a more secure supplier, this is quite understandable and reasonable." *MEES,* February 11, 1980.

17. *MEES,* May 19, 1980.

18. Ibid., June 16, 1980.

19. Ibid., September 29, 1980.

20. Ibid., March 31, 1980.

21. Ibid., June 7, 1976.

22. U.S., Congress, Joint Economic Committee, Subcommittee on Energy, *Hearings: Energy Independence or Interdependence, The Agenda with OPEC* (Washington, D.C., 1977), p. 3.

23. U.S., Congress, Senate, Committee on Energy and Natural Resources, *The Geopolitics of Oil: Staff Report* (Washington, D.C., 1980), p. 79.

24. Ibid., p. 80.

25. *MEES,* March 6, 1980.

26. Ibid., December 22, 1980.

27. Distinction should be made between production facility capacity and sustained capacity over a long period of time. The latter is usually considerably lower than the former.

28. *MEES,* April 23, 1979.

29. Ibid., July 2, 1979.

30. Ibid., December 31, 1979.

31. The major sources for Chapter 8 were: U.S., Congress, Joint Economic Committee, Subcommittee on Energy, *Hearings: Energy Independence or Interdependence*; U.S., Congress, Senate, Committee on Energy and Natural Resources, *Hearings: World Petroleum Outlook—1981* (Washington, D.C., 1981); idem, *The Geopolitics of Oil*; U.S., Congress, Senate, Committee on Foreign Relations, Subcommittee on International Economic Policy, *The Future of Saudi Arabian Oil Production: A Staff Report* (Washington, D.C., 1979).

9

A THIRD CRISIS—
FOR THE PRODUCERS

Various theories of the oil price, which were reinforced by the events of the 1979–1980 period, were advanced in OPEC councils. The moderates maintained that the oil price should reach a level that would make it competitive with the prices of energy alternatives but should climb gradually so that consumers could adjust to it. Because the costs of alternatives were constantly rising, the price of oil would inevitably rise as well. The more hawkish or radical members saw no limit to the price of oil, for the Western consumers had no choice but to depend on oil. They would have to pay whatever the producers exacted from them. They would have to adjust to the high prices and, in the process, would have no option but to transfer a considerable part of their wealth to the producers. Even in 1978, Jamshid Amouzegar of Iran predicted that after a few years the scarcity of oil would raise prices to such levels that OPEC would no longer be needed. This assessment was shared, at the time, by the Saudi Arabian oil minister.

Others advanced the business-cycle theory. Prices rose sharply in 1973–1974; consumers reacted by cutting consumption in 1975, but in 1976 the price rose again and increased further in 1977. Reaction set in and demand dropped in 1978, but in 1979 prices rose again. In 1981 demand went down, but after awhile the swing would come around and prices would climb again.

The process in which the producers had replaced the concessionaire companies began with producer participation in the upstream operation of production (as outlined in Chapter 4). The next push of the Middle East producers had been for the downstream operations: refining, transportation, and marketing. The building of local refineries, which had proceeded at a slow pace before the 1973–1974 crisis, was greatly accelerated after the crisis. Time is the most important element in the procedure of building refineries, so the rate of refining-capacity growth was not spectacular but steady. Transportation was greatly facilitated by the deep tanker crisis that set in in 1974. This had enabled the Middle East producers, singly or in groups, to acquire cheaply many idle tankers and to order new ones. The tanker fleets of the producers were growing rapidly, although they operated at a financial loss.

Marketing was the most difficult area. The distribution facilities of the great multinational oil companies were complex, worldwide, and very costly. The Middle East producers could not possibly duplicate the marketing facilities and outlets of the companies, and they despaired about it. Indeed, after the total takeover of the concessions, some producers retained their former concessionaire companies to dispose of their oil. However, the panic that engulfed the consumers in their mad rush for oil supplies during the second oil crisis changed the producers' marketing aim. Instead of attempting to build facilities on an international scale directly servicing the consumers, the producers began to market their oil on a government-to-government basis or a government-to-distribution (or -refinery) basis. In fact, they did not have to seek out the customers; the customer sought out the producers. A good percentage of the 1979–1980 production was disposed of by direct government sales. This not only eliminated the mediation cost of the companies but also established potential political maneuverability.

During the crisis years, the producers had revealed their true character. There was no group discipline and no consideration of consequences; each member acted separately and was concerned with its own individual advantages. Thus for two years, each member charged any price it wished for its oil; established its own credit terms; and set up its own differentials system. The producers acted as if this price orgy would go on. What they did not realize, however, was that regardless of price theories, certain cardinal facts could not be overlooked. The high oil prices, without any plots, without schemes, and without official policy decisions by the consuming governments, made consumers adopt very simple measures to reduce consumption. The entire life-style of energy-intensive practices changed—from the individual's habits of automobile driving, to home heating and home and office air-conditioning, to the technological engineering of the industrial energy structure. Conservation became a major feature in the life of Western regimes. This was reflected in the relation between energy consumption and economic growth. Prior to the 1973 crisis, a one to one ratio between consumption and economic growth had been an accepted axiom. Since 1973, the energy consumption half of the ratio had gone down drastically compared to economic growth.

The results

1981—RAPID DECLINE IN THE DEMAND FOR OIL

At the end of 1980 demand for oil began to decline, and from that time until March 1983 it dropped more rapidly than it had risen during 1979–1980. On the way down, OPEC members acted in the same selfish and reckless manner as on the way up. OPEC faced for the first time issues that could not even be mentioned before: controlled production, a production quota system, monitoring the quota system, credit time, a firm differentials system, and price reduction.

One of the most disturbing factors in the situation was the impact of the non-OPEC oil producers. OPEC producers, through their high prices, had made it possible for the non-OPEC producers, especially those in the North Sea (such as Great Britain and Norway), to enter the world oil markets. When demand for oil began to fall, the new producers were hungrier than the OPEC countries for the oil markets and became the really threatening competitors for OPEC.

The process of oil price increments since 1973 had brought about a complex international financial structure in which both the Middle East and the Western world were tightly and almost irrevocably related, making the two interdependent (Chapter 7 dealt with surpluses and recycling). A network of economic undertakings had emerged, based on the high oil prices, and the new realities in the oil market affected the entire structure. To be sure, if oil prices could be isolated by themselves, lower prices would in the long run correct all the ills that were the result of the high prices. But in the context of interdependence, a sudden sharp decline in oil prices could tumble the international financial system in which producer and consumer countries had become intertwined.

Early in January 1981, following the OPEC December Bali conference, the Gulf producers Kuwait, Iraq, and Qatar raised their official prices by $4 a barrel effective as of January 1. The marker crude was raised to $36 a barrel, but premiums of from $5 to $7 a barrel were added to the official charge. Although Iran officially raised its price by $2 to a total of $37, it was reported that at the time of the Bali conference Iran had offered crude-oil deliveries at Kharg Island at $28 a barrel, $7 below the official price. The discount was supposedly granted as compensation for the high insurance rate for lifting from Kharg because of the war risk.

After the release of the U.S. hostages in Iran, British Petroleum and Royal Dutch–Shell signed new contracts for crude with Iran for a nine-month period, from January 1981. They agreed to pay the official price of $37 a barrel plus a premium of $1.80 for the first three months, and thereafter only the official price; credit time was sixty days. There was no mention of a discount for the war-risk insurance rate for lifting at Kharg.

Demand continued to fall, and the glut in the international oil market became more pronounced. Some OPEC members were seriously discussing the need for reducing production. In April, Yamani was asked whether, in view of the oil glut, his country would lower prices. He replied, "Well, as a matter of fact, this glut was anticipated by Saudi Arabia and almost done by Saudi Arabia. If we were to reduce our production to the level it was at before we started it, there would be no glut at all. We engineered the glut and want to see it in order to stabilize the price of oil." He made price unification a condition for lowering the Saudi production level, but when he was asked whether a uniform price would be achieved at the forthcoming May OPEC conference, Yamani answered, "I am not that optimistic."[1]

Geneva Conference: May 25

When the regular midyear conference opened in Geneva on May 25, 1981, the glut in the oil market was the most outstanding issue. On May 1, Indonesia cut fifty cents a barrel from its premium charge. Nigeria's production dropped from 2.05 million barrels a day in 1980 to 1.94 million in February 1981, and in May it fell to 1.6 million barrels a day. Members expressed their belief that the only way to remedy the situation was to reduce production. Saudi Arabia, on the other hand, was reported to have tried its tactic again: The Saudis would be willing to increase the marker-crude price by $2 if the others reduced their prices and would also be willing to cut production.

After two days of discussion, the conference failed to reach agreement. It was decided, however, to freeze existing prices, which ranged from $36 to $40 a barrel. Saudi Arabia stuck to its $32-a-barrel price. For this decision Saudi Arabia made its routine demands on the United States—a change of U.S. policy on Israel and an end to stockpiling. The OPEC situation continued to worsen. Demand continued to fall, and revenue kept on dropping. A special consultative meeting was convened in Geneva.

Geneva Consultative Meeting: August 19–21

Saudi Arabia did not give up its effort and tried again. The Saudis were ready to raise their price to $34 a barrel if the others would come down to the same level, but this offer was rejected, and the Saudi price remained at $32. Because of the heavy drop in demand, Saudi Arabia announced a production cut of a million barrels a day for the month of September.

Yamani, in offering to raise the price to $34 a barrel, realized how unrealistic that price would be; in reply to a question as to what the real price of a barrel of oil should be, he said, "Ideally, to eliminate the glut the price of oil should come down to $28/B."[2] (It took twenty months for this to come true.)

The level of demand went from bad to worse. At the end of August it was reported that Nigeria's production had plummeted, Libya's output had gone down from 1.75 million barrels a day at the beginning of 1981 to 700,000 to 800,000 barrels a day at the end of August. Algeria's production level, which had been over a million barrels a day, came down to 700,000 to 800,000 barrels in August. Iran's output was reported to have dropped from 1 million barrels a day to about 600,000 to 700,000 a day. Kuwait's output was reported to be about 800,000 to 900,000 barrels a day.

After the failure of the Geneva conference, Nigeria cut prices on August 26 by $4 a barrel, from $40 to $36. This in effect eliminated the $4 differential. Nigeria was also reported to have extended credit time from thirty days to 120 days, which was essentially a reduction of about $1.50 a barrel. Nigeria was the hardest hit of all OPEC members, perhaps because of its almost exclusive dependence on oil revenue for a population of approximately 80 million. Although Nigeria belonged to the radical group in OPEC, by August 1981 it was the weakest member.

In an interview in London on September 8, Yamani asserted that if demand for OPEC oil were to fall to 15 million barrels a day by the early 1990s—as some analysts predicted—"it would be the end of OPEC and cause great economic difficulties for Saudi Arabia which relies basically on its revenue from oil." He added that if OPEC prices were unified, "Saudi Arabia's production would fall to much less than 8.5 million b/d, and this would lead to a deficit in budget."[3] Total OPEC production, according to Yamani, had gone down from 31 million barrels a day in 1979 to about 27 million in 1981. He asserted that oil production in both developing and developed countries had grown by about 2 million barrels a day, which reduced OPEC daily production to 25 million barrels, and noted that oil-stock drawdown and coal production accounted for another million barrels, bringing OPEC production down to less than 24 million barrels a day. He stressed that with the low production level, the pressure on OPEC supplies has eased and consequently, the world would witness a long period of comfortable supply/demand balance unhampered by shortfalls.

A Unified Price

The situation in the world market, in spite of Yamani's optimistic prediction, was growing worse by the day. An extraordinary OPEC conference met in Geneva on October 29. After its two abortive attempts in May and August, Saudi Arabia finally succeeded, and OPEC established a uniform price of $34 a barrel. Because of the critical situation in the world market, the other OPEC members agreed to lower their price to $34, to be frozen to the end of 1982. Saudi Arabia agreed to reduce production, on a permanent basis, to 8.5 million barrels a day effective November 1. The question of differentials was provisionally worked out and was to be revised from time to time. *Middle East Economic Survey,* November 2, 1981, stated, perhaps somewhat prematurely, that: "All in all, it would be no exaggeration to conclude that this week's Geneva agreement on price unification has saved OPEC as a functioning organization." The differentials question soon became a major issue at the year-end conference in Abu Dhabi, December 9–11. Because of the oil glut, the Africans wanted smaller differentials between their oil prices and those of the Gulf producers, but could not agree on one base. Three days were devoted to the differences between the Gulf and the African producers and among the African producers themselves.

1982—THE OIL GLUT CONTINUES

Even after the OPEC price was unified, the oil glut continued and demand kept on falling. At a consultative meeting on March 6, 1982, in Doha, Saudi Arabia announced that it had

Table 9.1 Saudi Arabian Light: January 1972–March 1983

	(dollars per barrel)		*(dollars per barrel)*
January 1, 1972	1.79	October 1975	11.51
January 20, 1972	1.91		
		January 1977	12.09
January 1973	2.05	July 1977	12.70
April 1973	2.17		
May 1973	2.55	January 1979	13.34
June 1973	2.77	April 1979	14.55
July 1973	2.75	June 1979	18.00
August 1973	2.85	November 1979	24.00
September 1973	2.86		
October 1973	2.80	January 1980	26.00
October 16, 1973	4.76	April 1980	28.00
November 1973	4.81	August 1980	30.00
December 1973	4.68	November 1980	32.00
January 1974	10.84	October 1981	34.00
November 1974	10.96		
		March 15, 1983	29.00

Source: Petroleum Economist, April 1983

Table 9.2 Saudi Arabian Oil Revenue, 1973–1983

Year	Amount (billions of dollars)	Percentage Change
1973	4.340	+58.1
1974	22.573	+520.
1975	25.676	+13.7
1976	30.754	+19.3
1977	36.540	+18.8
1978	32.234	−11.8
1979	48.435	+50.3
1980	84.466	+74.3
1981	101.813	+20.5
1982	70.479	−30.8
1983	37.120	−47.1

Source: Saudi Arabian Monetary Agency (SAMA), *Annual Report* (Jidda, 1973–1983)

reduced its oil production level from 8.5 to 7.5 million barrels a day for the month of March.

Vienna Conference: March 19–20

An extraordinary conference met in Vienna on March 19–20. Saudi Arabia declared that it was ready to defend the $34-a-barrel price by all means at its command. For the first time in its history, OPEC agreed to curtail production collectively and adopted a total production level of 18 million barrels a day. As a move of generosity or encouragement, Yamani announced that his country would cut production by 500,000 barrels a day for the month of April, thus reducing the OPEC ceiling to 17.5 million barrels a day. He stressed that this move was made in an effort to stabilize production but added emphatically that Saudi Arabia would not cut production any further. To save face, because Saudi Arabia had never acceded that OPEC had the power to control production, Yamani made it clear that the production cuts were voluntary moves of individual members. The conference agreed to base the differentials system on the 1978 pattern. A major problem within OPEC was Nigeria. A few days after the closing of the conference Nigeria reported that it had dropped its production level to 630,000 barrels a day, and that it was charging $35.50 a barrel, a differential of only $1.50 above the marker crude. Because Nigerian oil was far superior even to Saudi light, a differential of only $1.50 a barrel could eliminate Saudi light from the market.

The regular midyear OPEC conference took place in Quito on May 20–21. It decided to maintain, for the time being, the status quo of an overall daily OPEC production of 17.5 million barrels.[4] OPEC refused to admit that the glut was the result of its price policies and sought a scapegoat in the consumer countries, whom they blamed for drawing down their oil stock. Early in May, the UAE minister of petroleum, Mana Said al-Otaiba, called on the industrialized countries to halt the drawdown of their oil stocks in an effort to help stabilize the world oil market. First stockpiling had been blamed, then drawdown.

In the middle of June it was reported that total OPEC production was actually about 17.9 million barrels a day, some 400,000 more than the quota agreed upon. Iran, Nigeria, and Libya were producing above their quotas. Iran declared that it did not accept the quota of 1.2 million barrels a day that had been set for it and instead produced 2 million barrels a day. Iraq produced less than the quota because Syria had closed the pipeline (from northern Iraq to the Mediterranean, through Syria).

Vienna Conference, July 9–10

Production quotas and price differentials were the two major issues at the Vienna conference that met in July. Following very angry exchanges between the Iranian and Saudi Arabian delegates, the conference was suspended indefinitely on July 10, without arriving at any decisions. Nigeria, Iran, Libya, and Venezuela declared that they would produce more than the quotas set for them. Iran demanded a quota of 3 million barrels a day, with the difference coming from a reduction in Saudi Arabia's share. This demand was rejected by Saudi Arabia. According to the *Petroleum Economist,* Saudi Arabia found itself on the horns of a dilemma. In order to maintain the uniform price and their leadership in OPEC, the Saudis had to cut their own production and thus seriously reduce their revenue. Should Saudi Arabia reduce its price, as it had threatened to do, it would forfeit both leadership and income.

The Saudis were particularly disturbed by the differentials question. In 1978, before the Iranian debacle, the differentials between the Saudi light and the African lights had ranged from $1.20 to $1.50 a barrel. After the Iranian revolution the differentials jumped to from $8 to $9 a barrel. With the price unification in October 1981, differentials stabilized at between $3.50 and $2.50 a barrel. At the March 1982 OPEC meeting in Vienna it was agreed to reduce differentials to the 1978 levels. In May 1982, Saudi Arabia's output fell to 5 million barrels a day. The Gulf producers pressed the Africans to raise their differentials so that the Gulf producers could compete with the African crudes; Saudi Arabia asked for a $3 differential. A special committee set up to study the differentials question recommended in September that the differentials be raised from $1.50 to $2.30.

After setting up the production quotas, OPEC had established, in March 1982, a monitoring committee consisting of the UAE (chairman), Algeria, Indonesia, and Venezuela, which was to monitor the production levels of the members. The committee's function was limited because it had to rely on the reports of the members. Meeting on August 20 in Vienna, the committee decided that the issue of differentials should be studied by a group of experts and also stated that members had violated their quota limits.

Tension within OPEC was rising, as evidenced by a paper delivered by al-Otaiba before the Oxford Energy Seminar in September 1982. Al-Otaiba called for an extension of the price freeze to the end of 1985, as well as maintenance of the production ceiling of 17.5 million barrels a day, until the demand for oil pushed up again. He noted that some members granted price discounts and said,

> I want to lay the greatest possible stress on encouraging demand since my country is one of those which has large oil reserves for which we would like to find buyers. I do not want to be taken for a ride by some of our OPEC colleagues who not so long ago were calling for a very sharp increase in the price of oil and selling their oil at much higher than $40/b, while we were sticking to the official price and not going into the spot market. Now these same countries are going in reverse and pressing us from the other side by selling at a cheaper price and giving discounts amounting as much as $7–8/b. So we would like to see a healthy increase in demand for oil. We cannot live with the present level of production for long. We need to raise our production, we have new fields coming on stream.[5]

A similar charge against some members was made by the ruler of Kuwait, Jabir al-Ahmad al-Sabah: These members had increased their quotas and decreased their prices. Yamani made the same charges.

Vienna Conference: December 18–20

As the year-end OPEC conference approached, it seemed that both the quota system and the unified $34 price were in real danger. Yamani listed conditions for continued support of the unified price: restoration of price and production discipline, no discounting and other forms of price cutting, observance of production quotas and correction of the differentials structure. He warned that as long as the differentials remained uncorrected, Saudi Arabia would not be bound by the marker-crude price.

After two days of arguing, the conference decided to maintain the $34-a-barrel price and to take the necessary steps to stabilize the market and to defend the OPEC price structure, but it failed to agree on a production program. The total OPEC production level for 1983 was set at no more than 15.5 million barrels a day, but OPEC could not allot the individual member quotas, and these were left for "further consultations among the respective governments." (See above Yamani's prediction of disaster for OPEC if production were to fall to 15 million barrels a day.) The conference ended in total disarray, without succeeding in eliminating price discounting and without correcting the differentials structure. The discord continued. Algeria, Iran, Libya, Nigeria, and Venezuela insisted that Saudi Arabia should bear the necessary production reduction. Saudi Arabia refused to make the sacrifice and became, more than ever, convinced that it could no longer defend the $34 price.

Estimated OPEC production was 19 percent less in 1982 than in 1981 and 40 percent less than in 1979; OPEC's share of world oil production dropped in 1982 to 45 percent, from 65 percent in 1975. Instead of a surplus as in previous years, the OPEC countries' current account for 1982 was a deficit of $10 billion, and total oil revenue for the year dropped to $205 billion from $255 billion.

1983—OPEC REDUCES CRUDE-OIL PRICES

The question of differentials became a very thorny issue. A consultative meeting was convened in Geneva on January 23, 1983, to deal with the problem. The oil minister of Kuwait complained that his country could not sell the 1.2-million-barrel-a-day quota set by OPEC because of the unfair differentials set by other members and because of the discounts they offered. His country could sell only about half of its allotment. The meeting broke up the following day without arriving at any agreement either on differentials or on discounts.

While OPEC was struggling with its own members to bring some order to the chaos of both production levels and prices, the oil glut extended even beyond OPEC, and the non-OPEC producers despaired for markets as well. On February 18, 1983, the British National Oil Company (BNOC) officially announced a $3-a-barrel cut in contract sales, retroactive to February 1. On the same day, Norway announced a price cut of $3.25, and on the following day, Nigeria, whose oil, because of its quality, is competitive with North Sea oil, announced a drop of $5.50, down to $30 a barrel.

Six days later, consultations began among different OPEC members in Riyadh, Paris, Geneva, and London, among themselves and with Britain and Mexico, about oil prices and production levels, lasting until March 4. Ten days later an OPEC meeting opened in London.

London Consultative Meeting: March 14

This London conference was no doubt a fateful event in the history of OPEC. It decided to reduce the price of the marker crude from $34 to $29 a barrel; Nigeria was granted a fifty-cent cut below the North Sea oil price. The members reached an understanding about the differentials structure; Algeria and Libya were granted $1.50 differentials. All members gave firm commitments, though without sanctions, to abide by the production quota system, the total of which was set at 17.5 million

Table 9.3 Saudi Arabian Oil Production, 1973–1983

Year	Quantity (million barrels a day)	Percentage Change
1973	7.4	+27.8
1974	8.3	+12.1
1975	6.9	−17.0
1976	8.5	+24.6
1977	9.2	+8.2
1978	8.3	−9.6
1979	9.5	+14.5
1980	9.9	+4.2
1981	9.8	NA*
1982	6.5	−33.7
1983	5.0	−23.0

Source: SAMA, *Annual Report,* 1973–1983 (Jidda)
*Not available

Table 9.4 OPEC Total Production, 1973–1983 (thousand barrels)

1973	11,297,544
1974	11,198,849
1975	9,934,232
1976	11,240,215
1977	11,467,628
1978	10,914,165
1979	11,205,055
1980	9,848,499
1981	8,218,066
1982	6,751,708
1983	6,381,522

Source: Petroleum Economist, June 1984, p. 216; September 1984, p. 364

barrels. Although the total was the same, the apportionment was adjusted to increase the levels of the weaker members at the expense of Saudi Arabia.[6] Saudi Arabia agreed to be the "swing producer," which meant that the Saudis would adjust their output to the market conditions after the others had filled their quotas. Saudi Arabia was, therefore, technically not under a quota.

OPEC faced one of the most critical decisions of its existence. The glut, as indicated above, had affected OPEC and non-OPEC producers alike. To prevent a calamitous price war and consequent total collapse of the price structure, both OPEC and non-OPEC producers would have to cooperate. Although the non-OPEC producers, especially the North Sea producers, were much more vulnerable to the results of a price war (because of their very high production costs compared with the very low production costs of the Middle East producers), a price war would be ruinous and disastrous to both groups. The alternative was cooperation between the two groups on the issue of production and on the issue of price. Here emerges a note of irony.

The non-OPEC producers had been eager, long before the crisis, to work out an understanding with OPEC. On December 20, 1978, a spokesman of the British Energy Ministry had announced in London that a meeting between OPEC and non-OPEC producers was scheduled to be held in London in the first week in March 1979. OPEC was to be represented by the oil ministers of Saudi Arabia, Kuwait, and Venezuela; the non-OPEC group was to be represented by ministers of Britain, Norway, and Mexico. They were to discuss a wide range of questions, except price. In the middle of January 1979, the British energy minister had reported in Mexico that the three non-OPEC oil producers would meet in March with the OPEC members. The initiator for the meeting was Venezuela. However, in the middle of February it was announced that the March scheduled meeting had been postponed. The Arab participants had not been particularly keen on the whole idea, although the British energy minister, Anthony Benn, was anxious to promote it.

Then, in 1983, both groups were faced with the possibility of a catastrophic price war. The first to cut prices were Great Britain and Norway, to which Nigeria, an OPEC member, retaliated by undercutting Britain. The non-OPEC producers would have to react to Nigeria. So while OPEC members were busy negotiating and consulting among themselves, some were also hectically meeting with Britain, Norway, and Mexico, with two issues on the agenda: no price war and no production increases. Between them, the two groups could monopolize the world oil market. For mutual protection both groups agreed to stabilize prices. On the issue of production, Mexico agreed to cooperate with OPEC; Britain refused to commit itself and thus assured for itself the possibility of augmenting production as soon as the market improved. Britain wished to escape "OPECization." The OPEC negotiators had to be satisfied with what they obtained.

Meanwhile, OPEC leaders attempted to gain agreements with the other non-OPEC producers: the USSR (which exported 1.5 million barrels a day to the West), Egypt, and the People's Republic of China. The USSR and Egypt raised and lowered prices in line with OPEC decisions, but they did not respond to OPEC approaches. Late in March, Yamani declared, somewhat humbly yet shrewdly, "I think there is a growing feeling, even among the consumers, that OPEC is needed. You cannot leave the price of oil fluctuating up and down. It will definitely lead to disaster. So the strength of OPEC will come from the joint actions of the member countries and cooperation with the non-OPEC producers. We do have, fortunately, some cooperation with them which is highly appreciated by OPEC."[7]

Although observers were skeptical that OPEC members would abide by the March 1983 decisions, self-preservation no doubt guided members not to cheat flagrantly on prices, for that would immediately result in swift retaliation from the non-OPEC producers. As regards production, OPEC members might disregard the decisions and exceed their quotas as soon as the oil market improved, but in this they would find the North Sea producers open competitors.

Midyear and Year-end: Helsinki and Geneva

The regular midyear OPEC conference, which convened on July 18–19 in Helsinki, agreed for the time being to retain both the existing price system and production levels. The quotas, however, had not been strictly observed. On October 4, Chairman al-Otaiba of the Monitoring Committee reported that his group "noted that a number of countries have increased their productions and exceeded their quotas. That excess production is more than 1 million b/d above the 17.5 million b/d OPEC ceiling. In addition North Sea output has risen to an additional 500,000 b/d."[8] Nevertheless, when the year-end conference met in Geneva on December 7–9, tension within OPEC was high. The Geneva conference agreed to continue with the same prices and the same quotas.

It was assumed that the general economic recession would end, demand for oil would mount, and prices might even start climbing again. However, the disturbing fact was that, in spite of some economic improvement indicators, the demand for oil did not rise. The Dresdener Bank estimated that the current account OPEC deficit for 1983 was $20 billion. It was reported that OPEC members were being forced to reduce their foreign assets to replace the shortfall in revenue.

The Chase Manhattan Bank estimated the OPEC deficit at $33 billion; the Morgan Guaranty Trust Company estimated it as $40 billion; and the Marine Midland Bank estimated the deficit as high as $53 billion.[9]

1984—PRICES DROPPING

Time did not work for the OPEC producers. With the drop in demand, which had entered its fourth year; with the reduction in the price of oil and the lowered dependence of the Western consuming countries on Middle East oil; and with the huge shortfall in revenue, the Middle East producers had lost a great measure of their oil power and their money power. In an interview with the Cairo *Al-Ahram,* on April 11, 1984, Yamani observed, "There can be no doubt that the strength and influence of oil has diminished as a result of surpluses in the oil market and the inability of the oil producers to use this commodity as a political force at the present time. But the importance of Arab oil politically still exists, because the Western world could not exist without Arab oil. We believe that by the end of 1987 the picture will change and the political power of oil will again be as it was in 1973 and 1979."[10]

This dream was dashed by reality. Relations between Saudi Arabia and the Aramco companies changed radically. During the 1979–1980 crisis—when Saudi Arabian prices were below those of the other OPEC producers, and the spot market was even higher than the prices of the OPEC radicals—the Aramco companies had been reaping enormous extra profits, reaching about $8 to $9 a barrel, lifting the limits of their long-term contracts. The other lifters, including the major multinational oil companies, had to pay the very high OPEC prices, which created tensions between the Aramco partners and other oil companies. After OPEC prices collapsed, and spot market rates went down below OPEC prices, these other oil companies cancelled most of their long-term contracts. They gambled and bought their oil in the spot market. The Aramco companies were then at a great disadvantage because they were required to lift the Saudi Arabian oil at the highest OPEC prices. They therefore sought to be released from lifting considerable quantities of Saudi oil. Pressed by the Aramco companies to reduce their contract liftings as well as by some OPEC members to increase their quotas at Saudi expense (because Saudi Arabia was the swing producer), the Saudis were forced to reduce production drastically. As a result Saudi revenue dropped heavily.

Has the contribution of the non-OPEC producers to the stabilization of the oil market been equal to that of OPEC? The chairman of the OPEC Monitoring Committee, al-Otaiba, said on April 20, 1984, "We know that it is OPEC that has been bearing the brunt of measures to stabilize the oil market, whereas the non-OPEC producers in the North Sea and elsewhere have been producing to the maximum. They talk nicely to us, but I don't see what is their contribution to the stabilization of the market. Also, when the market was strong they charged the highest possible prices. This is reality and we have to face it."[11] These practices of the non-OPEC producers were identical with what the OPEC producers' practices had been when the market was strong.

In the middle of May, Yamani expressed disappointment with a British production increase from 2.3 million to 2.6 million barrels a day. He said that this increase was contrary to expectation and remarked bitterly, "It seems, that Britain cannot bring itself to cooperate with us unless and until the market deteriorates to the point where there is real danger of collapse. When they feel that this is imminent, they do cooperate. But as soon as the market firms up a bit, they take the opportunity to get whatever increase in output they can."[12] This plaintive complaint borders on hypocrisy. The British never committed themselves on production, while his OPEC colleagues were committed to production quotas, and they, according to al-Otaiba, exceeded their limits.

Vienna Conference: July 10–11

The midyear OPEC conference opened in Vienna in an atmosphere of gloom. The oil glut was greater than ever, and pressure to lower prices both in OPEC and outside OPEC was mounting. Britain had been forced, because of the refusal of its customers to pay the official price, to send a good portion of its oil to the spot market, where it was sold at $2 a barrel below the official price. The OPEC Monitoring Committee met in Vienna and recommended to the conference that it resist the pressure to lower prices.

After two days of closed-door debates, the conference decided to maintain prices and quotas at their existing levels (Iran, however, called for a $5-a-barrel increase in price). The major danger to the quota system was Nigeria, which was in desperate need of additional revenue. Nigeria could lower its price and disrupt the arrangement between OPEC and non-OPEC producers; it could also increase production unilaterally and menace OPEC itself. In a last-minute effort to prevent a possible OPEC breakup, Saudi Arabia—as swing producer—granted Nigeria (from the Saudi share) 100,000 barrels a day for the month of August and 150,000 barrels a day for the month of September, which augmented Nigeria's quota from 1.3 million barrels to 1.45 million barrels. But could Nigeria sell its oil at the official price? The conference concluded with a pathetic call on the non-OPEC producers—the USSR, Britain, and Mexico—to join in a common campaign to avoid new shocks in the oil market and keep the current prices.

In an interview with *Middle East Economic Survey* on August 20, Yamani stated that the turmoil in the world oil market would be over by the end of September, and that by October OPEC would be considering an increase rather than a cut in the oil output ceiling. "We expect that the last quarter of this year will witness an increase in oil consumption and demand which will raise OPEC's share of the crude oil market to 19 million barrels a day or more." On the same day King Fahd proposed that oil prices be "fixed for a specific number of years"[13] as a way to stabilize the market.

Extraordinary Conference—Geneva: October 29–31

In spite of Yamani's assurance, September came and went and the turmoil was not over. Then came October, and both Norway and Britain could no longer maintain their oil price. Demand continued to fall. Britain was forced to send its oil to the spot market where it was sold far below the official price. On October 15, Norway announced a $1.50-a-barrel price cut; Britain reduced its price by $1.35; and the following day, Nigeria cut its price by $2. OPEC was alarmed and called an extraordinary conference to meet in Geneva on October 29. The emerging pattern seemed to be a repetition of the early 1983 episode. Could OPEC stem the tide of price reduction through production curtailment? At whose expense? Or would the March 1983 drama be repeated? On October 21, it was announced that six OPEC oil ministers, headed by Yamani, were to meet on the following day in Geneva to prepare the agenda for the extraordinary conference.

For two days, October 22–23, the six OPEC oil ministers conferred, together with representatives of Mexico and Egypt, and decided to recommend that the conference maintain the current price structure. Yamani declared, "There will be no price change. We decided to restore the price of oil by cutting production."[14] It was reported in Geneva that the proposed OPEC cut might be 3 million barrels from the existing ceiling of 17.5 million barrels a day. The Saudi Arabian and Mexican oil ministers were to persuade Nigeria and Norway to restore their price cuts. To complicate the situation, Canada announced on October 25 that it had followed Britain, Norway, and Nigeria and had reduced its oil price by $1.33 a barrel, effective November 1.

The only issue before the extraordinary conference was that the OPEC price of $29 a barrel for Saudi Arabian light be maintained through any cut in production. A number of questions arose: First, the magnitude of the overall cut; second, the apportionment of the cut among the members; and third, would Nigeria restore the official price and agree to share in the production cut? The Nigerian oil minister, Tam David-West, declared that "cutting back is suicidal . . . oil is life to Nigeria."[15] When he arrived at Geneva for the conference he said that he had not come to negotiate either a Nigerian price increase or a production cut. The first decision of the conference was an agreement in principle—Nigeria dissenting—to reduce total production by 1.5 million barrels a day, from 17.5 million to 16 million barrels a day. The apportionment of the cut was the tough problem of the conference.

The UAE oil minister added another issue. Abu Dhabi, which had increased its oil production capacity, was desperate to acquire purchasers. It claimed that the OPEC differentials structure affected Abu Dhabi adversely and greatly benefited Saudi Arabia; that the differential between Abu Dhabi oil and Saudi Arabian oil was too high, and Abu Dhabi could not sell its oil, as allotted by OPEC. The UAE oil minister demanded that the differentials system be modified so that Abu Dhabi could compete fairly with Saudi Arabia. The issues were to be taken up again by the ordinary OPEC conference to be held in December in Vienna.

DECEMBER 1984 TO JULY 1985—
FURTHER DETERIORATION

The market situation grew worse for both OPEC and non-OPEC oil producers, and all producing countries were determined to increase or at least to retain their oil revenue. In spite of all the hopeful predictions and in spite of all the measures adopted to stabilize the market, demand for oil was dropping; as a result the efforts of the oil producers to dispose of their product became more desperate. The steady oil purchasers refused to commit themselves to long-term contracts at set prices and instead turned to the spot market for their oil needs. This prompted the oil producers—OPEC as well as non-OPEC—to resort to measures that would guarantee their oil income. OPEC members disregarded both production and price levels; and non-OPEC producers resorted to price cutting to bring their prices in line with those of the spot market. On November 11, 1984, Norway announced that it had temporarily suspended its official price system and would negotiate terms based on the free market (a more elegant term for the spot market).

Even at this point, Ahmad Zaki Yamani, the Saudi Arabia oil minister, was not yet ready to admit that the prolonged crisis was the direct result of OPEC high-price policies, and he sought to put the blame on consumers, who, he said, were drawing down their stock. On the same day as Norway's announcement—November 11—he declared in Riyadh, "We know that the price of oil will go up. There is no doubt about it."[16] Then, in an interview with the *Sunday Times* (London), published on November 25, 1984, Yamani said that the December demand for OPEC oil would far outstrip the supply and that "there could be a real panic in the markets. The situation is very alarming and very risky." Four days later, at a press conference in Kuwait he explained, "We expect sometime in the future, probably by the end of December an interruption inside consumer countries because inventory is too low and consumers are drawing so much from stock."[17]

The British never committed themselves on production lim-
itation. Their understanding with OPEC in March 1983 was
only on price. Real difficulties were created for the British
government by the practice of the British National Oil Company
(BNOC) of announcing the official price from time to time.
BNOC's official price was the basis of payment for the oil to
which it was entitled—up to 51 percent—from the producing
companies holding leases in the North Sea. The official price
worked well in times of shortage, and customers flocked to
purchase the oil on the basis of long-term contracts, but in
times of surplus oil supplies the official price boomeranged.
When oil was abundant, BNOC customers refused to pay the
official price, and BNOC was forced to dispose of its oil in
the spot market at at least $2 a barrel less than what it had
paid for it.

BNOC consequently accumulated deficits that the British
government had to cover; for the month of December 1984,
the government paid BNOC £45 million ($48 million). Finally
the British government announced in Parliament that it was
abolishing BNOC. This meant that the price of British oil
would be determined by the free market. Now that Britain and
Norway were selling their oil at the free market price, it was
inevitable that Nigeria would have to follow suit. The *New
York Times* of February 2, 1985, quoted the Nigerian oil minister
as saying: "My two feet are firmly in OPEC. But my two eyes
are on the North Sea."

Tension rose as the OPEC year-end conference approached.
Saudi Arabia felt that it was being pressed between OPEC
members and the non-OPEC producers. As the OPEC swing
producer, Saudi Arabia would incur the expense of whatever
cuts OPEC made in production level. Indeed Saudi Arabia
constantly complained that other OPEC members did not
comply with their quota limits and only Saudi Arabia continuously reduced its production level. In relation to the non-
OPEC producers OPEC played the role of swing producer; its
production levels were determined by what the market would
bear after non-OPEC production was set. On December 11,
1984, reacting to British and Norwegian intentions to follow
the free market price, Yamani stated, "Both King Fahd's gov-

ernment in particular and OPEC in general have fought against the idea of leaving prices to be determined by the vicissitudes of the market, and in this regard we made great sacrifices."[18]

In the midst of this discord the OPEC conference opened in Geneva on December 19. After two days of heated discussion, the conference adjourned to reconvene on December 27. During the recess the delegates were to obtain their governments' approval of measures to strengthen the discipline of members regarding prices and production levels. Among the proposals made by Saudi Arabia and Kuwait was the naming of a high-ranking ministerial council, above the monitoring committee, to supervise (by engaging professional auditing help) production and price operations of members. Yamani apparently despaired of the situation. In a quote that appeared in the *New York Times* on December 23, 1984, he declared that OPEC was "sick and dying" because of the failure of members to exercise production discipline. The former Kuwaiti oil minister, Abdul Muttaleb al-Kazemi, in an article in the Kuwait daily *Al-Watan* on December 25, 1984, wrote: "In the best evaluation, OPEC is currently dying. To be more optimistic, it is in the phase of absolute freeze."

On December 27 the conference reconvened. After two days of further debate it decided to adopt the proposal on differentials, reduced the price of Saudi Arabian light oil to $28 a barrel, and named a five-member Ministerial Executive Council, headed by Yamani, to supervise price and production levels of members. It also decided to meet again on March 28 in Geneva to review the functioning of the auditing system and its ability to enforce member discipline on production and prices.

On December 29, after the closing of the conference, Yamani held a press conference in Geneva. When asked what he would want the North Sea producers to do, he replied, "I hope they don't go to what we heard they wanted to adopt—that is the spot market formula. I think it is time for them to look at the level of production and protect their long-term interests as well as short-term interests." Behind this polite general statement was the implied threat of possible retaliation. He declared that the North Sea producers should realize that the situation was extremely serious. When asked why they should do so as long as OPEC was propping up prices, he answered, "Because if we start a price war—and we have every intention of doing so if we have to—the revenues of the UK, for example will drop sharply. If there is a price war, there will be real chaos in the market. When we enter that war we will not create a stable lower price for oil. We will just go up and down and hit whatever floor we want to hit. I think the damage will be very serious, not only for the UK, but for banks in the U.S. Mexico could not service its debts even with rescheduling—even if that were possible. If the price falls to $27/B, they cannot even ask for rescheduling. As a Mexican friend told me, this is not a worry for the Mexicans, it is a worry for the American banks."[19]

A careful analysis of the total world oil situation will reveal that this threat of a price war is just bluff and bluster. Saudi Arabia could not and would not start a price war. Theoretically, because the cost of oil production in Saudi Arabia is ridiculously low compared to the cost of production in the North Sea, a price war could totally ruin the oil industry of the North Sea— with possible disastrous consequences to Britain's economy. But practically, a wild price war would be as disastrous to OPEC producers, including Saudi Arabia, as it would be to the North Sea and Mexican oil producers and to U.S. banks. As it is, OPEC is very seriously smarting from lowered prices and reduced production; how much more calamitous would the situation be if a reckless price war broke out. Neither OPEC nor Saudi Arabia is ready to proceed with a price war. This threat, like many of Yamani's threats over the last fifteen years, made in the name of his country, both inside OPEC and outside OPEC, was nothing but bluff. The non-OPEC producers were not deterred by Yamani's threat of a price war.

The impact of the oil crisis on OPEC members has been far-reaching. An estimate at the end of 1984 by Salomon Brothers, the New York brokerage firm, calculated that declining revenues had wiped out $91 billion that the OPEC have-nots boasted at the end of 1981. Libya's oil revenue in 1980 amounted to $22.6 billion; in 1984 it dropped to $9 billion. The United Arab Emirates' revenue in 1984 fell to $4.4 billion, down from $7.4 billion in 1983. Saudi Arabia's oil revenue dropped from $113 billion in 1981 to $43 billion in 1984; in 1985 it was running at the rate of $25 billion a year. Some 1,500 Saudi firms have gone bankrupt or sought government assistance. The Gulf Cooperation Council countries have decided to cut one million jobs during the coming five years; Saudi Arabia alone was to cut its manpower by 600,000.

Only some twelve days after Yamani's threat of a price war, Norway abandoned official pricing in favor of negotiating secret agreements with its oil customers. The major U.S. oil companies—Texaco, Gulf, Mobil, Exxon, and others—lowered their crude purchasing price to $27.50 a barrel. Canada reduced its oil price by $1.89 a barrel. It looked as if the non-OPEC producers had taken the lead in determining world oil prices. The *Petroleum Economist* of January 1985 noted that OPEC spokesmen, rather than blaming the inability of OPEC members to exercise collective will to observe official production quotas, blamed two external causes for the market's weakness: abnormal drawing down of stocks by the consuming countries and the high level of North Sea production.

Tension among the OPEC members was rising, and an emergency conference was convened on January 28, 1985, in Geneva. The first day of the session was stormy. The UAE delegate, Mana Said al-Otaiba, greatly upset about the inability of his country to sell its oil, accused Nigeria of stabbing OPEC in the back and of undermining the price structure by producing oil above the agreed quota. He stormed out of the meeting and said that he was going home. Later in the day Yamani and the Nigerian delegate Tam David-West visited al-Otaiba in his hotel and brought him back to the meeting.

The conference had to deal with two major issues: differentials structure and price stabilization. The differentials issue has troubled OPEC ever since the beginning of the present crisis. Right after March of 1983, the price structure was: Saudi Arabian light, $29; better light, 56 cents above; and Arab heavy, $2 below—a price spread of $3.50; Nigerian light was $1 above the marker crude. After Norway reduced its price by $1.35, Nigeria reduced its price by $2. This disrupted the entire differentials structure. In December, a compromise was worked out to reduce Gulf light crudes by 25 cents and increase the price of heavy crudes by 50 cents, thus narrowing the price spread to $2.80. But the compromise did not work. The pattern of the price structure between light and heavy crudes had been radically changed. When oil prices were low, refineries, as a rule, were built to refine the light crudes. Very few refineries were handling heavy oils. However, when the price of oil skyrocketed, many refineries installed facilities to handle heavy crudes. Because the difference in price was considerable, the demand for heavy oil increased and the demand for light oils decreased. The only alternative was to reduce the price of the light oils and increase the price of the heavy oils. This created discord among OPEC members.

On January 31, after three days of discussions, the emergency conference arrived at a partial agreement to cut prices by an average of 29 cents a barrel. Four members, Algeria, Libya, Iran and Gabon, rejected the agreement. UAE oil (light) was reduced by $1.41 to $28.15 a barrel; Saudi Arabia's light was down $1 to $28 a barrel; Indonesia's oil was cut by $1 to $28.53 a barrel; Nigeria was to increase its price by 65 cents to $28.53 a barrel. All other members were to keep prices at the current level. The *Financial Times* of London of February 4, 1985, reported that the military leader of Nigeria warned that if Britain's North Sea oil prices dropped, Nigeria would have to follow suit. "We will have to do that to survive." The *New York Times* of February 2, 1985, reported that nine out of the thirteen members of OPEC agreed to a $1-a-barrel cut in the official price of Saudi light crude. This was a concession to the fact that members were selling oil at even sharper discounts in the spot market.

On the issue of price stabilization, the discord between OPEC members was deeper than ever. In spite of the monitoring committee headed by al-Otaiba and in spite of the Ministerial Executive Council headed by Yamani, there was widespread cheating on both price and production levels. The conference was incapable of adopting any controlling measures. Egypt, which was an observer at the conference, withdrew, and its representative stated that his country's cooperation with OPEC was in doubt.

The march of price cuts continued. On February 3, 1985, Egypt cut its oil prices by 50 cents a barrel, and its top-grade

Suez blend was set at $27.50. On February 10, Venezuela announced an average cut of $1.75 a barrel of its light crudes, and Mexico reduced its light Isthmus blend by $1.25 to $27.25 a barrel. Mexico also decided to increase its production level from 1.4 million to 1.5 million barrels a day. On the same day Iran cut its prices by $1.05 a barrel. At the end of May, Norwegian oil was selling at $26.50 a barrel, and early in June British Brent blend slumped to $25.50 a barrel.

How did OPEC members cheat? In an interview with *Al Sharq al-Awsat,* on September 8, 1981, when OPEC officially regulated only prices, Yamani outlined the methods by which OPEC members tried to move their oil. They began by giving large discounts to their customers "either openly or under the counter." He explained that this was done in several ways: through processing deals, whereby oil was sold in product form at a net back below official crude prices (OPEC regulated only crude prices); via barter deals in which the goods bartered for oil had inflated price tags; through extending the credit period for oil payments; or through reductions in the level of taxes and royalties of the concession-holding companies. By 1984 the magnitude of these methods of cheating on both price and production levels grew in proportion to the pressures of the distressing financial needs of OPEC members.

Saudi Arabia itself was a major practitioner. By the end of 1983, Saudi Arabia had organized Norbec, a company that secretly acquired a number of large oil tankers, anchored in Saudi Arabian territorial waters outside the Gulf and used to store huge quantities of crude oil. In February 1984, the *Petroleum Economist* reported that Norbec had some estimated 40 to 45 million barrels of Saudi crude. At first, observers believed that the storage outside the Gulf was a precautionary measure against a possible closure of the Strait of Hormuz in the Iran-Iraq war. But later some of the Norbec tankers were found in Caribbean and Far Eastern ports. It was never made clear whether the oil stored in the Norbec tankers was within or without the OPEC production limits for Saudi Arabian oil.

After the stormy consultative OPEC conference on January 23–24, 1983, Yamani was asked what the production level of his country was. He said, "It is very low. We are much below

5 mn. b/d. The problem is not our financial needs, it is far greater than this. The problem is gas production. We produce sweet water and electricity from natural gas, and it is associated gas. If production of Arabian light falls below that it is now, then we are in trouble. We have to produce enough Arabian light to produce gas in order to have water and electricity."[20] Some saw in this stored Norbec oil in different parts of the world, a "waiting position." Should the opportunity present itself for selling it, the oil would be available.

The barter exercise was widespread and involved Saudi Arabia, Nigeria, and other OPEC members. These barter deals were very large in scale and were not on a direct procedure between the oil producer and the supplier of the imported products, as had been the practice during the first oil crisis. A new technique had been developed, called countertrade. The oil producer transfers crude oil to a trading company; the trader sells the oil on the spot market and puts the proceeds into an escrow account. This account is used to pay cash for the goods being provided in return for oil. On paper the oil may be transferred at official prices; the price of the goods, however, may be artificially inflated to offset any loss of the resale of the oil.

At the end of February 1985, it was reported that Saudi Arabia signed a $1.2 billion contract with Boeing to provide Saudi Arabia with ground components for an early-warning system. In mid-March 1985, it was reported that Saudi Arabia was about to conclude a large barter deal involving oil worth $2 billion for an undisclosed number of French Mirage jet fighter planes. A Venezuelan senator declared that the deal would make the world oil market even weaker and push prices further down. The deal was to involve 73 million barrels of oil. On August 13, 1984, *Business Week* reported that Saudi Arabia had been confounding the oil trade: "The Saudis in recent weeks radically increased output and suddenly unloaded nearly $1 billion worth of oil on the spot market in barter for 10 Boeing 747s." The oil was sold on the spot market at $2 below price.

On March 18, 1985, *Newsweek* reported that Nigeria concluded a contract with Brazil to supply 40,000 barrels of oil daily for twelve months in exchange for $500 million worth of sugar, chemicals, paper, and machinery. The *International Herald-Tribune* of May 16, 1985, reported that Nigeria had reached agreement for an oil-barter deal with France worth $500 million for assembly kits of Peugeot cars, refined sugar, and other products. A similar agreement was reached between Nigeria and Austria in which $200 million in oil was traded for machinery, steel, and other products. On June 16, 1985, Nigeria signed an agreement with Italy for 40,000 barrels of oil a day for twelve months, worth $400 million, in exchange for chemicals and Fiat car kits.

Iran, Algeria, and Libya were also involved in barter deals. On May 1, 1985, the Kuwaiti oil minister Ali al-Khalifah al-Sabah voiced grave concern over OPEC countries using barter deals to sell their oil. He said that these deals posed the greatest threat to OPEC. By June 1985, the situation in OPEC seemed to have gone from bad to worse. The conflicting interests among members were sharper than ever—conflicts between the Gulf and the African producers, between the Gulf producers themselves, and between the African producers themselves.

Meanwhile the demand for oil continued to drop. Crude-oil imports to the United States dropped to the lowest level in many years. The largest share of the drop was experienced by OPEC. In 1977 OPEC's share of U.S. crude imports had been 83.4 percent; in 1984 it went down to 42 percent; and during the first quarter of 1985 it fell to 33 percent. In 1977 Saudi Arabia shipped to the United States a daily average of 1.4 million barrels; in the first quarter of 1985 Saudi Arabia shipped a daily average of 97,743 barrels. The average of all U.S. daily imports of crude in 1977 was 6,694,700 barrels; in 1984 it went down to 3,605,813; the average for the first quarter of 1985 was 2,719,954 barrels. Prices were falling, and ever-greater quantities of oil were traded through the spot market.[21] Cheating by OPEC members, both on price and production levels, was rampant. All the measures adopted by the conferences to check and stop cheating were ineffective.

Saudi Arabia saw its oil production continuously declining and its revenue shrinking while other OPEC members were cheating both on price and production levels at Saudi expense. It, therefore, changed its position as swing producer and demanded that its production level be increased through the reduction of other members' production levels. The demand was accompanied with the threat that Saudi Arabia would increase production and decrease prices unilaterally—the same threat it had made to non-OPEC producers. When the Ministerial Executive Council, created to supervise production and prices under the chairmanship of Yamani, met in Taif, the Saudi summer capitol, on June 2–3 for informal consultation, Saudi Arabia stated its case.

On June 1, on the eve of the council meeting, Yamani was interviewed in the daily *Al-Sharq al-Awsat*. In response to a question as to whether he expected that the Taif meeting would succeed, he said, "Do we have any choice in the matter? Either we succeed in maintaining prices and in correcting mistaken practices or we face a collapse of prices and chaos, from which no one will be immune and which will hit the undisciplined harder than the disciplined." The average daily production level for the month of May in Saudi Arabia dropped to 2.44 million barrels, and the same level was expected for the month of June.

At the opening of the Taif meeting, Yamani read a letter from King Fahd. The king declared that there was no reason why OPEC resolutions should be respected by some members and violated by the majority; either discipline was maintained in OPEC ranks, in which Saudi Arabia would fully cooperate, or else Saudi Arabia would feel free to follow the practices adopted by other members. If other members increased production above their quotas, Saudi Arabia would increase its production; and if other members granted price discounts in one form or another, Saudi Arabia would openly sell its oil in line with prevailing market prices. Then, in view of the disturbed situation in OPEC, the council decided to advance the scheduled July 22 OPEC meeting to June 30.

The July Conferences

July 5–7. It was in this atmosphere that the mid-year conference, rescheduled for July 5, opened in Vienna. The issues that had dominated the December 1984 and January 1985 conferences continued with greater intensity to occupy the July meeting. The pressure to lower prices was increased. Intra-OPEC conflicts, involving, among other issues, the differentials structure, as well as relations with non-OPEC producers, prevented the conference from arriving at any solutions.

Mexico, the most cooperative non-OPEC producer in both price and production policies, warned that it would defend its national interests if OPEC failed to take decisive action to stem the world decline of oil prices. The Mexican oil minister declared that his country might reduce its oil prices as early as July 10. Yamani was reported to have made clear, on July 6, that his country was determined to increase its oil output. He warned the members that they would have to choose between accepting the lower prices that would result from an overall increase in production or reducing their own quotas to offset a Saudi increase. The very critical issues facing OPEC were formulated as: declining demand for OPEC oil; increasing oil production by non-OPEC producers; and widespread violations of OPEC established prices through secret agreements with purchasers, basing prices on spot market rates. Although the official overall OPEC production ceiling was 16 million barrels a day, members reportedly could sell only 14.1 million barrels a day. Some members were producing more than their quotas and were offering discounts of as much as $4 a barrel below the official price. Although Saudi Arabia's official ceiling was 4.3 million barrels a day, it actually was producing only 2.1 million barrels. The efforts of OPEC to obtain the cooperation of the non-OPEC producers—Britain, Norway, Mexico, and Egypt—failed. These all lowered their prices below OPEC levels.

Nigeria, Ecuador, and Venezuela exceeded their quotas in a desperate effort to earn revenue. Because of its low production level, Saudi Arabia had one of the largest deficits in its balance of payments and was drawing down its reserves at the rate of $20 billion a year to finance the already heavily curtailed Saudi development programs.

After three days of acrimonious discussions the conference was unable to arrive at any solutions and decided to meet again on the original designated date, July 22, in Geneva.

July 22–25. During the two weeks between the closing of the conference in Vienna and the opening of the 74th OPEC conference in Geneva on July 22, matters did not improve; in fact, they worsened. A U.S. task force studied the possible impact of a drop in oil prices on international financial institutions and on the relations of the United States with some oil producers. The task force reported that a 23 percent drop in world oil prices to about $20 a barrel, from the current $26, could be tolerated by crucial U.S. allies that depend on oil exports for their revenue as well as by international banks that had granted loans of billions of dollars to those countries. Venezuela and Indonesia could live with such price cuts; Mexico and Egypt would need some U.S. financial support. This report was not encouraging news for OPEC and especially for Saudi Arabia.

OPEC had seen in the establishment of the International Energy Agency the very antithesis of its aims and purposes and had opposed it vigorously. Now it was seeking a dialogue with the IEA in an attempt to save its own existence. OPEC Deputy Secretary General Fadhil al-Chalabi met with U.S. officials and broached the idea of an OPEC price cut in return for a cooperative effort to increase purchases of oil from OPEC members. He pleaded for a dialogue with IEA to explore cooperation on oil prices and consumption. The ultimate aim of IEA was a meeting of oil consumers and oil producers for mutual cooperation, as envisioned by former Secretary of State Kissinger. Now the plea of OPEC for this very aim was rejected. At the IEA meeting in July 1985 in Paris, the IEA president, M. Van Ardenne, declared: "We don't see what interest we could achieve from an institutionalized dialogue with [OPEC]."[22]

Yet OPEC did not give up the effort and tried again. The July 22 conference issued a call for cooperation of the world's other oil producers to support the crumbling structure of oil prices. OPEC's President Subroto, the oil minister of Indonesia, said that it was time that non-OPEC producers, such as Britain, Norway, the USSR, and the United States, as well as major oil companies, helped to halt the slide. "The situation has deteriorated to the point where I must regretfully state in very clear and unequivocal terms that oil market stability is at the crossroads. My message to those non-OPEC producers is clear. We must all cooperate so that all of us can reap the benefits of market stability, or we will all suffer."[23] This declaration and plea, after twenty-five years of OPEC's existence and hectic operations, must be taken as an admission of OPEC's failure. No response came from the non-OPEC producers.

The tension within OPEC continued. On the one hand, Saudi Arabia, as the leader of the rich conservative members, was determined to increase its own production level to 4 million barrels a day and to reduce the quotas of the other members of OPEC. At the same time, as a producer, with Kuwait, of heavy crudes, Saudi Arabia insisted on a deep cut in the price of the heavy crudes. On the other hand, Algeria, a producer of light crude, leader of the poor members and a radical, was equally determined not to permit a serious reduction in the price of the heavy crudes and not to allow Saudi Arabia to increase its production level; instead, some of the poorer members should be granted increases in their production quotas.

Saudi Arabia came to Geneva with its two demands backed by a threat to increase its oil production and thereby flood the oil markets. Yamani apparently had instructions from King Fahd to press hard for the Saudi demands. When the conference opened, the two major items on the agenda were production levels and price reduction. After two hours of discussion of the production issue, during which Qatar, Iraq, Ecuador, and Gabon asked for increases in their quotas, it became clear that if the issue was pressed to a conclusion OPEC would collapse. It was, therefore, decided to postpone discussion of production levels until a special conference to be convened in September.

The July conference then turned to the question of price cutting of the heavy crudes. The proponents advocated a cut of about $1.50 a barrel; the opponents resisted any price cuts. Behind the Saudi Arabian demand for the cut was its threat to flood the market. The opposition—Algeria, Libya, and Iran—challenged the Saudi threat. After four days of rancorous debate, the 74th OPEC conference decided, on July 25, to reduce the price of heavy crude by 50 cents a barrel and the medium oils by 20 cents a barrel. This lowered OPEC's average oil price to $27.82 a barrel, a reduction of .5 percent. The decision was presented as a victory for Saudi Arabia and its oil minister,

Ahmad Zaki Yamani, and a supposed defeat for Algeria, the leader of the opposition. In reality the winner of the battle was the opposition. Saudi Arabia failed to exercise its threat. According to both Saudi and U.S. sources, King Fahd sent last-minute instructions to Yamani rescinding his previous orders to go into battle. Saudi Arabia saved face with the .5 percent drop in the OPEC price of oil. The average price in the spot market was $25.88 a barrel—$2 below the new official OPEC price.

CONCLUSIONS

The third crisis lasted for almost four years; in 1985, the end was not yet in sight. It would appear that OPEC members had not fully appreciated the causes of the crisis and continued to live in the false hope of soon regaining their old positions and power.

The first, foremost, and major factor in the crisis was the high prices. These brought about the inescapable reaction of the consumers: reduction of their dependence on OPEC oil by broad conservation regimens. Again, through their high prices the OPEC producers created their own Frankenstein's monster—the non-OPEC oil producers that arose to compete with and threaten OPEC. The inflated oil prices contributed greatly to the economic recession that engulfed both the United States and Europe and that decisively depressed the demand for oil. The resultant adjustment that the consumers made was not to the higher prices, as the OPEC radicals had anticipated, but to lower consumption levels. These lower consumption levels, it seems were not temporary expedients that would be abandoned when economic prosperity returned but became permanent features in the Western economies. Thus, although economic recovery was reported in the later part of 1984 in the Western countries, demand for oil had not risen; indeed, oil prices of both crude oil and refined products were reported to have fallen. Another factor was the activation, on a small scale at first, of energy alternatives, especially in the generation of electricity. This, of course, negatively affected the demand for OPEC oil.[24]

Of no small importance were the differences and difficulties within OPEC. When prices were high and supply was short, all OPEC members, small and large, moderates and radicals, had reaped enormous revenues and indulged in grandiose economic development projects and general expansion in all areas of government operations. (Saudi Arabia adopted an economic development program for the five-year period 1980–1985 to cost $243 billion covering only civilian projects.) Moreover, the members believed that they had in their hands oil power and money power and could dictate their terms to the Western world. These ideas were preached by the big Middle Eastern oil producers and were believed by the small ones. As long as prices climbed and supply was short, they all took advantage of the situation. But when the reaction set in, and demand fell and glut replaced shortfall, the internal OPEC conflicts widened.

When the pressure of overproduction began to build up, the small producers resented the curtailment of their production through the quota system, which radically diminished their incomes. The demand, most vociferously made by Iran, was that all production reductions should be made at the expense of the biggest and richest producer, Saudi Arabia. Saudi Arabia resisted this demand but without success; to prevent a total collapse of OPEC, Saudi Arabia had no choice but to yield and, as the swing producer, reduced its production level.

Kuwait, a big producer, complained bitterly about its reduced production rate. The UAE oil minister, al-Otaiba, declared in June 1982, "The OPEC production ceiling should be regarded as a temporary measure, not a permanent fixture. It was designed to remedy a certain problem, that is the glut or what I refer to as the 'stock war.' As soon as this problem is over, there will be no further need to keep the OPEC ceiling, and my country will not join in any production programming once the present crisis is ended."[25] Since al-Otaiba made that statement more than three years have passed, and the oil glut is still with us and so is the OPEC crisis.

The glut in fact—in spite of the quotas and the other devices meant to reduce it—is still, late in 1985, very menacing.

Ironically, what eases somewhat the pressure of the oil glut is the Iran-Iraq war, as the war prevents an additional 4 or 5 million barrels a day from reaching the world markets. The stalemate of the war is, in a sense, a "blessing" for the oil producers within OPEC and for the non-OPEC producers as well. Curiously, the frequent scares that the war would explode and spread further among the Gulf countries or even that the Strait of Hormuz might be closed have caused little panic buying of oil; the spot market reacts comparatively calmly to these scares.

It would definitely appear that the oil glut persists and that instead of easing, it is intensifying. The inevitable result would be drastic price cutting. In the middle of June 1985 it was variously reported that prices might come down to $15–20 a barrel. The results of such an eventuality could bring disaster to many of the economic and financial structures of the Western world, because the economies of many developed and developing countries are currently based on high oil prices. Many production companies and service concerns invested large amounts in undertakings based on oil-price returns. A number of oil-producing countries borrowed heavily from banks and other financial institutions with the hope of repaying the indebtedness from their high oil revenue. The entire oil industry in Britain, Norway, and Mexico would collapse if oil prices should descend to $15 a barrel. If oil prices dropped that low, practically all OPEC countries would experience deep deficits, not only in their economic development programs but in their ordinary government budgets. The U.S. and European companies that depend largely on contracts from the Middle East oil producers for gigantic economic development projects, and which have invested billions of dollars in joint-venture enterprises in the producers' lands, would face possible calamities.

In light of the history of the last two oil crises, it is obvious that OPEC possesses staying power and supposedly is capable of weathering all storms. This is mainly because of the nature of OPEC as a collection of sovereign entities. However, the exaggerated hysterical fear that the Middle East oil producers possessed almost unlimited power, felt by many who dealt with the issue of OPEC, was not only unjustified but revealed a lack of basic understanding of economic and political processes. The conflicting interests of the various OPEC members, as exposed in the last two crises, had made OPEC almost mortally vulnerable to any measures adopted collectively by the consuming countries. The survival of OPEC has not been due to its own positive strength so much as to the weaknesses of the consuming countries.[26]

Is the present OPEC setback permanent, and has the energy question been solved? Or is the third crisis a temporary phase, and will the Middle East producers return to wield their influence and power as they did in 1973 and 1979, as Yamani predicted? The possibilities for the future are discussed in Chapter 10.[27]

NOTES

1. NBC's "Meet the Press," April 19, 1981; *Middle East Economic Survey (MEES)*, April 27, 1981.
2. *MEES*, August 31, 1981.
3. *Al Sharq al-Awsat*, September 8, 1981; *Wall Street Journal*, September 8, 1981.
4. Production quota set in Quito, 1982 (barrels per day):

Algeria	650,000	Libya	750,000
Ecuador	200,000	Nigeria	1,300,000
Gabon	150,000	Qatar	300,000
Indonesia	1,350,000	Saudi Arabia	7,000,000
Iran	1,200,000	UAE	1,000,000
Iraq	1,200,000	Venezuela	1,500,000
Kuwait	800,000	Total	17,500,000

MEES, March 21, 1983.
5. Ibid., September 20, 1982.
6. Production quota set in London, 1983 (barrels per day):

Algeria	725,000	Libya	1,100,000
Ecuador	200,000	Nigeria	1,300,000
Gabon	150,000	Qatar	300,000
Indonesia	1,300,000	Saudi Arabia	5,000,000
Iran	2,400,000	UAE	1,100,000

Iraq	1,200,000	Venezuela	1,675,000
Kuwait	1,050,000	Total	17,500,000

Ibid., March 21, 1983.

7. Ibid., March 21, 1983.

8. Ibid., October 10, 1983.

9. Leaders in the Middle East threatened, and some analysts in the United States and Europe maintained, that the major Middle East producers would be satisfied to live on their other income rather than lower prices and let down their colleagues, the small producers. On March 10, 1983, the ruler of Kuwait, Jabir al-Ahmad al-Sabah, declared that Kuwait did not intend to use its investment income to make up for any shortfall in revenue. "Income from investments has always been considered a supporting element in the country's economy, but it was never regarded as an alternative to the revenues for oil." Ibid., March 14, 1983. Yamani voiced his country's concern that the drop in production had caused a serious deficit in the budget.

10. Although Yamani repeatedly stressed the political aspect of the oil weapon, when such a tactic was not convenient oil became a purely economic and commercial commodity. At the end of January 1977, in an interview with Agence France Presse, King Khaled was asked whether his country's petrodollars would be used to oppose the accession to power of the Communist parties in France and Italy. He replied, "Oil is an economic and commercial problem which should not be brought into political questions." Ibid., January 31, 1977. On June 3, 1979, Yamani told the Saudi Arabian *Al-Jazirah* that Saudi Arabia had no intention of cutting back production as a means of applying political pressure on the Western countries to arrive at a comprehensive settlement of the Arab-Israeli conflict. On November 19, 1981, in answer to a question of whether oil was likely to lose its power as a political weapon, Yamani replied, "No, I think oil is a political power. No one can argue that. But at a time when there is glut in the market you don't talk about an embargo, and that's what people call the political weapon." *MEES*, November 21, 1981.

11. Ibid., April 23, 1984.

12. Ibid., May 14, 1984.

13. Ibid., August 27, 1984.

14. *New York Times*, October 28, 1984.

15. *MEES*, November 5, 1984; *Wall Street Journal*, October 30, 1984.

16. *Wall Street Journal*, November 12, 1985.

17. *MEES,* December 3, 1984.

18. Ibid., December 17, 1984. On January 12, 1982, Yamani stated about production levels: "We will leave it to market forces to determine level. . . . If there is a serious drop in demand, we think Saudi production will be affected; and it will come down not by our decision but by the decision of the market forces. . . . From the beginning our policy has been based on using the price mechanism in OPEC to work as a built in system for production programming." Ibid., January 18, 1982.

19. Ibid., January 7, 1985.

20. Ibid., January 31, 1983.

21. The rapid increase of the spot-market operation is illustrated by Japan. In 1981 Japan bought 5.6 percent of its total imports in the spot market. In 1982 that proportion increased to 9 percent; in 1983 it went up to 17.9 percent; in 1984 it rose to 22.6 percent; in January 1985 it increased to 26.9 percent; and in March 1985 it jumped to 39.1 percent. Ibid., June 10, 1985.

22. *Wall Street Journal,* July 22, 1985.

23. On October 14, 1975, at a symposium in Bonn, Yamani explained the nature of OPEC. The general rule in cartels is that the strongest member "has to carry weaker members on its shoulders. It will eventually tire of its burden and refuse to bear it any longer, and, therefore, any cartel will come to an end and collapse. However, this is not the case with OPEC. In most cartels the strongest member seeks to sell as much of its goods as possible, but Saudi Arabia's interest lies in selling less of its oil." *MEES,* October 17, 1975.

24. This process was steadily expanding both in the United States and in Europe. France for instance, which in 1973 imported oil earmarked for electricity generation at 250,000 barrels a day, has reduced such imports to 16,000 barrels a day. In 1975, the bulk of French electricity generation was produced by nuclear power. *Business Week,* August 27, 1984.

25. *MEES,* June 7, 1982.

26. The Saudi Arabian minister of oil and mineral resources, Ahmad Zaki Yamani has been very much quoted throughout the book, more than any of the other personalities involved in the Middle East oil story, for two reasons: (1) He represented, in OPEC and in the world, the wealthiest oil-producing country with the greatest oil reserves; (2) as the most articulate, polished, and eloquent spokesman not only for his country but for all the Middle East producers, he did most of the talking in the councils of OPEC and interpreted OPEC to the outside world. Through his personality, tactics, strategies, and standards

we gain an appreciation and understanding of the Middle East oil drama. The petroleum ministers of the UAE and Kuwait have been his seconds in command.

27. The major sources for Chapter 9 were: U.S., Congress, Senate, Committee on Energy and Natural Resources, *Hearings: World Petroleum Outlook—1981* (Washington, D.C. 1981); U.S., Comptroller General, *Report to the Congress: Critical Factors Affecting Saudi Arabia's Oil Decisions* (Washington, D.C., 1978); British Petroleum, *Statistical Review of the World Oil Industry 1978.*

10

POSSIBLE SOLUTIONS

The Western world has been experiencing an energy—in reality a Middle East oil—crisis since October 1973, with ups and downs, a very acute and prolonged down beginning in 1981. This persistent crisis has wrought deep changes in the economic and financial patterns of Europe, the United States, and Japan. It has affected economic and even political relations among Western countries, and as the Middle East played an important role in the superpowers' global strategic struggle, with the outbreak of the energy crisis the struggle intensified. As a result of developments following the 1973 crisis, the position of the oil-producing countries vis-à-vis the West radically changed. During this period, the Middle East producers took over the petroleum industry—from production through marketing—from the foreign companies. They eliminated the concessionaire companies and all their power and influence; they, and they alone, determined prices; they acquired the power to control and even to stop supplies completely. Oil consumers, willy-nilly, had to transfer a goodly portion of their wealth to oil producers; oil prices were more than twenty times what they had been before October 1973. These radical changes brought in their wake economic and financial consequences: deficits in the balances of payments, devaluation of currencies, a drop in economic growth, an increase in unemployment and inflation. In spite of the devices of recycling, which had no doubt greatly eased the impact, in 1985 the Western economies are still ailing.

From the very beginning it was obvious that a two-phase solution would have to be found to the energy crisis: a long-

213

range solution to guarantee energy supplies for the future, and a short-range solution to meet the current very urgent energy needs. Because oil is, by any definition, an exhaustible resource, and as the rate of consumption was constantly rising, it was clear that one day output would reach its peak and thereafter would begin to decline rapidly. If exact figures on the availability of oil resources and the rate of consumption were established, the approximate date of the peak and the subsequent decline could be predicted with some degree of accuracy. However, there is no valid assessment of how much oil will be available, say, in the year 2000. Some determinants are unknown, and a number of others are overlaid with variables that make accurate evaluation very hazardous. Any prediction would, therefore, be speculative.

The first question pertains to the extent of oil reserves. Do we have definite geological information as to the quantities of oil to be found in our globe? We more or less know the extent of the reserves—regardless of the definition of reserves (published proven, possible, or probable)—in the areas where oil is being produced today. But are these all the major available resources? On this issue specialists have been sharply divided. One school has maintained that all the possible major oil fields have already been discovered. The finds of the last thirty years have been so small they they could not possibly change the general picture and could not fill shortages to be expected in the not-too-distant future. Compared to the great Texas and Saudi Arabian fields, the oil resources of both Alaska and the North Sea are minor. Hence, among the experts of this school there are some who predicted that the crucial year is 1985; others moved the date to 1995; and the more optimistic have put the date as 2005. Another group, small in number, has maintained that only a small area of our globe has so far been explored for oil, and the greater portion of it is yet to be explored. With proper development and adequate financing, new discoveries could expand reserves immensely and enlarge output for many years. The main concern should not be supplies, but exploration—both onshore and offshore. This group has assured us that there is a plentiful supply of oil waiting to be found. It sees no cause for anxiety and no need for alternatives.

In the various studies and projections of the majority there are a number of factors that would invalidate their conclusions. The first is the rate of oil consumption in relation to economic activity. As was mentioned in Chapter 9, the old assumption of a one-to-one ratio between oil consumption and economic growth had proven wrong during the crisis period. Hence the projections of all the different studies, most of which had three scenarios each, have already been invalidated. It is possible, through the widening process of conservation, that the ratio of consumption to economic activity might even become negative. Another factor involves technological advances, made since 1974, affecting the percentage of a well that can be exploited. Before the 1973 crisis the normal amount of oil that could be pumped from a well was up to 30 percent. If the crude yield could be raised to 60 percent of contents, then total reserves would be doubled. In addition, conservation is a much larger factor in consumption projections than has been assigned to it in all the different studies.

Nevertheless, even with all these reservations and limitations, whether the crunch comes in 1988 or in 1995 or even 2015, it would still seem to be a matter of the highest priority that the Western consuming nations plan intensively and with great urgency to activate the production of alternatives to oil. It should be emphasized that there is no one single miracle alternative that when activated could solve the energy problem. A group of different energy sources would have to be brought into operation simultaneously and in a very coordinated fashion by all the major consuming nations. These would include: atomic, coal (both solid and gaseous), shale, geothermy, heavy oils and oil sands, solar, biomat, wind, and ocean energy sources. To prevent a further deterioration of the Western economic structure, oil alternatives would have to be activated not only for the long-range solution of the energy supply problem, but also for the short-range objective of relieving the total dependence of the oil consumers in both price and supply on (and thus, vulnerability to political pressure from) the Middle East producers. But the three major consumer groups (the United States, Western Europe, and Japan) have not yet taken the combined necessary steps to activate the available alternatives and search for new ones.

Right after the outbreak of the crisis late in 1973 and early in 1974, the United States announced Project Independence, which aimed to make the United States practically independent of Middle East oil. In view of U.S. resources in technology, finance, manpower, and know-how, this aim could have been realized within a reasonable number of years. But calmer consideration showed that the activation of alternative energy would be exorbitantly costly compared even to the high prices of oil resources. Without the full and wholehearted cooperation and participation of all the other consuming groups, the result would be a united front of the Middle East producers and the other Western consumers against the United States. The various inhibitions—economic, financial, and political—of the consuming countries to come to grips with the long-range solution of the energy problem have been discussed in the preceding chapters. These inhibitions still appeared to prevail in 1985.

Now to the short-range solutions. Early in the crisis period in about 1975, a number of threats were made by the United States of a military invasion of the Middle East oil fields—should the conditions resulting from either the high prices or from a cutoff of supplies cause "economic strangulations" (Kissinger's phrase)—in order to insure the flow of the oil at reasonable prices.[1] These threats, which were first made by Secretary of State Kissinger and by President Gerald Ford, were very general and did not specify ways or means of executing the possible invasion, nor did they propose methods of activating the oil industry after such an invasion. But commentators and scholars attempted to fill in the many and varied particulars and tried to persuade world public opinion that a military invasion was a practical possibility. It seemed clear that those who sent up the trial balloons of an invasion were aware of the insuperable political and technical difficulties involved in executing such an undertaking and would, therefore, never trouble to go into operational details.

Perhaps, although not certainly, from a purely theoretical and technical point of view such an invasion might have been possible, but it is improbable that the complex Middle East oil industry—with its many branches and phases, from production to marketing—could have been activated afterward in a hostile environment. Moreover, the very idea of a military invasion does not seem feasible in view of the relations between the United States and Western Europe. The sad and bitter experience of the United States with the airlift in the October 1973 war indicates the magnitude of the problem. From a realistic point of view, only the United States could think seriously—merely in terms of resources and logistics—of an invasion scheme, and it would be inconceivable to assume that it would undertake such a project considering the prevailing relations.

In spite of all the gloomy predictions that U.S. policymakers made about the ever-growing dependence of the United States on Middle East oil, the fact remained that in case of an emergency the United States could manage without Middle East oil. It does not seem plausible that the United States would go out of its way thousands of miles to the Gulf to invade the oil fields there in order to save Western Europe and Japan from economic strangulation, when these very countries refused to be saved. Such an invasion would cost hundreds of billions of dollars, which would make oil produced under such circumstances more expensive than possible energy alternatives. Moreover, it is unthinkable that the Soviet Union would stand on the sidelines and allow the United States, its rival superpower, to do as it pleased in one of the most important global strategic regions, in which the Soviets were also struggling to gain a degree of control. An attempt to invade the Middle East oil fields would have been an open invitation to World War III.[2] The conclusion must be drawn that the threat of a military confrontation between the oil-consuming countries (in fact, only the United States) and the oil-producing countries was more a psychological tactic than a practical possibility. For all intents and purposes, it was a complete fiasco.

To achieve a practical short-range solution, logic would dictate that both producers and consumers come to some understanding and workable arrangement in stabilizing prices and supplies in a contest—not confrontation—between the two economic blocs, both of which have at their command important economic assets. The producers have the oil supplies that the consumers need and want, but the consumers—all three groups—also possess tremendous resources that the producers need and want, resources not less powerful than the oil of the producers. Only the consumers have the technology that the producers desperately desire; they furnish the various and multifarious products, from ordinary everyday items to heavy industry and most sophisticated armaments; they provide the expanding markets for the producers' oil, crude and refined, they are capable of absorbing the money surpluses of the producers in good and safe investments; and they provide for the producers the international complex of financial institutions. The economic and financial structures of the producers as well as their economic development programs are based on their relations with the consuming countries. The consumers, especially the United States, possess all the resources—technical, managerial, and financial—to develop and activate alternatives to oil.[3]

But, over the crisis years, the consuming countries have not entered the contest with the producers because they were split and hopelessly divided into groups of conflicting interests and objectives; they were powerless to take measures that could bring some sense of balance to the situation. The producers, in contrast, and in spite of the various groupings and divisions among them, have nevertheless been able to survive as a united body. Despite the many crises, especially the most severe last one in 1981, the producers have achieved wonders since 1973. The real strength of the producers' unity was never contested by the consuming countries.

Throughout the crisis years, one school of thought among Western conservative economists, especially in the United States, and commentators and analysts advocated that nothing be done about the energy crisis. Purely economic determinants[4] would straighten out the temporary maladjustments that the excesses of the producers caused to the Western economies. These observers pointed to the 1975 drop in demand, the 1978 reduction in consumption, and the third crisis, which practically deprived the Middle East producers of their power. As far as this school of thought is concerned, the energy crisis is over, normalcy has returned, and its proponents have been vindicated. But should the most recent crisis, which has now lasted almost four years, prove to be as passing an interlude as the short crises for the consumers that occurred in 1975 and 1978, then the latest relaxation that has overtaken the consumers, lulling them into a false sense of security, could turn into a consumers' disaster. Should prosperity return and oil consumption increase, the glut would soon turn into a shortage, and the West would have learned nothing. A fourth crisis would be worse than the second, as the second was worse than the first. This, in a sense, is the hope of the producers, as Yamani expressed it—a return to 1973 and 1979.

On the other hand, if the conservation regimen that has emerged in the last seven years, since 1978, should become a permanent aspect of Western life (and in time the process could widen and deepen), consumption—even with intensified economic activity—would continue to decline, and the power of the oil producers would be weakened. It would take a number of years for the complex symbiotic relationship between the producers' and consumers' economies to become disentangled, a process that would be very painful and costly to both. To guarantee a secure supply of energy resources, the consumers would have to continue more vigorously and determinedly with the development and activation of alternatives to oil.[5]

NOTES

1. *Business Week,* January 13, 1975; *Middle East Economic Survey* (*MEES*), January 10, 1975.

2. The French foreign minister, Jean Sanvagnargues, stated on January 19, 1975, in an interview in *Le Monde,* that even if U.S. military intervention in the Middle East was possible from a military point of view, "it would be difficult to conceive of it politically, since the consequences would be extremely grave." Drew Middleton of the *New York Times* reported on January 12, 1975, that senior U.S. and Western European military officers considered the seizure of selected Middle East oil fields militarily possible but politically disastrous.

3. The U.S. Comptroller General, in his *Report to the Congress: More Attention Should Be Paid to Making the United States Less Vulnerable to Foreign Oil Price and Supply Decisions* (Washington,

D.C., January 3, 1978), listed as U.S. strengths, "This is the home country of five of the seven multinational major oil companies, which provide much of the expertise integral to the production, transportation, refining, and marketing of crude oil from OPEC countries.

"The U.S. market for foreign oil represents about 20 percent of OPEC exports—already large enough to be important to OPEC countries' sales. The U.S. is a leading innovator and supplier of high technology and managerial know-how. It offers large and secure opportunities for capital investments. It occupies a leading, often commanding position in the international flow of loans, loan guarantees, and it has the capability to offer security to other nations."

4. U.S., Congress, House, Committee on Interstate and Foreign Commerce, *Report: Energy Conservation and Conversion Oil Policy Act of 1975* (Washington, D.C., 1975), stated: "Neither the world nor our domestic market is free! The market price is not a function of consumer bargaining but a matter of agreement among the OPEC nations. The four-fold increase in crude oil prices experienced in the last two years should serve as a stark witness to the absence of a 'free' market."

5. The following are selected works dealing with some of the issues in Chapter 10:

Desprairies, Pierre. *La Crise de l'energie: le mal, le remède.* Paris, 1982.
Energy Policy Project of the Ford Foundation. *Energy: The Next Twenty Years.* New York, 1979.
Ion, D. C. *Availability of World Energy Resources.* London, 1976.
Jordan, Amos A.; Haydan Bryan; and Michael Moodil. *Facing the International Energy Problem 1980–2000.* New York, 1980.
Odell, Peter. *Oil and World Power.* London, 1981.
Odell, Peter, and Kenneth E. Rosing. *The Future of Oil.* London, 1980.
Odell, Peter, and Luis Vallenilla. *The Pressures of Oil.* London, 1978.
O'Neill, Bard. *Petroleum and Security: The Limitations of Military Power in the Persian Gulf.* Springfield, 1978.
Rowan, Henry, et al. *Options for U.S. Energy Policy.* San Francisco, 1978.
Veziroglu, Nejat, ed. *Miami International Conference on Alternative Energy Sources.* Coral Gables, Fla., 1977.

Workshop on Alternative Energy Strategies. *Energy: Global Prospects 1985-2000*, Massachusetts Institute of Technology Study. New York, 1977.
World Energy: Looking Ahead to 2000. Guilford, Surrey, 1978.
Yergin, Daniel, and Martin Hillenbrand, eds. *Global Insecurity: A Strategy for Energy and Economic Renewal*. New York, 1982.

11

EPILOGUE—DEVELOPMENTS BETWEEN JULY 1985 AND MARCH 1986

After the Geneva OPEC conference (July 22–25, 1985) the world oil situation continued to deteriorate, Saudi Arabia being especially hard-hit when the decline in demand caused oil production to drop in August to about 2 million barrels a day. Although all OPEC members suffered from the drop in the demand for oil,[1] the impact on Saudi Arabia—if only because of the huge dimensions of previous Saudi production and the accordingly enormous revenue—was most severe. Officially, OPEC refused to reduce prices and attempted to maintain the overall production ceiling; Saudi Arabia was forced to reduce its production to a level that it considered unacceptable. In order to meet its budgetary requirements, it was forced to draw upon its financial reserves at the rate of $20 billion a year. Many of its economic development projects were curtailed, and the country experienced a very large deficit in its balance of payments.

King Fahd, Oil Minister Yamani, and other Saudi spokesmen asserted that their country would not tolerate the cheating that other members of OPEC carried on at Saudi Arabia's expense and threatened to resort to the same devices. The OPEC conferences—both regular and extraordinary—were practically paralyzed because members could not agree on either price or production levels. As demand continued to drop, most OPEC

222

members as well as the non-OPEC producers[2] began to use the
spot market price in determining their prices.
What was the full impact of the oil crisis on Saudi Arabia?
In August 1985 the British National Westminster Bank predicted
that Saudi Arabia's 1985 balance of payments deficit would be
among the largest in the world, second only to the United
States. This forecast was based on the assessed oil revenue of
less than $30 billion and investment income of $8 billion. It
suggested that Saudi Arabia's total financial reserves had been
run down to only $100 billion from the 1980–1981 peak of
$150 billion. The implication of the balance of payments deficit,
according to the bank, was that Saudi Arabia would have to
reduce further its foreign assets, repatriate foreign loans, and
restrict imports, all of which would lead to a drop in the gross
national product and to higher inflation.

The Saudi Ministry of Finance and National Economy, to
be sure, refuted the bank's forecast. On September 22, addressing
the University of Umm al-Qura in Mecca, King Fahd denied
the validity of the forecast and added, "By the way, when the
bank was questioned it was discovered that the report was
compiled by a worthless member of the bank's staff and was
summarily dismissed and the matter was closed."[3] The fact that
Saudi Arabia adopted drastic measures to safeguard its economy
right after the bank's forecast raises questions about Saudi
Arabia's denials.

The issues of both price and production levels were becoming
more acute as the extraordinary conference planned for October
3 approached. As mentioned previously, Saudi Arabia functioned
as the swing producer in OPEC and did not have a production
quota. However, at the October 1984 conference, Saudi Arabia
formally abandoned its role as swing producer and opted for
a quota of 4.35 million barrels a day.[4] This created a new crisis,
for not one of the members would reduce its quota to accom-
modate Saudi Arabia. The immediate crisis was averted as Saudi
Arabia continued as swing producer. However, in September
1985 Saudi Arabia increased production to fulfill the quota it
had claimed.

Another issue involved the netback technique, which was a
new addition to the long list of cheating devices. Because

OPEC's control of price and production levels was limited to crude oil, Saudi Arabia negotiated, first with major oil companies in the United States, later with companies in Europe, and ultimately even with companies in the Far East, to arrange netback price deals. The netback price was calculated for specific markets by taking the spot market realization from product sales (based on an agreed refining yield) and subtracting refining expenses and crude freight and insurance costs incurred at the port of loading. The netback of Arabian light was, at the time, $2 to 3 below the official OPEC price. The entire structure of regulated prices and production was steadily breaking down.[5]

VIENNA: EXTRAORDINARY CONFERENCE OF OCTOBER 3–4, 1985

It was in this tense atmosphere that the extraordinary conference opened, and the two major issues were still production quotas and price structure. Iran and Iraq were virtually under-quota producers because the Iran-Iraq War had damaged their loading and transportation facilities, limiting their production capacities. Nevertheless, after Saudi Arabia granted Iraq the right to share Saudi pipeline and terminal facilities, Iraq demanded a 500,000 barrels-a-day increase in its quota. Whereupon Iran immediately threatened to request double the amount requested by Iraq. The Iranian oil minister, Mohamed Gharazi, insisted that the additional 1.5 million barrels that the two quota increases constituted be subtracted from the quotas of Saudi Arabia and Kuwait because these countries had aided Iraq in the war.

The conference ended without the adoption of any decisions on either price structures or production quotas. The attending countries agreed only to maintain the overall production ceiling of 16 million barrels a day. The members, according to the conference president, Dr. Subroto of Indonesia, discussed the netback issue and decided to consult with each other bilaterally and multilaterally prior to a full discussion of the issue at the next meeting in December. The October 7 issue of *Middle East Economic Survey* (*MEES*) concluded that the conference was a failure. OPEC held two cards, price and production; the price card disappeared "under the impact of the demise of the official price system," and the production card was about to be lost.

As tension in OPEC was rising, demand for oil was declining, and members resorted to a variety of devices to bypass the production quotas and the official prices. The United Arab Emirates (UAE) minister of oil, Mana Said al-Otaiba, appeared on Abu Dhabi television on October 31, 1985, and declared: "Since the last OPEC meeting (in Vienna on 3–4 October) every producing country, whether OPEC or non-OPEC, has had complete freedom in setting whatever price it sees fit for its oil. We are thus relieved of those obligations which at the same time benefited the non-OPEC producers who pushed their output to the maximum by selling at market related prices." He concluded by proclaiming: "As of now each producer is free to produce his quota and sell it at whatever price he can get in the market. We have only one remaining obligation which is the question of production and determining quotas."[6] This assertion by al-Otaiba that OPEC's role as price regulator had been eliminated caused strong reaction from various quarters. On November 3, al-Otaiba was interviewed by *Emirates News,* and he reiterated what he had stated on television.

The big issue was the production level; the real villains, according to OPEC spokesmen, were the non-OPEC producers. The only way to stabilize oil prices was for the non-OPEC producers to join OPEC. The only alternative to joint action by OPEC and non-OPEC producers was a ruinous price war. Joint action would involve a just distribution of production quotas "in light of market circumstances and without discrimination among producers, whether they are OPEC or non-OPEC."[7]

The theme of a stock drawdown conspiracy among oil-consuming countries was dropped, and all OPEC spokesmen saw the answer to the current crisis in the joining of the non-OPEC producers with OPEC to convert the organization into a world oil cartel. Speaking on October 14, 1985, at a conference in Rimini, Italy, OPEC President Dr. Subroto pointed out that non-OPEC output had risen from 14.4 million barrels a day to 22.6 million barrels a day, which was one and one-half times the OPEC production level. He very strongly urged the non-OPEC producers to join OPEC for the benefit of all concerned. In a television interview in London in mid-July, the Kuwait oil minister, Ali Khalifah al-Sabah, admitted that OPEC was experiencing very serious difficulties but said he felt that there still was an opportunity to gain control over prices if the non-OPEC producers joined OPEC. He warned that if OPEC should lose control "prices will drop dramatically."[8] He urged the non-OPEC producers to join the organization for their own sake.

After Saudi Arabia claimed its quota of 4.35 million barrels a day, the big question was how to dispose of such a huge additional quantity in the already glutted market. Even before the October 3–4 conference in Vienna, Saudi Arabia's oil minister had declared at the end of September that it was clear that OPEC members could not sell 16 million barrels of crude oil a day at the official prices. All the other countries had boosted sales by offering discounts of one kind or another; Saudi Arabia had at last decided to follow suit.

At the Oxford Energy Seminar session on September 14, 1985, the Saudi oil minister stated: "If non-OPEC producers do not cooperate with OPEC in stabilizing the market and we in the Organization do not discipline ourselves, then I expect there will be a price war, and under that assumption alone I would expect the price would drop to a level between \$15/B and \$18/B after the winter."[9] In an interview with the *International Herald Tribune* on November 8, 1985, Yamani said that oil prices could temporarily drop below \$20 a barrel. This was a warning to both OPEC and non-OPEC producers. He cautioned that a price war could be avoided if the non-OPEC producers cooperated with OPEC, but he noted that the non-OPEC producers did not seem to be ready for such cooperation.

All OPEC spokesmen realized that the organization's efforts to stabilize prices through self-discipline among the members had failed and that the only other way to stabilize prices was by using the threat of a price war to coerce the non-OPEC producers, including the United States and the Soviet Union, into joining OPEC which would lead to regulation of the world oil industry. But the non-OPEC producers refused to be intimidated. On July 16, 1985, Britain's energy minister, A. Buchanon-

Smith, told the House of Commons that the government ruled out any possibility of production cutback by the United Kingdom to help OPEC stabilize prices in the world oil market. On October 25, 1985, U.S. Secretary of Energy John Herrington met with OPEC President Dr. Subroto to discuss OPEC's suggestion that the non-OPEC producers cooperate in stabilizing oil prices. Herrington dismissed the possibility of a dialogue between the United States and OPEC, saying: "I think when you agree to a world-wide price it is not good economics."[10]

As the December 7, 1985, conference was approaching, the oil price structure was rapidly crumbling. Venezuela proposed that crude prices be tied to a "basket" of chosen crudes and products. It also proposed that production ceilings and quotas be flexible to adjust to seasonal changes in demand.

GENEVA: DECEMBER 7–9, 1985, CONFERENCE

When the conference opened, it became clear that not one of the thirteen members was willing to reduce production. Defiantly, the oil ministers of Iraq and Nigeria declared that their countries planned to produce as much oil as they could sell. Eleven out of the thirteen members were producing more than their official quotas. The Saudi Arabian oil minister repeated his prediction that oil prices could fall below $20 a barrel during the next year unless OPEC and non-OPEC producers cooperated in limiting oil supplies. OPEC could no longer stabilize the oil market by itself.

The conference was as paralyzed as the previous four 1985 conferences. It did, however, decide "to secure and defend for OPEC a fair share of the world oil market consistent with the necessary income for member countries' development." For this purpose, a committee headed by the new president, Arturo Hernandez Grisanti of Venezuela and including Indonesia, Iraq, Kuwait, and the UAE was named "to examine the ways and means to achieve this objective and recommend to the conference the course of action to be taken in this respect."[11] *MEES* noted optimistically that this decision marked a momentous turning point in the history of the oil industry. OPEC had decided to break out of its straitjacket role as the residual supplier (swing producer) for the world oil and energy market. Defense of a minimum market share would, for the time being at least, take precedence over price maintenance as the primary objective of the member countries. Only prices competitive with the non-OPEC producers' prices would guarantee OPEC's market share.

Yamani stressed the fact that although OPEC had not yet defined its "fair share" of the oil market, it would have to be "well above 16 mnb/d." He warned that in the event of a price collapse, OPEC output might reach 20 million barrels a day or even higher[12] and that only a cooperative arrangement between OPEC and non-OPEC producers could prevent a price collapse. He singled out Great Britain as the "number one" candidate for cooperation with OPEC in this connection. If the price and market situations deteriorate, he said, "we are heading towards something unknown. So anything can happen."[13] OPEC's decision to abandon the price issue, combined with the threat of a price war, caused oil prices to drop throughout the world.

It would seem that the world reacted rather calmly to this development. To properly assess the situation I should note a statement made by Saudi Oil Minister Ahmad Zaki Yamani on June 1, 1985: "The Kingdom has the economic power in the world oil market to exercise a near monopoly. We are blessed with the largest reserves in the world, the lowest production costs and a high production capacity." If Saudi Arabia would reduce the price and increase production, "many oil producing countries, both OPEC and non-OPEC, would exit from the world oil market. Many banks which are involved in large loans to the oil producing countries would collapse. It would thus shake the world economy, not only in the oil market, but also in the financial markets. The countries of the world are financially and economically interdependent, and any such rupture would lead to a major depression."[14]

The other OPEC leaders, Ali Khalifah al-Sabah of Kuwait, Mana Said al-Otaiba of the UAE, and OPEC President Dr. Subroto of Indonesia, concentrated their attacks on the non-OPEC producers and predicted disaster should the non-OPEC producers refuse to cooperate with OPEC in stabilizing prices by cutting production.

As, on the one hand, Saudi Arabia substantially increased its oil production and export rate to almost 5 million barrels a day, and on the other hand Britain and the other non-OPEC producers continued with their production, the battle between OPEC and non-OPEC producers was inevitably drawn.

The Saudi threat of a price war with all its grim consequences was primarily aimed at Britain. The British accepted the challenge stoically. Only a few days after the Geneva conference, on December 12 Nigel Lawson, chancellor of the exchequer, presented the British government position to the House of Commons. He acknowledged that a decline in oil revenue might affect planned tax cuts in the following year's budget but stressed that, short of an oil price collapse, there was "no threat to the British economy." He said, "Even now, at its peak, oil accounts for only 6% of GDP, and we are a substantial oil consumer as well as a substantial producer. What we stand to lose on the swings we stand to gain at the roundabouts." He categorically declared: "There is no way in which the United Kingdom will become a country member of OPEC."[15] On the following day, *The Times* (London) carried the headline "Why the Oil Slide Need not be Bad for Britain"; the newspaper took the same position as the chancellor of the exchequer.

On January 26, 1986, Prime Minister Margaret Thatcher appeared on the BBC television program "Face the Press." She pointed out that it was quite absurd to equate the United Kingdom with countries that are entirely dependent on their oil revenue: What Britain lost as a producer of oil it would regain as an oil consumer. When the prime minister was asked whether the government would take action to regulate production, she replied that production rate decisions were primarily in the hands of the companies that have concessions to operate the oil fields. The government would not interfere.[16] Two days later the prime minister was asked in the House of Commons whether the government, in view of the drastic drop in oil prices, would help stabilize prices by cutting production. She replied: "No, I do not think so."[17]

The *New York Times* of December 10 urged the United States not to squander the opportunity offered by OPEC's loss. The price fall "would be just deserts for a greedy cartel as well as a striking lesson in the capacity of the industrialized world to resist economic strangulation." Five days later the newspaper, reporting that "Saudi Arabia and its followers" had threatened the non-OPEC producers with either joining OPEC or preparing for a price war, noted: "The British have neither panicked nor knuckled under." After detailing developments since the December 7 Geneva conference, the newspaper summarized: "OPEC threatened a price war, saying it would abandon attempts to control prices in favor of maintaining a fixed share of world oil markets. Calls to other countries to cut production were rebuffed, and some analysts doubted whether OPEC was strong enough to wage an all out price war. Oil prices plummeted in hectic trading after OPEC's announcement, but stabilized as traders calmed."

The United States, although a major oil producer (the second in the world after the Soviet Union, which would be deeply affected by heavy reductions in the price of oil), had readily accepted the prospects with a sigh of relief. On January 11, 1986, President Ronald Reagan declared in a radio broadcast that U.S. economic measures had "shaken up oil prices and brought OPEC to its knees."[18]

The Saudi Arabian maneuvers within OPEC to increase Saudi oil production and threaten the non-OPEC producers with a price war resulted in a continuous, rapid drop in oil prices that negatively affected the smaller OPEC producers. The situation became a vicious circle. The more the price fell the more production had to be increased in order to obtain the minimum revenue; the more production increased the greater the glut in the market became; and the greater the glut in the market became, the lower the price fell. Thus, the radical members of OPEC saw in Saudi Arabia the cause of their difficulties. They therefore opposed both Saudi Arabia's production increase and its policy based on the threat of a price war, which Saudi Arabia openly avowed was aimed at the OPEC cheaters as well.

By the end of January 1986, Iran, Libya, and Algeria had publicly dissociated themselves from the official OPEC policy of securing and defending a fair share of the world oil market. Instead they advocated production cuts by the OPEC members to steady the market.[19]

Meanwhile oil prices continued to fall in the Middle East, Europe, the Far East, and the United States, reaching early in March about $12 a barrel. The two antagonists, Saudi Arabia and Britain, made no changes in their public positions. However, while Britain continued with its production policy, Saudi Arabia, in spite of its threats, did not proceed with the price war. Instead, Saudi Arabia seems to have adjusted to the lowered prices by resorting to various methods of disposing of ever-greater quantities of oil.

The oil-consuming world has accepted the price reduction as a most welcome development, one that will reestablish a sane balance in international economic and financial orders that were seriously and dangerously disrupted by the reckless OPEC oil price hikes of the last thirteen years. As a result of the heavy drops in oil prices, some countries, especially oil producers, will experience or already are experiencing great economic and financial hardships. Others will be forced to make hard and very painful adjustments. But the overall result will be beneficial to all countries, both producers and consumers. Indeed, for the first time, oil prices are, and one would hope will continue to be, determined by economic forces.[20]

NOTES

1. In September 1985 it was reported that OPEC's share in the world's total petroleum production, including natural gas liquids and products, during the first half of 1985 amounted to 29 percent, a drop from 33 percent in 1984 and the smallest share since 1960. *Petroleum Economist,* September 1985, p. 322.

2. In April 1985, the two North Sea producers, Britain and Norway, switched over to market-related prices. *Middle East Economic Survey* (*MEES*) commented: "Britain and Norway have served notice, once and for all, that they have no intention—either now or in the future— of moderating their dedication to the full maximization of oil output

or cooperating in any way, with OPEC for the defense of price levels."
MEES, April 22, 1985.

3. *MEES*, September 30, 1985.

4. After the July 5–7, 1985, Vienna conference, Yamani stated at a press conference: "I made it clear to the Vienna meeting that Saudi Arabia is no longer swing producer. We did act as swing producer after the London agreement of March 1983, when the Kingdom was not allocated any fixed quota. But since the November 1984 decision we have had a fixed quota and are, therefore, no longer the swing producer. In line with this decision the Saudi quota is 4.3 mnb/d." *MEES*, July 15, 1985.

5. The *Petroleum Economist* (July 1985, p. 258) explained: "As oil products do not come under the jurisdiction of OPEC price controls, the move into downstream markets effectively gives Saudi Arabia the opportunity to evade official prices, and to dispose of volumes of oil which it could not sell in unprocessed form in the currently glutted market."

Between October and November of 1985, Saudi Arabia contracted netback deals with various companies totaling 1.27 mnb/d. In January 1986, *MEES* reported that Saudi Arabia's target output for netback deals was 3 mnb/d: 2 mnb/d for Western destinations and one mnb/d for Far Eastern markets. *MEES*, October 28, 1985; *MEES*, November 1985; *MEES*, January 27, 1986.

6. *MEES*, November 4, 1985.

7. *MEES*, November 11, 1985.

8. *MEES*, July 22, 1985.

9. *MEES*, September 23, 1985.

10. *MEES*, November 4, 1985.

11. From the official OPEC communiqué in *MEES*, December 16, 1985.

12. In an interview in the Kuwaiti *Al-Anba* on December 12, 1985, Ali Khalifah al-Sabah, Kuwait oil minister, stated that the OPEC market share to be defended should be no less than the previous 16 mnb/d and could be as much as 18 mnb/d." The Nigerian oil minister, Tam David-West, said on Nigerian television on December 16 that the figure was 18–20 mnb/d. *MEES*, December 23/30, 1985.

13. *MEES*, December 16, 1985.

14. *MEES*, June 3, 1985.

15. *MEES*, December 16, 1985; *MEES*, December 23/30, 1985.

16. *MEES*, February 3, 1986.

17. Ibid.

18. *MEES*, January 20, 1986.

19. *MEES*, February 3, 1986. Late in February, Iranian Oil Minister Gholamreza Aqazadeh traveled through the Gulf countries to persuade them to adopt the policy of cutting production. While in Abu Dhabi, he claimed that his plan for drastic cuts in production by OPEC was supported by other members in addition to Algeria and Libya.

20. Assessing the impact of the rapid development in OPEC, Barnaby J. Feder, in the *New York Times* of December 12, 1985, observed: "The lost revenues would accelerate a trend strongly felt in international financial circles—the declining importance of OPEC's overseas investment. The always exaggerated vision of Middle Eastern oil sheiks buying up huge chunks of the United States and Europe, not to mention influencing United States foreign policy, has faded. Indeed, in the last three years, OPEC nations have used almost $23 billion of their treasure to cover trade deficits."

SELECTED BIBLIOGRAPHY

This bibliography is highly selective and concentrates on U.S. congressional investigation publications and other official U.S. works. No articles are listed. A full list of publications up to 1973 can be found in *Middle East Oil and the Great Powers* (Westview Encore Edition, 1985), pp. 551–604. At the end of Chapter 10 of this book is a list of books dealing with the overall issue of the oil problem.

Abolfathi, Farid, et al. *The OPEC Market to 1985*. Lexington, Mass.: D. C. Heath & Co., 1977.

Al-Chalabi, Fadhil J. *OPEC and the International Oil Industry: A Changing Structure*. London: Oxford University Press, 1980.

Alexander, Sidney. *Paying For Energy*. New York: McGraw-Hill Co., 1975.

Al-Farsy, Fouad. *Saudi Arabia: A Case Study in Development*. London: Kegan Paul International, 1982.

Anthony, John Duke, ed. *The Middle East: Oil Politics and Development*. Washington, D.C.: American Enterprise Institute for Public Research, 1975.

Badger, Daniel, and Robert Belgrave. *Oil Supply and Price: What Went Right in 1980's*. London: Policy Studies Institute, 1982.

Ben Shahar, Haim. *Oil: Prices and Capital*. Lexington, Mass.: D. C. Heath & Co., 1976.

Blair, John M. *The Control of Oil*. New York: Pantheon Books, 1976.

Bohi, Douglas R., and W. David Montgomery. *Oil Prices, Energy Security and Import Policy*. Baltimore: Resources for the Future, Johns Hopkins University Press, 1982.

Bohi, Douglas, R., and Milton Russel. *U.S. Energy Policy: Alternatives for Security.* Baltimore: Johns Hopkins University Press, 1975.

Conant, Melvin A. *The Oil Factor in U.S. Foreign Policy 1980–1990.* Lexington, Mass.: D. C. Heath & Co., 1982.

Danielson, Albert L. *The Evolution of OPEC.* New York: Harcourt Brace Jovanovich, 1982.

Desprairies, Pierre. *Short and Long Terms Prospects for the Energy Market.* Surrey: Surrey Energy Economics Centre, 1983.

Kelly, J. B. *Arabia, the Gulf and the West.* New York: Praeger, 1980.

Klinghoffer, Arthur Jay. *The Soviet Union and International Oil Politics.* New York: Columbia University Press, 1977.

Krämer, Hans R. *Die Europäische Gemeinschaft und Die Ölkrise.* Baden Baden: Nomus Verlagsgesellschaft, 1974.

Manfold, Peter. *Superpower Intervention in the Middle East.* London: Croom Helm, 1978.

Maull, H. *Oil and Influence: The Oil Weapon Examined.* London: International Institute for Strategic Studies, 1975.

Mendershausen, Horst. *Coping with the Oil Crisis: French and German Experiences.* Baltimore: Resources for the Future, Johns Hopkins University Press, 1976.

Mossavar-Rahmani, Bijan, and Fereidun Fesharaki. *OPEC and World Oil Outlook.* London: Economist Intelligence Unit, 1983.

Paust, Jordan J., and Albert P. Blaustein. *The Arab Oil Weapon.* Dobbs Ferry, N.Y.: Oceana Publishers, 1977.

Pearce, Joan, ed. *The Third Oil Shock: The Effect of Lower Prices.* Henley-on-Thames: Routledge & Kegan Paul, 1983.

Seymour, Ian. *OPEC: Instrument of Change.* London: Macmillan Press, 1980.

Stobaugh, Robert, and Daniel Yergin. *Energy Future: Report of the Energy Project of the Harvard Business School.* New York: Random House, 1979.

Stone, Russel A. *OPEC and the Middle East.* New York: Praeger, 1978.

Turner, Louis. *Oil Companies in the International System.* London: George Allen & Unwin, 1978.

Udovitch, A. L., ed. *The Middle East: Oil, Conflict and Hope: Critical Choices for Americans.* Lexington, Mass.: D. C. Heath & Co., 1976.

United Nations Economic Commission for Western Asia. *Arab Energy Prospects to 2000.* New York: McGraw-Hill, 1982.

United States Central Intelligence Agency, National Foreign Assessment Center. *The World Oil Market in the Years Ahead.* Washington, D.C.: Government Printing Office, 1979.

U.S., Comptroller General, *Report to the Congress: Critical Factors Affecting Saudi Arabia's Oil Decisions.* Washington, D.C.: Government Printing Office, 1978.

————. *Report to the Congress: More Attention Should Be Paid to Making the United States Less Vulnerable to Foreign Oil Price and Supply Decisions.* Washington, D.C.: Government Printing Office, 1978.

————. *Report: The U.S.–Saudi Arabian Joint Commission on Economic Cooperation.* Washington, D.C.: Government Printing Office, 1979.

U.S., Congress, Congressional Budget Office. *The Effect of OPEC Oil Pricing on Output, Prices, and Exchange Rates in the United States and Other Industrialized Countries.* Washington, D.C.: Government Printing Office, 1981.

U.S., Congress, House, Committee on Foreign Affairs. *New Perspectives on the Persian Gulf.* Washington, D.C.: Government Printing Office, 1973.

U.S., Congress, House, Committee on Foreign Affairs, Staff. *The United States Oil Shortages and the Arab-Israeli Conflict: Report of a Study Mission to the Middle East from October 22 to November 3, 1973.* Washington, D.C.: Government Printing Office, 1973.

U.S., Congress, House, Committee on Foreign Affairs, Subcommittee on Foreign Economic Policy. *Hearings: Foreign Policy Implications of the Energy Crisis.* Washington, D.C.: Government Printing Office, 1973.

U.S., Congress, House, Committee on Foreign Affairs, Subcommittee on Foreign Economic Policy and Subcommittee on the Near East and South Asia. *Hearings: Oil Negotiations, OPEC, and the Stability of Supply.* Washington, D.C.: Government Printing Office, 1973.

U.S., Congress, House, Committee on Government Operations. *Hearings: Alternatives to Dealing with OPEC.* Washington, D.C.: Government Printing Office, 1979.

U.S., Congress, House, Committee on Interstate and Foreign Commerce. *Report: Energy Conservation and Conversion Oil Policy Act of 1975.* Washington, D.C.: Government Printing Office, 1975.

U.S., Congress, House, Committee on Interstate and Foreign Commerce, Subcommittee on Energy and Power. *A Study: Oil Imports, a Range of Policy Options.* Washington, D.C.: Government Printing Office, 1979.

U.S., Congress, House, Committee on Ways and Means. *Report: Energy Conservation Act of 1975.* Washington, D.C.: Government Printing Office, 1975.

U.S., Congress, Joint Economic Committee. *Hearings: The Economics of the President's Proposed Energy Policies.* Washington, D.C.: Government Printing Office, 1978.

U.S., Congress, Joint Economic Committee, Subcommittee on Energy. *Hearings: Creating Jobs Through Energy Policy.* Washington, D.C.: Government Printing Office, 1978.

_____. *Hearings: Energy Independence or Interdependence, The Agenda with OPEC.* Washington, D.C.: Government Printing Office, 1977.

_____. *A Strategy of Oil Proliferation: A Study.* Washington, D.C.: Government Printing Office, 1980.

U.S., Congress, Joint Economic Committee, Subcommittee on International Economics. *Hearings: Economic Impact of Petroleum Shortages.* Washington, D.C.: Government Printing Office, 1974.

_____. *Hearings: The International Monetary Situation and the Administration Oil Floor Price Proposal.* Washington, D.C.: Government Printing Office, 1975.

_____. *Report: The State Department's Oil Floor Price Proposal: Should Congress Endorse It?* Washington, D.C.: Government Printing Office, 1975.

U.S., Congress, Library, Congressional Legislative Reference Service. *The Arab Oil Embargo and the United States Shortages, October 1973 to March 1974.* Washington, D.C.: Government Printing Office, 1974.

U.S., Congress, Library, Congressional Research Service. *Congress and the Nation's Environment.* Washington, D.C.: Government Printing Office, 1975.

_____. *Oil Fields as Military Objectives: A Feasibility Study.* Washington, D.C.: Government Printing Office, 1975.

_____. *Project Independence: U.S. World Energy Outlook Through 1990.* Washington, D.C.: Government Printing Office, 1977.

U.S., Congress, Senate, Committee on Energy and Natural Resources. *Access to Oil: The United States Relationships with Saudi Arabia and Iran.* Washington, D.C.: Government Printing Office, 1977.

_____. *The Economic Impact of Oil Import Reduction.* Washington, D.C.: Government Printing Office, 1979.

_____. *The Geopolitics of Oil: Staff Report.* Washington, D.C.: Government Printing Office, 1980.

_____. *Hearings: Geopolitics of Oil,* Parts 1 and 2. Washington, D.C.: Government Printing Office, 1980.

_____. *Hearings: World Petroleum Outlook—1981.* Washington, D.C.: Government Printing Office, 1981.

U.S., Congress, Senate, Committee on Energy and Natural Resources, Subcommittee on Energy Conservation and Regulation. *Hearings: Crude Oil Pricing Amendments of 1977.* Washington, D.C.: Government Printing Office, 1977.

U.S., Congress, Senate, Committee on Finance. *World Oil Developments and U.S. Oil Import Policy.* Washington, D.C.: Government Printing Office, 1973.

U.S., Congress, Senate, Committee on Finance, Subcommittee on Energy. *Fiscal Policy and the Energy Crisis.* Washington, D.C.: Government Printing Office, 1973.

U.S., Congress, Senate, Committee on Finance, Subcommittee on International Finance and Resources. *The International Monetary Crisis.* Washington, D.C.: Government Printing Office, 1973.

U.S., Congress, Senate, Committee on Foreign Relations. *Data and Analysis Concerning the Possibility of a U.S. Food Embargo as a Response to the Present Arab Oil Boycott.* Washington, D.C.: Government Printing Office, 1973.

———. *The Middle East: A Report by Senator Charles H. Percy.* Washington, D.C.: Government Printing Office, 1975.

———. *The Middle East Between War and Peace, November–December 1973: A Staff Report.* Washington, D.C.: Government Printing Office, 1974.

———. *Saudi Arabia: A Report by Senator Mike Mansfield.* Washington, D.C.: Government Printing Office, 1975.

U.S., Congress, Senate, Committee on Foreign Relations, Subcommittee on International Economic Policy. *The Future of Saudi Arabian Oil Production: A Staff Report.* Washington, D.C.: Government Printing Office, 1979.

U.S., Congress, Senate, Committee on Foreign Relations, Subcommittee on Multinational Corporations. *Chronology of the Libyan Oil Negotiations 1970–1971.* Washington, D.C.: Government Printing Office, 1974.

———. *A Documentary History of the Petroleum Reserves Corporation 1943–1944.* Washington, D.C.: Government Printing Office, 1974.

———. *Hearings: Multinational Corporations and United States Foreign Policy.* Washington, D.C.: Government Printing Office, Parts 4, 5, 6, 7, 1974; Parts 8, 9, 1975.

———. *The International Petroleum Cartel: The Iranian Consortium and U.S. National Security.* Washington, D.C.: Government Printing Office, 1974.

――――. *Multinational Oil Corporations and U.S. Foreign Policy: Report Together with Individual Views.* Washington, D.C.: Government Printing Office, 1975.

――――. *U.S. Oil Companies and the Arab Oil Embargo: The International Allocation of Constrained Supplies.* Washington, D.C.: Government Printing Office, 1975.

U.S., Congress, Senate, Committee on Government Operations. *Petro-Politics and the American Energy Shortage: Report by Senator Abraham Ribicoff.* Washington, D.C.: Government Printing Office, 1979.

――――. *Preliminary Federal Trade Commission Staff Report on Its Investigation of the Petroleum Industry.* Washington, D.C.: Government Printing Office, 1973.

U.S., Congress, Senate, Committee on Government Operations, Permanent Subcommittee on Investigations. *Materials Shortages: Selected Readings on Energy Self-Sufficiency and the Controlled Materials Plans.* Washington, D.C.: Government Printing Office, 1974.

――――. *Staff Study of Oversight and Efficiency of Executive Agencies with Respect to the Petroleum Industry, Especially as It Relates to Recent Fuel Shortages.* Washington, D.C.: Government Printing Office, 1973.

U.S., Congress, Senate, Committee on Interior and Insular Affairs. *Consideration in the Formulation of Energy Policy.* Washington, D.C.: Government Printing Office, 1971.

――――. *Energy Policy Papers.* Washington, D.C.: Government Printing Office, 1974.

――――. *Highlights of Energy Legislation in the 94th Congress.* Washington, D.C.: Government Printing Office, 1975.

――――. *Implications of Recent Organization of Petroleum Exporting Countries (OPEC) Oil Price Increases.* Washington, D.C.: Government Printing Office, 1974.

U.S., Congress, Senate, Committee on the Judiciary, Subcommittee on Antitrust and Monopoly. *Competitive Aspects of Energy Industry.* Washington, D.C.: Government Printing Office, 1970.

――――. *Hearings: Government Intervention in the Market Mechanism.* Washington, D.C.: Government Printing Office, 1969.

U.S., Congress, Senate, Select Committee on Intelligence. *U.S. Intelligence Analysis of the Oil Issue.* Washington, D.C.: Government Printing Office, 1977.

U.S., Department of Energy. *Technical Analysis of the International Oil Market.* Washington, D.C.: Government Printing Office, 1978.

U.S., Department of Energy, Energy Information Administration. *Analysis Memorandum: Petroleum Supply Vulnerability, 1985.* Washington, D.C.: Government Printing Office, 1979.

U.S., Federal Energy Administration. *The Economic Impact of the Oil Embargo on the American Economy.* Washington, D.C.: Government Printing Office, 1974.

———. *New Energy Outlook.* Washington, D.C.: Government Printing Office, 1976.

———. *Oil: Possible Levels of Future Production: A Taskforce Report for Project Independence.* Washington, D.C.: Government Printing Office, 1974.

———. *Project Independence: Blueprint Final Taskforce Report.* Washington, D.C.: Government Printing Office, 1974.

U.S., Federal Energy Commission. *The Relationship of Oil Companies and Foreign Governments.* Washington, D.C.: Government Printing Office, 1975.

United States Information Service. *Statements on the Middle East, November 29, 1973–June 24, 1974.* Washington, D.C., 1974.

Vernon, Raymond, ed. *The Oil Crisis.* New York: W. W. Norton & Company, 1976.

Yergin, Daniel. *Global Insecurity: A Strategy for Energy and Economic Renewal.* Boston: Houghton Mifflin and Company, 1982.

SELECTED PERIODICALS

Annual Report, British Petroleum	(London)
Annual Report, Saudi Arabia Monetary Agency	(Jidda)
Business Week	(New York)
Daily Radio Broadcasts, BBC	(London)
Economist	(London)
Events	(London)
Financial Times	(London)
Foreign Affairs	(New York)
Hadashot Haneft	(Tel Aviv)
International Herald-Tribune	(Paris)
Jerusalem Post	(Jerusalem)
Maariv	(Tel Aviv)
Middle East Economic Digest (MEED)	(London)
Middle East Economic Survey (MEES)	(Beirut, Nicosia)

Newsweek   (New York)
New York Times
Oil and Gas Journal   (Tulsa, Okla.)
OPEC Review and Record   (Vienna)
Petroleum Economist (*Petroleum Press Service*)   (London)
Petroleum Intelligence Weekly   (New York)
Statistical Review of the World Oil Industry,
   British Petroleum   (London)
Statistical Summary, Saudi Arabia Monetary Agency   (Jidda)
Sunday Times   (London)
Time   (New York)
The *Times*   (London)
Wall Street Journal   (New York)
Weekly News Bulletin, Iraq National Oil Company (Baghdad)
World Financial Markets, Morgan Guaranty
   Trust Company   (New York)
World Oil   (Houston)

INDEX